I0797015

READING THE HINDU AND CHRISTIAN CLASSICS

RICHARD LECTURES FOR 2017

READING THE HINDU AND CHRISTIAN CLASSICS

Why and How Deep Learning Still Matters

FRANCIS X. CLOONEY, SJ

University of Virginia Press
CHARLOTTESVILLE AND LONDON

University of Virginia Press

Printed in the United States of America on acid-free paper

First published 2019

ISBN 978-0-8139-4311-4 (hardcover)
ISBN 978-0-8139-4312-1 (ebook)

9 8 7 6 5 4 3 2 1

Library of Congress Cataloging-in-Publication Data is available for this title.

For those who taught me to love reading and to read carefully, patiently, and well: my parents, Irene and James Clooney; the Presentation Sisters at St. Christopher's School on Staten Island, New York; and my Jesuit and lay teachers at Regis High School in Manhattan, New York

Contents

Foreword

On Monday, January 25, 1830, Johann Eckermann talked, as he often did, with Goethe, who was, it seems, enjoying one of his lighter moments. "He then joked upon the difficulty of reading," Eckermann says, "and the presumption of many people, who, without any previous study and preparatory knowledge, would at once read every philosophical and scientific work, as if it were nothing but a romance. 'The good people,' continued he, 'know not what time and trouble it costs to *learn to read.* I have been employed for eighteen years on it, and cannot say that I have reached the goal yet.'"[1]

Just over half a century later, a sage of a quite different stripe, although another (and utterly different) master of the German language, reflected on his new book, *Morgenröte* (1881). Nietzsche observed:

> It is not for nothing that I have been a philologist, perhaps I am a philologist still, that is to say, a teacher of slow reading:—in the end I also write slowly. Nowadays it is not only my habit, it is also to my taste—a malicious taste, perhaps?—no longer to write anything which does not reduce to despair every sort of man who is "in a hurry." For philology is that venerable art which demands of its votaries one thing above all: to go aside, to take time, to become still, to become slow—it is a goldsmith's art and connoisseurship of the *word* which has nothing but delicate, cautious work to do and achieves nothing if it does not achieve it *lento.* But for precisely this reason it is more necessary than ever today, by precisely this means does it entice and enchant us the most, in the midst of an age of "work," that is to say, of hurry, of indecent and perspiring haste, which want so "get everything done" at once, including every old or new book—this art does not so easily get anything done, it teaches to read *well,* that is to say, to read slowly, deeply, looking cautiously before and aft, with reservations, with doors left open, with delicate eyes and fingers.[2]

Two things have changed significantly since Goethe and Nietzsche lived and wrote. On the one hand, reading has been developed to a very high level, while, on the other hand, our culture, including our educational culture, moves at vast speed, more so than what Nietzsche noticed, seeking to assimilate masses of visual and written information, so that there is little incentive to read slowly and, alas, many reasons to read all too quickly.

One index of the way in which culture and speed have been linked will suffice. In 1974 when Leonardo da Vinci's *Mona Lisa* (*c.* 1517) was loaned by the Louvre in Paris to the National Museum in Tokyo, the museum administrators in Japan allowed each group of admirers "an optimum time" of seven seconds to view the great painting. As one local commentator on Japanese culture ruefully observed, "It is not surprising, then, that two or three seconds suffice for the Bridge of Heaven. Mount Fuji generally rates five or six and the Second Coming of Christ will merit ten."[3] This reaction to the speed with which culture, even religious culture, is to be consumed was written over thirty years ago, and the situation to which it responds has gotten worse, not better, not only in Japan but also everywhere.

Yet in the West at least the early decades of the twentieth century reveal a new stress on slowing down our learning in the humanities. If we look at the history of reading over the last hundred years, we find the New Critics deviating rather sharply from the noted literary critics of the generation before, people such as George Saintsbury (1845–1933) and Edmund Gosse (1849–1928). With T. S. Eliot's "Tradition and the Individual Talent" (1919) and I. A. Richards's *Practical Criticism* (1929), the stage was being set for closer attention to the language of poetry, in particular.[4] And when the performance commenced, it was nothing if not memorable. To read William Empson's *Seven Types of Ambiguity* (1930) was to wonder what people had been doing with poetry beforehand.[5] One might be forgiven for thinking that they had not been reading it at all or that "reading" had significantly changed its meaning in recent times. Certainly, it had become an activity that would take a good deal of time. Not everyone deemed that the change was for the better; some scholars felt that a proper distance from the poem being considered had been forsaken, and that a microscope had been substituted for a decent pair of glasses. Others felt that reading was in danger of subsuming the broader category of learning, which included attention to history and culture, as well as linguistic meaning. Yet the new criticism flourished, despite reservations. Empson's study of ambiguity was published in the United States in 1947, the same year that Cleanth Brooks's *The Well Wrought Urn* appeared.[6] Ambiguity, paradox, skepticism about the importance of the author's intentions, combined with dire talk of "the heresy of paraphrase," as Brooks put it, launched a period of intense close reading, based primarily on lyric poetry, that was to remain in departments of English well into the 1970s.

Some twenty years after the *annus mirabilis* of the New Criticism, though, we find that the frontier of slow reading has passed to France. This frontier was not, as one might think, *la nouvelle critique,* which followed the publication of Roland Barthes's *Sur Racine* (1963). American and British critics who looked to Paris tended to think that the French were merely catching up with what had been going on at home for quite some time, yet they were soon to be surprised. For Jacques Derrida (1930–2004) changed the stakes of reading with his early publications. To be sure, his first book went almost completely unnoticed by Anglophone readers. Had it been read at the time, however, his *Introduction à la "Origine de la géométrie" de Edmund Husserl* (1962) might have made the New Critics reflect on some of their fundamental assumptions about reading, especially the sort of texts that would respond to close reading. Only with his further study of Husserl in *La voix et le phénomène* (1967) and his examination of Jean-Jacques Rousseau in *De la grammatologie* (1967) did it become apparent to literary critics what close reading could do or, perhaps more accurately, what it could undo: all manner of assurances about presence, unity, and foundations. In some ways Derrida was returning us to Goethe's and Nietzsche's reflections on reading, for his focus was at first on philosophy, not literature, and even when he later attended to poetry he remained concerned with philosophical assumptions about the relations of poetry and philosophy.

Derrida's first publications were taken to announce a program that the humanities in the United States would substantially follow for two decades or more. Curiously, it was largely confined to departments of English and comparative literature and was mostly drained of its philosophical reference and almost all of its philosophical subtlety.[7] Departments of philosophy, drawn to analytic philosophy, which promised high standards of clarity and rigor, much as presumed in the natural sciences, paid little attention to the new development, partly because the North American version of Derrida's work was riven with philosophical howlers and partly because analytic philosophy is not particularly interested in the reading of philosophical texts. Nor was Derrida adopted at first in departments of theology or religious studies. He was taken to be hostile to religion, especially so toward Christianity, and it took some time to distinguish the views of his North American admirers, who were often alienated from religion, from Derrida's own views, which were far more nuanced; more importantly, it took time to discern what his ideas meant for the study of religion.[8]

At least in his first maturity, Derrida's interest in religion was confined to part of William Warburton's *The Divine Legation of Moses Demonstrated* (1742), a defense of the revelation given to Moses on the ground that Torah does not affirm an afterlife and is therefore distinctive in the religions of the Middle East.[9] It is a peculiar piece of writing, and one hardly read by Anglophone theologians these days or even all that often by students of eighteenth-century British literature. Why then did Derrida brood in "Scribble (pouvoir /écrire)" on the *Divine Legation* of all theological treatises? Because in Book IV section 4 of the work Warburton proposes a theory of writing designed to show that hieroglyphs establish the antiquity of Egypt, and the young Derrida was deeply concerned with philosophical issues arising from inscription. For Warburton, the "mystery and secrecy" associated with hieroglyphs befall the act of inscription, as though from outside; and Derrida shows that things are not so simple: "the *veil* of mystery and secrecy," on which priests and religious hierarchy depend, is necessary and inevitable.[10] "Scribble" was never collected in one of Derrida's many volumes in French or in English. One of his most interesting works remains hardly read in either language.

Meanwhile, of course, Scripture was receiving minute attention from the "lower criticism," which sought to establish the most reliable early text of any given biblical book. This is editing of a modern, rigorous kind, though not "reading" as it came to be practiced with respect to literature and Derrida's inflection of phenomenology. It would be a mistake of the first order, however, to think that Christianity had not been practicing slow reading of one kind or another for a very long time indeed. To give only the barest indices: we might think of Bernard of Clairvaux's *Sermons on the Song of Songs,* which, in eighty-six homilies, comments on several pages of the biblical book; we might recall, also, Thomas Aquinas's commentary on the Gospel of John, which devotes a hundred or so pages to the first chapter of the book; and of course we might recur to Origen's commentaries on the Song of Songs and John, which are nothing if not voluminous, even when condensed into Latin translation.[11] *Allegoresis,* whether unrestrained, slightly restrained, or highly restrained, generates ways of closely reading Scripture that, if not quite to our taste today, nonetheless testify to very slow reading indeed. Not that practices of slow reading are confined to Christianity. We can point to the Babylonian and Jerusalem Talmuds in Judaism, to Averroes's commentaries on Aristotle in Islam, and in Hinduism to Sāyaṇa's commentary on the *Ṛg Veda,* among many other similar works.

Reading the Hindu and Christian Classics by Francis X. Clooney, SJ, begins to come into focus for us when we see it as a new contribution to slow reading or, better, its correlative, slow learning. Nowhere do we find the names of Goethe, Nietzsche, or Derrida, and the tradition to which I have alluded by way of Origen, Aquinas, and Bernard of Clairvaux is not his primary focus. If anything, he looks to Wittgenstein for support; but he is no card-carrying follower of Wittgenstein, and he has no philosophical program in the back of his mind that we need to identify and evaluate. His concerns are far from ancient or modern theories of reading, even from theories of "religious reading," and yet a quiet affirmation of the need to slow down the process of how we learn of and from religion, especially reading important (yet sometimes decidedly difficult) texts of one's religious tradition is everywhere apparent in his project in general and in this contribution to it in particular.[12] Clooney's slow reading is not done in detail on the page; it has been mostly done in his study, and only the fruits of it are given to the reader. I think of Pierre Hadot (1922–2010), who would carefully translate Greek or Latin texts into French simply as preparation for lecturing or commenting on them. Like Hadot, Clooney has an eye and an ear for important texts that get overlooked or bypassed in the modern academy. Peter Lombard's *Sentences* are essential to the Latin Catholic tradition, but all too few people, including theologians, read them with the care that they require. Peter Canisius's *The Greater Catechism* is less central to the same tradition, and Louis de Montfort's *The Admirable Secret of the Most Holy Rosary* even less so; yet sometimes it is only by looking to the side that one can understand what is central.

That said, Clooney's project in general, and this study in particular, comes even more sharply into focus when we name it and ponder it. The expression we need to consider is "comparative theology," which names an approach to theology of which Clooney is the primary begetter, at least in modern times. But this is not the first use of the expression. To find that, we need to go back to Church of Scotland divine James Garden's *Discursus Academicus de Theologia Comparativa* (1699), which was rendered into English in 1700. Its main claim is that there is an important yet neglected distinction between absolute theology and what is coined there as "comparative theology." Absolute theology, Garden tells us, "considers its object only as revealed and enjoined, or instituted by God; and its business is, to find out those things which are proposed to us in the Scriptures to be believed or practiced, and to discern and distinguish them from all others." He then goes on to define "comparative theology"; it "ponders the weight of importance, and observes the order, respect and relation of things belonging to religion; whether they be points of doctrine, or precepts, or sacred rites; and teaches to distinguish and put a difference between the *accessories* of religion and the *principles,* the *circumstantials* and *substantials,* the *means* and their *ends.*"[13] Garden was motivated by what he took to be a serious decline in Christian belief and practice, one prompted by prizing the niceties of Orthodox doctrine over pious Christian practice. Influenced by Quietism, he stressed repentance and humility by way of mortification and self-denial as the path back to God. Only if we recognize what is essential to the faith will we become true Christians, Garden argues, and comparative theology will help us to do just that.

Clooney also is eager that Christians build up our faith by doing comparative theology, but his project includes far more than that and does so by quite other means. As a placing shot, we might begin to understand comparative theology by sitting it beside comparative literature. Even those of us who do not pursue comparative literature in a scholarly way often read poetry or narrative in another language for consolation, pleasure, wisdom, or knowledge. If I read Baudelaire, Mallarmé, Rimbaud, René Char, and Yves Bonnefoy, I do not thereby lose my familiarity with English-language poetry from Wordsworth to Basil Bunting and Geoffrey Hill; if I am attentive, I will find that my sense of what can be done and cannot be done in English and American poetry is deepened and finessed simply by reading French poetry. I might even find hidden paths that go from the one literature to the other, but I will certainly not forget literature written in English.

Similarly, if I immerse myself in the texts of another religion, I will become more attentive to aspects of texts in my own religion; and, more than that, I might develop a finer sense of liturgical, pastoral, and theological possibilities in my own tradition. Looking over a border turns out also to be a way of looking more deeply within as well as actually learning something about the practices and beliefs of others. So comparative theology is invested in Christianity, if one is a Christian (and in Hinduism if one is a Hindu, and so on), in a way that the practice of comparative religion is not. The aim of comparative religion, from Max Müller (1823–1900) to Mircea Eliade (1907–86) and beyond, is scholarly examination of various beliefs and practices in order to reach a more profound understanding of those things, to emerge with a more nuanced grasp of what the human engagement with religion is all about. Comparative theology, however, is not tied to the myth of neutrality that is assumed (and usually not investigated) in comparative religion.

Nor, though, is comparative theology quite the same as the theology of religions, not even in the inflection of it proposed by Karl Rahner (1904–84), Clooney's distinguished confrere in the Society of Jesus. Before Vatican II (1962–65) and well after it, theologians have mostly approached the theology of religions from the viewpoint of soteriology, asking themselves: Can a Hindu, a Muslim, or a Buddhist be saved? Always, the primacy of Christianity has been presumed. For Rahner, the good Hindu, the good Muslim, the good Buddhist, even the good atheist, can experience God by way of their own moral acts. This experience is not thematic, and it offers no ecstasy or consolation; it comes in ordinary human interactions one with another. He calls it "transcendental experience," because, by his lights, it is one with the very possibility of intersubjective human experience. Those in the great religious traditions of the Earth, as well as those who on principle do not follow any religious tradition, are from the Christian perspective "implicit Christians," Rahner says, or, as he also puts it, "anonymous Christians."[14] To be sure, Rahner understands that, from the viewpoint of a Hindu, he must be regarded as art]an implicit or anonymous Hindu. Yet a threefold worry persists. First, Hindus committed to their traditions may well object to being assimilated to another faith tradition in this way. Second, Christianity is a public confession of belief with nothing anonymous about it; and the situation remains the same mutatis mutandis with respect to other religions. And third, in Christianity salvation comes only in and through Christ: for a Christian, the symmetry of being an anonymous Hindu is cosmetic. Comparative theology does not seek the eschatological grandeur of Rahner's theology of religions; it remains modestly and solidly on the ground, in the careful study of practices and traditions, that, over time, will enrich one's response to one's own religion as well as that of other persons by unobtrusive, persistent work in two or more traditions.

Rahner's theology of religions resonates powerfully with the temper of Vatican II: both *Lumen gentium,* the dogmatic constitution of the Church, and *Gaudium et spes,* the pastoral constitution of the Church, express hope for the salvation of those who have not heard the Gospel, even if the former document also stipulates that having heard the Gospel one must enter the faith or risk the final displeasure of God. The shortest of the documents of the council, *Nostra Aetate,* the declaration on the relation of the Church with non-Christian religions, expresses an openness to all that is good and true in the other world religions, beginning with the other members of the Abrahamic family; and, if anything, this openness has been encouraged during the pontificate of Francis I (2013–). Clooney's comparative theology proceeds in the same spirit of responsiveness, and the slowness that characterizes it in all ways is perhaps beneficial: in the world of interreligious dialogue knowledge and understanding of texts, practices, and traditions is invariably required. And not just knowledge but also self-knowledge: we get nowhere in such discussions without a decent sense of our limits and, more than that, an awareness of epistemic humility with regard to God, that is, a conviction of how little we really know for sure about God, even if we cling devotedly to a particular tradition.

Reading the Hindu and Christian Classics is an appeal to slow learning, a kind familiar in tradition but too often forgotten today. In some ways Clooney is drawing us back to a very old characterization of theology proposed by Anselm (1033–1109): *fides quaerens intellectum,* "faith in quest of understanding," a quest that was never meant to be completed in an hour, a day, a week, a year, or even a decade. Comparative theology augments the old adage by asking us to see that our own faith can understand more of its own tradition by seeking to apprehend more of the traditions of others. Also, comparative theology quietly draws, in its own way, from the long tradition of contemplation in the West, with its many correlatives in the East: "slow reading," here, is not a matter of technique to make more of a text or to undo its philosophical claims; it is a response to other traditions and, perhaps, to the otherness of one's own tradition. The quest that is comparative theology is itself only in its first stages; it will take generations of work before it has even commenced breaking the ground that needs to be cultivated.[15] This new book by Francis X. Clooney takes us further on the quest, one that in the study of religion is as exciting as any I know today.

Kevin Hart
University of Virginia
May 1, 2018

Preface

Due to many commitments at Harvard and as director of the Center for the Study of World Religions from 2010 to 2017, *Reading the Hindu and Christian Classics* has taken longer to complete than otherwise I might have hoped. Fast times indeed, leaving little space for slow and reflective reading. So this book has been at least six years in the making. But in retrospect I can see that I have benefited from this delay, since it gave me more time to practice the slow reading that is at the book's core, to learn from various stops and starts, sidetracks and dead-ends, to pursue new leads arising along the way, and above all to ponder the problems arising when slow reading is possible and fruitful, but no one has the time for it.

The delay also gave me the wonderful opportunity to try out the ideas underlying this project more amply in the format of the James W. Richard Lectures, which I gave at the University of Virginia, October 24–26, 2017.[1] Yet, I also found that turning the lectures into this book was not a straightforward matter.[2] It is one thing to make a plausible statement in a lecture and to leap in speaking from one point to another; it is another to write in a way that reads well and coherently on the page. The many notes and the bullet points in my PowerPoint presentation needed to be turned into sentences and paragraphs, and that in itself was a painstaking process. But the heart of the project remained constant: we are in danger of losing our bearings as individuals and communities and whole societies, because we are no longer in sufficiently deep and dense living intellectual contact with our own religious traditions—because we no longer read the great books that have formed our traditions, and because we no longer have the patience, humility, and dispositions to read slowly, for as long as it takes, without any craving for immediate results. If we cannot go deep into our own traditions, neither will we be able to engage the traditions around us: forgetting how to learn our own traditions, we will hardly be in a position to learn from our neighbors. Ignorance of self and other can fuel violence; benign ignorance may show us merely to be out of touch with all that has given us religious grounding and direction over the millennia. So this slow little book, like the quiet lectures that led to it, is sounding an alarm for those willing and able to hear the call.

Like the six texts I discuss and the examples I choose, *Reading the Hindu and Christian Classics* as a whole plays a transitional role, intensely wrought and hoping for committed readers—but only for a time. In writing this book as such—situated between the whole of texts to be read thoroughly and some heartfelt opinions about how we ought to be learning religiously—my goal has been to win over willing readers to the great work of reading religiously and interreligiously, in a way that satisfies and nourishes mind and heart. I labored to find exemplary passages in all six books, so as to offer initial satisfaction in learning, even as I wanted to encourage some readers to move beyond my book and go to the books themselves and read them all the way through, for a richly variegated Hindu and Catholic education.

I make a great deal of my six chosen texts (introduced properly in chapter 1) on ritual and legal reasoning, catechesis in the basics of the faith, the subtleties of a nondualist view of reality, the profound mysteries of doctrine, the recitation of familiar prayers, and songs that yearn for the essence of true love for God: *these* books need to be read, since through them do readers really enter the great worlds of learning they condense and intensify, so as to be transformed in accord with the disciplines of instruction, doctrine, and participation. Yet at the same time, I have no reason to insist that *only* these six (and others like them in other traditions) can do the work I envision. In chapter 6 I remind readers that substitutions are perfectly fine, since what they can learn from me regarding how we ought to read can be tried out and tested with other texts too. But I still urge readers to follow my example, even if they shift to texts of their own choosing: seek to be instructed and transformed by sustained acts of reading that take as long as they need to take; do not cut corners or settle for the general ideas that excuse you from reading; trust that your reading in your own tradition and another tradition will bear fruit, when the time is ripe for it.

There are many to thank for their help and listening along the way. That there is a book at all is due to the good will and assistance of many friends and colleagues here and in India. Early parts of the project took shape regarding the urtext underlying the book, the *Garland of Jaimini's Reasons* by the fourteenth-century scholar Mādhava, in lectures at the Kuppuswami Sastri Research Institute in Chennai, India, in January 2014, the Bhandarkar Oriental Research Institute in Pune, India, in February of that same year, and at Cornell University, New York, in April 2016.

At the University of Virginia, where I resided in the fall of 2017 as I prepared and gave the Richard Lectures, I am grateful to Martien Halvorson-

Taylor, cochair of the Page-Barbour and James W. Richards Lectures Committee, for watching over the arrangements, and to doctoral students Lucila Crena and Meghan Hartman, for their great help and advice before, during, and after the actual lectures. Kurtis Schaeffer, chair of Religious Studies, was a gracious host, facilitating my contacts with students and various faculty. Chuck Mathewes was a singularly welcoming friend and colleague during my stay at UVA, arranging events and sharing the occasional beer too. Michael Allen, a friendly face from the days of his Harvard doctoral studies, offered the introduction to my second lecture, was likewise supportive throughout, and happily was my nearest neighbor on campus. I owe especially great thanks to John Nemec, who facilitated my stay in Charlottesville in every way, and was a thoughtful and considerate host and friend throughout my whole visit, beginning to end. He also introduced my first lecture and later offered valuable comments on the whole of the manuscript. I likewise offer deep thanks to Kevin Hart, who first raised with me the possibility of giving the Richard Lectures and then proposed my name to the selection committee. He too was a very good colleague and friend throughout my stay. His introduction to the third lecture now serves as a very welcome foreword to this book, enhancing all that follows.

I cannot name everyone who made my stay in Charlottesville a good one, but I must mention the welcoming community at the Church of the Incarnation, where I helped out with Masses on the weekends and some weekdays. Father Gregory Kandt and Deacons Chris Morash and Tom Healey were supportive of my work and were kind enough to attend my lectures and encourage parishioners also to come. I was pleased likewise to meet devotees from the nearby Yogaville ashram, who came up for all my lectures. The whole event of the Richard Lectures turned out to be a happy crossover between the academic and church communities, and a sure basis for the writing of this book.

During the spring semester of 2018, I was a senior fellow at the Institute for Advanced Study at the University of Notre Dame. It was in that welcoming and supportive setting that I enjoyed the time and ideal environment in which to turn the Richard Lectures into this book. I am indebted to Brad Gregory, director of NDIAS, for his warm welcome, and to Donald Stelluto, associate director of NDIAS, and Carolyn Sherman, events and fellowships program manager, for their extraordinary solicitude at every moment of my stay there. My undergraduate research assistant, Salonee Sucharan, patiently read through an early draft of the manuscript, offering candid reflections and a fresh eye on the unusual ideas I was (and am) proposing.

The NDIAS staff also helped arrange, in collaboration with Peter

Casarella of the Theology Department, a most helpful seminar dinner discussion in April 2018, at which an extraordinary group of about thirty faculty and grad students came together to discuss the manuscript with me, offering helpful comments and raising pertinent questions that have greatly improved the final product. I cannot name all the participants here but wish to acknowledge the discussants at the seminar, Peter Casarella, Robert Gimello, David Bentley Hart, and Thomas Tweed, and doctoral students Alison Fitchett Climenhaga and Lailatul Fitriyah. In addition, Atalia Omer, professor of religion, conflict, and peace studies and a core member of the faculty of the Keough School of Foreign Affairs, David Burrell, CSC, professor emeritus of theology, and visiting NDIAS fellow Harvey Brown, professor emeritus at the University of Oxford, all offered very invaluable insights into my project and the emerging manuscript.

Lastly, I am grateful for the University of Virginia Press's interest in publishing my Richard Lectures as this book, to the anonymous readers who made a number of important and helpful suggestions; to Eric Brandt, assistant director and editor in chief, University of Virginia Press, for his support during the publication process; to Helen Marie Chandler and the excellent staff at the Press for guiding the manuscript through production and into print; and to Dorie Goehring, staff assistant at Harvard's Center for the Study of World Religions, for her invaluable assistance in proofreading the galleys and preparing the index.

Nearer to the end of my career than its beginning, I am increasingly mindful of those who were there at the very beginning of my education, who taught me to read and read well: my parents Irene and James Clooney, the Presentation Sisters at St. Christopher's School on Staten Island, New York, and the fine array of Jesuits and lay faculty who challenged me to read deeply and well in English and French, Latin and Greek, at Regis High School in Manhattan. To them I dedicate this book.

Francis X. Clooney, SJ
Cambridge, MA
October 15, 2018

READING THE HINDU AND CHRISTIAN CLASSICS

ONE

Remembering How to Learn in a Forgetful World

On My Shelf: A Fourteenth-Century Hindu Casebook of Ritual Law

Between 2012 and 2017 I had spent a great amount of time reading the *Garland of Jaimini's Reasons* (on which I say a lot more below), a particularly difficult Sanskrit text, a digest of Hindu ritual law from around 1400 CE. The work of reading it and translating it was most rewarding to me as a scholar and perennial student, since it opened up a vast world rich in ideas and insights on how to read, how to perform, how to think religiously. But the reading was hard work and the insights deeply imbedded in that hard work. It soon became clear to me that few others would be able or willing to learn patiently from the work I was doing, unless they repeated the act and read the whole of the *Garland.* The more I learned, the less confidence I had that the reading would bear fruits commensurate with the work I put into my reading: I could write a fine book on the *Garland* and its world of rites, laws, and rules—but who would read it?

The beginning of all this had been rather simple. I was finishing the project that became *His Hiding Place Is Darkness*—itself an intense reading of passionate mystical poetry in the Hindu and Christian traditions, as much as I could manage also by learning from premodern commentators in both traditions. One day then I was sitting at my desk, surveying my shelves for books that might help instigate my next project. I often start out this way, picking a book, not a theme, studying the book, and seeing where it leads. I have enough on my shelves to fuel a writing career over many lifetimes. My eyes soon rested upon a set of three nineteenth-century volumes from India, once sturdily bound, but now rather brittle: the *Jaiminīyanyāyamālā* (the *Garland of Jaimini's Reasons,* henceforth the *Garland*) of Mādhavācārya (1297–1388; Mādhava the teacher, henceforth Mādhava). He was a learned scholar, highly respected in his times, who wrote a number of erudite works, of which the *Garland* was the most well known.[1]

This is a work that summarizes several millennia of the interpretation of ritual texts and actions, solving the most arcane of interpretive problems, as carried out in the school of Indian thought known as *Mīmāṃsā* (more or less, "the intense desire to know precisely"). The books had sat on my shelves for many years, undisturbed except for an occasional dusting. But I started to read the first of them, intrigued and then caught up in a slow learning process that even now is not quite finished, since I've still to read 15 percent of the work, scattered sections I never got to. But I have learned much in the reading, and when I am done, I will have to start over again, to understand better the parts I read first.

The *Garland* covers the standard set of instances of Vedic text and practice where ambiguities and problems threatened the notion that the sacred texts were always clear and always made sense. Such cases had been collected first in the *Mīmāṃsā Sūtras,* a brilliant but extremely laconic text attributed to the sage Jaimini, who flourished around 200–300 BCE. More than a millennium of commentary and elaboration of the cases and the rules included in them led to the accumulation of a very large set of commentaries, too much for almost any reader. Mādhava's *Garland* sought to distill that tradition compactly, preserving the core problematic of each case while excising every unnecessary word. One *śloka* (two-line verse, henceforth "verse") would suffice for most cases, rendering the problem, positions, and conclusions as simply as possible, nothing missing.

Throughout the *Garland,* the search is for the interpretive key, the reason (*nyāya*) key to resolving each particular case. After first cases are explored, their conclusions are regularly extended and tested with reference to other ambiguous texts in religion and law.[2] Like most *mīmāṃsā* reasoning, the *Garland* is unsparingly rational and focused on nothing but the problem at hand at the moment. It is devoid of sentiment and of mystical insight (unless of course there is a mysticism deep in relentless religious reasoning. The price of focus on cases and their reasons is a diversion from much of what might be of interest to us in the ancient Vedas: stories of the gods, creation myths, reports (even if indirect) on human experiences of the divine, and the rubrics of how actually to do sacrifices. All this was left aside, and historical and social concerns of the kind we might hope for rarely arise, and not in the forms we expect. The cases considered and the classic positions regarding them form a canon well rooted in the tradition, yet ready for instructive study by the students of generations to follow.

In verses that appear in the introduction to the *Elaboration* (*Vistara*),[3] we hear the account of the composition of the text, Mādhava undertaking the task at the request of King Vīraśrībukkabhupati.[4] Perhaps Mādhava did his work too well, since the *Garland* immediately required prose paragraphs to explain more fully its dense verses. Some seem to have come to the *Garland* innocently, taking it to be a work of introduction, while others marveled at its elegance:

> From (his teacher) the revered Bhāratītīrtha Yati facing in four directions like Indra, Mādhava received unimpeded mercy and was beyond any parallel. After composing this *Garland of Jaimini's Reasons* that gives bliss to the learned, Mādhavācārya elaborated it, for the enlightenment of beginners.
>
> Protector of the revealed word, tradition, and good practice; earlier he had explained traditional wisdom for the benefit of all, and now for the benefit of the twice-born this work on the revealed word came forth: he is Mādhava the wise.[5]

I found the *Garland* be a wonderful text, hard but rewarding.[6] Though 1,536 verses long, the *Garland* is also manageably brief, compared with the 2,644 *sūtras* (brief or extensive, but quite often obscure statements) of Jaimini, some very short, some as long as a long sentence or fragments thereof, then surrounded with the commentarial literature that accumulated over time. And so, in 2013 I took up studying, and largely for my own sake translating, the verses of the *Garland.* Of necessity, I referred regularly to its prose *Elaboration,* though only rarely did I write out translations from that large prose text. I plodded along, a case at a time, gradually picking up speed in my reading. I learned something of the *Garland*'s style, engaged the problems presented one by one, and learned slowly to think through the cases as posed, delving as needed back into the commentarial tradition behind the *Garland.* In this way, I was studying Mīmāṃsā ritual analysis from the ground up, so to speak, according to the cases that shaped Mīmāṃsā reasoning throughout its long history. I have studied Mīmāṃsā for more than thirty-five years on and off, so I was not starting from zero. But the *Garland* was, I found, the most elegant and complete rendering of the tradition, yet still in a manageable form and, in its own dry and deliberate manner, still riveting in its promise of a totality of knowledge in a short form.

On the Art of Reading Mīmāṃsā Ritual Reasoning, Case by Case

But let us back up for a moment, and say a little more about Mīmāṃsā itself, the greater tradition that Mādhava seeks to condense and introduce.[7] These pages will be slow going, I am sure, but are important if we are to have a feel for the act of slow reading.

As a discipline, Mīmāṃsā is well over two thousand years old, but even as such it is following upon a much older tradition of text and sacrificial practice collected under the title of "Veda," the orthopraxy of ancient India. The sacrificial realm included simpler and more complex fire sacrifices, wherein offerings to a pantheon of deities occurred as solid or liquid, vegetarian or animal, offerings into fire, offered by sacrificial patrons employing learned brahmins to perform the rites, reciting the correct mantra, etc. The goals of these sacrifices could be celestial rewards or the satisfaction of mundane needs. Some sacrifices were simply mandatory, others the product of complicated balance between duty and desire. By plan, customs, and accident, the sacrifices grew more complex and diverse over time, and myriad puzzles confronted those who tried to see the harmony among texts and in practice. Mīmāṃsā is one of the key ancient supporting disciplines (*vedāṅga*) of Vedic word and practice, and has even been thought of as the reasoning inherent in the Veda, its inherent reasoning (*veda-tarka,* Veda-reasoning). Mīmāṃsā reaches a level of coherence deeper than the stories told, hymns sung, commands given, or actions undertaken.

The *Mīmāṃsā Sūtras* of Jaimini (second century BCE) is the founding text of the tradition. At the *Sūtras'* very start, the activity of *mīmāṃsā* is characterized as an "inquiry into *dharma*" (I.1.1), into the order and intelligibility of the world as ordinarily seen but, to those who can see (who can read), also rich in a deeper and enduring significance that is not esoteric, but simply a rearrangement of ordinary things for the sake of extraordinary sacrificial work. "To do *mīmāṃsā*" is to engage in "intense reflection," "enquiry, theoretical discussion (sometimes removed from practice)," fulfilling in that way "the desire and effort to know in proper measure."[8] The *Sūtras* proceed by way of 907 cases, a set of problems, textual and ritual, laconically posed in the nearly 2,700 brief statements (*sūtras*) that add up to the *Sūtras* as a whole. In turn, these were elaborated by Śabara Swāmi in his always indispensable commentary, which itself was then explicated in the commentaries of Kumārila Bhaṭṭa and Prabhākara Miśra and others.

It is hard to say briefly what Mīmāṃsā in general or the *Sūtras* in particular are about, given Mīmāṃsā's resolute focus on particular cases and rules regarding them. Imagine summarizing a casebook of common law problems and precedents, in lieu of actually studying the cases. But it will helpful to see a list of the rules and approaches that over the centuries have been taken to characterize the twelve books (*adhyāya*) of Jaimini's *Sūtras.* Here is my rendering of traditional accounts:[9]

1. the authority in the form of injunctions, commendatory statements, etc. (Book I);
2. the distinction among actions, sacrifices, gifts, etc. (Book II);
3. the status of the fore-sacrifices, etc., as accessory to the new and full moon sacrifices, etc. (Book III);
4. decisions regarding motives, that is, which actions are done for the sake of the ritual, and which are for the sake of the person, as ritual performer or more generally in his ordinary life (Book IV);
5. constraint in terms of order, etc., even if this is mentioned but not explicitly enjoined (Book V);
6. the fact that there is ritual eligibility for all who desire happiness, but not for those ineligible due to various deficiencies, though some deficiencies can be remedied (Book VI);
7. transfer of details from an amply described ritual to one merely sketched or named, by explicit statements and by statements inferred with reference to the names of various sacrifices, etc. (Book VII);
8. special cases of transfer, according to which mode of procedure is followed, which deities or materials substituted, etc. (Book VIII);
9. there is modification of rites in their adapted forms, by the changing of the name of deities receiving the offering, materials offered, etc. (Book IX);
10. there is the blocking of no longer relevant details in adapted rites, as when the threshing cannot be applied to gold coins, etc. (Book X);
11. there is the common performance of subordinate helps, such as the fore-sacrifices, once but serving multiple rites (Book XI);
12. the incidental help of subordinate rites, such as the fore-sacrifices, brought in to help the primary animal rite, but also contributing to related rites. (Book XII).

Each of these topics, illustrated and worked through by cases, is subjected to rigorous analysis in search of rules that can govern but not erase sacrificial materiality and plurality. It is in the relatedness of particular words and acts, carefully ruled, that the heart of Mīmāṃsā lies.[10]

Mīmāṃsā shows how these rules play out by proposing and arguing concrete ritual cases. Each is to be understood first of all on its own by identifying the rule or reason (*nyāya*) unlocking that particular case and dispelling an uncertainty or seeming contradiction. When the interpretive reason is detected, revelation's intelligibility too becomes evident in a concrete case. Subsequent cases often build on what has been resolved by further exploring related sacrificial matters, handling further objections that have arisen, or highlighting exceptions that however do not disprove the basic rules already in place. The cases are never repetitive, since the contexts and problems are always shifting; indeed, Mīmāṃsā hates mere repetition, and it would be unacceptable were any case merely to repeat the wisdom of the one before.[11] Mādhava's *Elaboration* on his *Garland* lists a number of ways in which the cases can follow one another:

> Connection by way of a clarifying objection (*ākṣepa*) to the decision made in the preceding case;
>
> Connection by way of an example (*dṛṣṭānta*) that shows the implausibility of the preceding case;
>
> Connection by a counter-example (*pratyudāharaṇa*) that in turn proves to be an exception even regarding an example adduced in the preceding case;
>
> Connection by what is incidental (*prāsaṅgika*), where an argument made in the course of the preceding case, though not central to it, prompts a new case to be argued;
>
> Connection by what is introductory (*upodghāta*), that is, such that the preceding case exists only to set the stage for the one that follows;
>
> Connection by way of exception (*apavāda*) that, while not disproving the judgment in the preceding case, is nevertheless a genuine exception for which space must be allowed.[12]

There is no smooth sequence of cases, merely illustrative of a theme. Nor are later cases merely further specifications of preceding cases. Every new case serves a purpose that cannot be entirely predicted by an understanding of the case or cases preceding it. Students must therefore work through the cases, one by one, in the given sequence, if they are to learn properly.

This case reasoning also sheds light on the project of *Reading the Hindu and Christian Classics.* I chose the six texts and the examples from each with care, but not with the idea that they all prove the same general point. Like Mīmāṃsā cases, my examples move forward precisely as case reasoning, extending or stretching or standing as exceptions to one another. There is rarely a theme that is simply being illustrated; nor do the examples add up to a proof of this or that tenet meant to be demonstrated. Rather, each example, small and large, does its work, challenging readers to read this way, then that way, and perhaps also to double back and try again. It is a wonderfully educative process that at first may also be terribly frustrating. But the key point will, I hope, be clear: while *Reading the Hindu and Christian Classics* has turned out not to be a book about the *Garland,* my deep appreciation for its case reasoning is at work everywhere in it.[13]

Beginning to Read the *Mīmāṃsā Sūtras*

Rather than just talking about Mīmāṃsā, however, it seems necessary to venture into the *Sūtras* and then the *Garland,* to see what it is like to read such texts. Otherwise, I would be in danger of talking about slow learning without actually doing it. Readers wishing to orient themselves first with an overview of what I am up to may however skip over these next several sections, move directly to the section entitled "But Who Wants to Learn Such a Dharma? A Productive Crisis," and come back to the actual reading later on.

I present here the relatively easier opening cases that start off the *Sūtras* by asking whether this manner of study is possible, necessary, and worthwhile. The *Sūtras* for the most part deal with very specific instances of text and practice, but they open with a self-critical reflection on whether such close and dense study can be fruitful or not. Here are key *sūtras* in I.1, beginning with reflection on the meaning of *dharma:*[14]

> Next, then, the enquiry into *dharma.* (case 1: *sūtra* I.1.1)
>
> *Dharma* is that meaning/purpose that is defined by injunction. (case 2: *sūtra* I.1.2)
>
> This is an investigation of the conditions of knowing *dharma.* (case 3: *sūtra* I.1.3)
>
> Perception is the birth of understanding by the conjunction of human senses with an existent object. But such is not the condition for knowledge of *dharma,* since it perceives only what is present. (case 4: *sūtra* I.1.4)
>
> The relationship of words with their meaning/purpose is innate. Knowledge of their relationship comes by teaching. Regarding its unperceived objects, such teaching is never unreliable, says Bādarāyaṇa, because it is independent (of factors leading to error). (case 5: *sūtra* I.1.5)

The next cases discuss the eternity of words, the authority and efficacy of Vedic sentences:

> Some say that a word is only conventionally (connected to its meaning), because it is seen to be such . . .
>
> No. In fact, a word must be unchanging in its relation to its meaning, since its utterance is for the purpose of communication with another. It is simultaneously communicative everywhere. (case 6: *sūtras* I.1.6, 18–19)

> But even if the connection of word and meaning is innate, words are not expressive of the meaning/purpose of *dharma,* since such are not the conditions for such knowledge.
>
> No. There is a handing down together of words regarding *dharma,* for the sake of action. This is the condition for coming to know that meaning/purpose. (case 7: *sūtras* I.1.24–25)

But isn't the Veda as a whole simply human words, speculations about things beyond human capacity? If so, they are hardly authoritative:

> Some say that the Vedas are human compositions, because they are named after persons, and because we also find ephemeral things mentioned in them.
>
> No. We have already explained that a word is prior to any particular usage. The names refer to the expounders, and not the composers of texts. (case 8: *sūtras* I.1.27–30)

At issue throughout these *sūtras* is a fundamental question: Are the intense deliberations of Mīmāṃsā needed, such that by study we can come to understand the transcendent reality of *dharma?* Or are we caught merely in a web of words about ordinary human experiences beyond which we cannot reach? Or, by way of an intellectual letdown, perhaps the *dharma* in its sacrificial form is always perfectly clear. Those for whom it matters already know what to do, and no special inquiry is required. Perhaps even for newcomers it is knowable by observation and thus again in need of no particular manner of religious study. Or, on the other extreme, perhaps it is to be known only by extraordinary means, for example, by revelation alone, simply given and accepted, not really thought through at all. Finally: perhaps it cannot be known at all, in which case too, there is nothing to study.

But if the investigation is necessary and worthwhile, then the extraordinary labor of the ensuing nine hundred–plus cases becomes plausible, a worthwhile effort to grasp *dharma* in action, even when ambiguity or contradiction seems likely. Here and elsewhere, the *Sūtras* set forth a middle way by pointing to the injunctions found in the Veda: they give instruction in how to act properly in the sacrificial setting. They instigate actions, not what is, but what is to be done, and so in this particular way they go beyond perception and inference. Since these injunctions can be grammatically and contextually analyzed in relation to other injunctions and to descriptive statements, study is necessary and worthwhile.

Sūtras of this kind give us in a very succinct fashion a sense of what is going on, even if there will always be more to be said, as further questions quickly arise. Indeed, from the start, the *Sūtras* expected oral elaboration. Indeed, the many individual *sūtras* are best thought of as prompts for teachers wishing to cover a set range of topics: if not so simple as a set of teacher's notes, they are something close to that. Once written down, they still needed teachers-as-commentators to fill in the blanks and elaborate at length what Jaimini meant. It is taken for granted that *dharma* has to do with right action; that perception, inference, and instructive texts are complementary; and that there is no supreme deity who promulgates the revelation. But all this needs explanation, lest matters seem unduly abbreviated or endlessly extended. Balancing succinctness with extreme clarity is what Mādhava contributes in his *Garland.*

How Mādhava Read Mīmāṃsā and Kept It Short

As a teacher writing more than a millennium later, Mādhava sought to fill out Jaimini's treatment of the cases, to regularize the style of the topics—and at the same time to summarize in a most economical way the consensus of the long ensuing commentarial tradition. Here then is Mādhava's complete rendering of the same opening cases, each beginning with the articulation of plausible alternatives between which students are asked to choose.

First, is learning through study something that can be enjoined? Study, however one goes about it, leads to knowledge, so why enjoin any particular form of it? Case 1 addresses this question:

> In accord with the usage of the injunction, "Personal study must be undertaken," is this reflective study not to be undertaken, or is it? Thus the doubt.
>
> Some say: Study is known from ordinary experience to be a means to understanding something. There is no restriction, just as with threshing. For this reason, it is not plausible that this study be enjoined.
>
> No. As with the unprecedented result (*apūrva*) of a new moon sacrifice, this command is restrictive with respect to an unprecedented result for ritual action, and this is determinative of its meaning/purpose. For this reason what is enjoined is indeed to be undertaken.

When the texts say, "Personal study must be undertaken" (*svādhyāyo 'dhetavyaḥ*), it must be something new and without precedent that is enjoined. We learn that to study in a particular way leads to particular and salutary results. As the commentaries tell us, the goal is to study with an authorized teacher, as his authorized student. Ordinary activities, such as threshing rice, have a clear and commonsense goal, and whatever means lead to it serve the purpose. But here, apart from a Vedic injunction imbued with particular meanings, we would have no way of knowing the particular desired results and the path to them.

Whether *dharma* can really be known, however one studies, is the topic of the second case:

> Is *dharma,* the topic of reflective study, devoid of definition and of reliable means of knowing it, or is it equipped with both? This has now to be carefully thought through.
>
> Some say: What could be a definition of *dharma,* if it lacks perceptible form? There is doubt regarding whether there are any reliable means, since perception, etc., do not work regarding what is too distant (as is the transcendent *dharma*).
>
> No. Its form is understood by injunctive force. If there is a referent, then there can be a definition too. Hence, injunctive force is the reliable means, in this instance, for knowledge of *dharma.* What more need be said?

The subject matter of Mīmāṃsā is therefore the study of injunctions, detecting the actions they command and what is brought about by those actions.

Need injunctive force, such as takes the form of particular injunctions, be closely studied? Why not simply do what is commanded? It would seem then that injunctions are so very clear that no hard study is required:

> It has been explained that the reliable means of knowledge that makes *dharma* known is injunctive force. Is this not to be examined—or is it to be thoroughly examined?
>
> Some say: If this reliable means of knowledge is taught explicitly, then the object of knowledge is clear. What then the need for inquiry?

The answer is brief, an appeal to tradition and to the very idea of what *mīmāṃsā* as a form of study is:

> Not so. This is a tradition of reflective study, so how could inquiry be neglected?

Readers are asked to turn aside skepticism, so as to undertake the necessary work at hand. There are many precedents for the arduous study of injunctions, and this is a tradition that can hardly be overturned. What

Mādhava might have added is simple: work your way through the nine hundred cases to follow, and you will understand the need for this study!

That there is no other way to know *dharma* than by study of injunctions is worked out in the next cases. The fourth case asks how *dharma* is to be known:

> Is *dharma* known by perception, etc., or only by injunction?
>
> Some say: Because the senses are reliable means of knowledge any *dharma* that is knowable can be perceived.
>
> No. The eye has as its sole object what is present, while *dharma* is that which comes to be (through acts of sacrifice). Inference and other reliable means of knowledge too depend on the senses. But *dharma,* as action, is known solely by injunction.

But the fifth case gives Mādhava, following Jaimini, a chance to argue the value of reading injunctions in context:

> But is injunction not informative, or informative?
>
> Some say: It is not, since the application of its powers to the extraordinary *dharma* is too difficult.
>
> No. The application of its powers works regarding *dharma* when *dharma* is taken in context.
>
> To conclude: That injunction is informative and a reliable means of knowledge is settled, since nothing is lacking.

Again, the focus is on reading: there is no other way to know *dharma* than to study the text.

The sixth, seventh, and eighth cases deal with the authority of words, sentences, and the Veda as a whole. Here Mādhava turns to the second set of questions raised already by Jaimini. Is it possible to think that words, ordinary or Vedic, are reliable, rather than merely human conventions?

> Are the words used in injunctions, etc., changing or imperishable?
>
> Some say: Changing, because words are formed of letters, and thus we see their origin in letters (and not in eternal speech).
>
> No. Due to the force of the unconflicted recognition, even these letters are unchanging. They are inflected merely in the effort to communicate, but they have no origin.

Second, aren't sentences merely conventional?

> Is a Vedic sentence not a reliable means of knowledge, or is it?
>
> Some say: It is not a reliable means of knowledge, because there is a need for a particular and conventional interconnection among its words,

> and so we rule out the notion that this is settled without any need for further context, etc.
>
> No. Regarding the meaning of the sentences of the Veda, there are not, as in ordinary speech, further particular interconnections that need to be apprehended. Hence, its sentences are independently a reliable means of knowledge.

Third, aren't whole Vedic texts merely humanly composed groups of sentences?

> Are Vedic texts human or not?
>
> Some say: They are human, because such texts have authorial names—Kāṭhaka, etc.—and because the Veda is composed of sentences, as are other texts.
>
> No. Those names are the names of teachers (Kaṭha, etc.), so the notion that these are ordinary texts should be ruled out. There is no evidence of authors, and hence we conclude that they are not humanly made.[15]

All these cases are elaborated by Mādhava beyond the minimalist statements of the *Sūtras,* but in a verse form that adds as few words as possible. I have found, and hope my readers may agree (now or after some further slow rereading of the cases), that we are gradually getting to the heart of things—the *reason* for decisions long established in tradition.

By further study, there will be almost no end to what one can learn by studying the *Garland.* It is brilliant in the economy of what it does say and also in what it leaves out, since deciding on inclusions and omissions requires a decision about what matters most in the tradition. An adornment—indeed, a garland—for Mīmāṃsā, the *Garland* is also one of the very best introductions to Mīmāṃsā in its completeness and actual practice.[16] It is brief enough that it makes possible a comprehensive study of and engagement with the *whole* of the Mīmāṃsā, in a way no other text does. It is written in such a way that through the words of its carefully crafted verses, readers can learn to think accordingly.

We can now cautiously generalize. The *Garland* also achieves a goal surely unanticipated by Mādhava: it affords to the truly outside readers some access to a vast body of knowledge and ways of thinking through and about that knowledge, not by mastery of the whole, but by the gleaning of insights that find meaning precisely at difficult points in text and practice. The price to be paid, however, is working it through, case by case. Readers must keep at it, persisting in taking up the cases in order to understand them. Practice matters.

But Who Wants to Learn Such a Dharma? A Productive Crisis

Thus some first examples from Mīmāṃsā. More follow in chapter 3, which is dedicated to the way our great texts instruct us. For now, though, I wish to make a different point. This very appreciation for the *Garland's* case reasoning made me realize how it was necessary also to move beyond the *Garland* to other examples. Greater than the issue of the complexity within traditions is the challenge of the complexities—ambiguities, seeming contradictions, unruled terrain, and so forth—among traditions, beyond the particular comprehensive worldviews of each. Here the set of possible readings becomes overwhelming. Such learning requires us to slow down a great deal, to ponder what it means for us to study one text, and then with a certain freedom of the imagination to move to the second, and the third, and so forth, patiently traveling a path that does not allow for skipping ahead and leaving things out. There are so many texts available for our learning—more than enough to occupy any given community of interreligious scholars for their lifetimes and beyond.

Yet the prospect of ever more deep and slow learning provokes a dilemma: so much learning, so wonderful, so immediate to the genius of a religious culture so distant in time and space—definitely worthy of a book—but for whom? Granting that such learning is available to those willing and able to do the work of acquiring it, and granting that this acquisition surely changes deeply how one thinks about ancient India and its continuing Hindu traditions, what are the prospects that more than a very few people might read such a text, or the book about it that I thought I might write? And then go on to read other such texts? That almost all readers lack the interest and probably the patience to read *Garland* is not surprising. But what if the wider human community loses hold of its classic sources and becomes unable and uninterested in reading the great texts of philosophy and theology?

This came to appear to me as the more important dilemma, and accordingly *Reading the Hindu and Christian Classics* could no longer be a book just about the *Garland*.[17] Convinced of the necessity of learning from more than one tradition, I have pondered how to present and justify reading in several traditions, not according to historical influences or according to large themes, but lining up the texts as cases that now follow upon one another, their differences as well as their similarities made obvious. Shortly I will introduce the set of six texts that count as the cases to be worked through one after the other in this book.

Widening My Horizons: A Young Catholic's Catechism

How to move beyond the *Garland* without forgetting it or the lessons learned from it turned out to be an intuitive path, step by step finding my way into the current project and the six books we read here. Reflecting on the *Garland* unearthed childhood memories. Though new to me, it reminded me of things old and familiar. The notion that a text has instructive force and was intended to "get inside" the heads of students, to form them intellectually and morally, was not new. I am a child in 1950s New York, and my Catholic grammar school education guaranteed that I would be well versed in the catechetical instruction of the pre-Vatican II Church. This learning, deeply inserted into our minds, and in some preliminary way understood, was achieved by the mastery of questions and answers by repetition, memorization, and recitation. As appropriate to our age and year in school, we were given the smaller, intermediate, and (in the end) still greater catechisms. For the youngest, things began simply, with great questions taken up in a simple manner:

> *Is there only one God?* Yes, there is only one God.
>
> *How many Persons are there in God?* In God, there are three Persons—the Father, the Son and the Holy Ghost.
>
> *What do we call the three Persons in one God?* We call the three Persons in one God the Trinity.
>
> *How do we know that there are three Persons in one God?* We know that there are three Persons in one God because we have God's word for it.[18]

We memorized such answers to such questions. We repeated the answers aloud and in unison in class, and we were repeatedly quizzed, expected to get the words exactly right. I remember mainly the memorization and tests, but I suppose that the good sisters in my Catholic grammar school also tried to get us to understand and assent to what we were memorizing. The whole process was a mixture of the dull and the intimidating and at first glance was unlikely to stimulate fresh thinking even on the doctrines that were taught. But as catechesis instilled Church teachings into my young mind and memory, also inculcated was the idea that the ultimate truths were complex but always harmonious if understood within the life and practice of the Church. This was a serious and solid grounding, on the basis of which I could later proceed from the Catholic to a host of other orthodoxies found globally.

My Catholicity did not depend entirely on the catechism. Such books only reflected the larger life of the Catholic community. Outside of school, too, Catholic life was envisioned to be all of a piece, even amid the changes already sweeping the Church and world in my grammar school years (1956–1964), and despite scandals and abuses seething and rotting beneath the surface in those days. Being a practicing Catholic shaped religion, culture, and individual life. Even politics and engagement in public life were expected to grow out of the dense particularity of Catholic practice and the Catholic way of seeing things. The catechism worked because it was an articulated marker of a whole Catholic way of life. It was not merely a book about what Catholics believed, but rather a basic articulation of a larger whole. Mādhava would understand this, and although his *Garland* is in many ways unlike a catechism, it too functioned within community and as memorized made possible a whole way of life. It seemed timely to me, early on in the writing of this book, to read after and with the *Garland* a great Catholic work of instruction. And so, in chapter 3 we study for a time the greater *Catechism* (*Catechismus Maior*) of Peter Canisius (1521–1597), the Jesuit theologian, preacher, and popular writer.

This is an apt choice because of the immense learning behind it, and because of its pedagogical intention: instruction by question and answer, mostly depending on familiar texts such as the Lord's Prayer and Hail Mary, the Ten Commandments, and the Apostles' Creed. Striking too is Canisius's attention to audience; his *Catechism* appeared in Latin and German (and quickly, other vernaculars too), and in several greater and smaller versions. It is thus an admirable work of catechesis, the summation of a tradition, and writing eager to communicate truth in a most accessible form. As we read Canisius (very selectively), we will be particularly interested in how he condenses the teachings of the Bible and tradition into stylized questions and answers, each simple point supported by weighty sources from the Bible and tradition. After studying the *Catechism,* we return to the *Garland,* for a second and more sustained look at what it tells us, in the course of its cases, about the meaning and value of the human.[19]

Humbly Learning, but with a Skeptical Edge

A word of caution is required here. In the twenty-first century we cannot hold up as exemplary a sixteenth-century catechism (or a fourteenth-century Hindu manual), as if to fit ourselves smoothly back into its questions and its answers. Times have changed greatly, and the most committed scholars and the best teachers of religious education have found new and fruitful ways of teaching and passing down the faith in today's diverse world. We no longer accept the catechism in an uncritical manner.

Nor should we. Looking back now on the catechisms used in the 1950s and 1960s, I see better some of the sharp edges concealed there. Taken-for-granted right answers ruled out in advance other answers, new answers. Consider the teachings related to the first commandment, "I am the Lord your God, thou shalt not have strange gods before me." Stipulating that this forbids the worship of false gods (n. 198),[20] the instruction goes on, positively, to enjoin that we "worship God by acts of faith, hope, and charity, and by adoring Him and praying to Him" (n. 200). After instruction on these points (nn. 204–6), Catholics are admonished rather absolutely to safeguard the faith, "by making frequent acts of faith, by praying for a strong faith, by studying [their] religion very earnestly, by living a good life, *by refusing to associate with the enemies of the Church, and by not reading books and papers opposed to the Church and her teaching*" (n. 204) Conversely, one sins "*by apostasy, heresy, indifferentism, and by taking part in not-Catholic worship*" (n. 205), the last of these forbidden because the Catholic who does this "*professes belief in a religion he knows is false*" (n. 206)[21]

Taken by themselves, such strictures communicate a closed-mindedness and disregard that are simply unacceptable in the majority of Christian communities today. Sharp edges are necessary if we are to resist efforts to rob the faith of its vitality and deep value; but if we are not really aware as to what the edges are edges of—in the living community of faith that cannot divide itself entirely from the world around it—only the exclusion remains, sure and sterile. To set boundaries is necessary, but we must be wise and well-informed when we do so.

We are not far here from the dynamics of Vedic orthodoxy: sharp boundaries around a truly deep, rich, and vital well of truth and wisdom. Miss the wisdom, and the sharp edges will appear unthinking, cruel, and impossible to accept. My proposal here is to balance depth and conviction by a serious engagement in learning deeply and in a sustained fashion from another religion; the sharp edges of each make this both interesting and difficult, but in the end those boundaries cannot prevent learning that crosses beyond them.

Instruction, Doctrine, and Participation: Through Six Hindu and Catholic Classics

This book unfolds by the chemistry of my prolonged and painstaking reading of the *Garland,* as complemented by my remembrance of the catechetical study fundamental to my Catholic childhood. Reading the

Garland reopened for me the dynamics of learning catechism. The *Garland* now has a partner, the *Catechism.* By facing up to two slow-moving pedagogies, I found myself better prepared to learn newly and broadly across religious boundaries. This book as a whole is fueled by this particular chemistry.

As we study, we become more deeply rooted in the traditions to which we belong. But it is also true, and crucial to this book, to recognize that in the twenty-first century, this manner of instruction enables us also to engage in interreligious learning in a sophisticated manner, since it is those who remember the complexity and integrity of their own traditions who are better equipped to recognize and learn from religious others in similar depth. But the possibility and difficulty of such study also fuels my concern about the relevance of such instructive traditions in today's world and about our loss of the ability to learn in this way, slowly, patiently, and for the long term. Knowing only my own tradition or knowing no tradition at all are gloomy options if we wish to have a humane and spiritual future.

But we must be careful not to stop short, lest an emphasis on slow learning among many religions leave the impression that we need to care only about method and interpretation, as if slow learning is no more than character building: as if to say, read anything, just read it well.[22] Slow reading is indeed a virtue and a precious habit to cultivate, but it is not merely an end in itself. Content matters, and its truth confronts us. Claims about the world and its truth ought not be passed over. Catechisms are explicit in the statement of truths. The *Garland* is oblique, but it shows us in practice why the Veda, in its words and deeds, is always free of conflicts and ever the reliable source of the highest knowledge.

That is to say, slow learning is also a matter of truth, as we are tutored in truth in texts, truth in its doctrinal form. In chapter 2 then we move directly to the slow study of two great instructive and doctrinal texts, the *Collection of Right Perspectives on Our Position* (*Siddhānta Leśa Saṃgraha,* Sanskrit) by Appayya Dīkṣita (1520–1593) and *Sentences Articulated in Four Books* (*Sententiae in Quattuor Libris Distinctae,* Latin) by Peter Lombard (1100–1160).[23] Each of these classics of doctrinal theology aims at clarifying and teaching the consensus of its tradition and delving into it, enduring truth.

The *Perspectives* offers a doctrinal summary focused on issues key to the system of the *Sūtras* and the Advaita reading of the *Sūtras.* It confirms over and again the nondualist view of realities divine, cosmic, and human, yet with a striking equanimity it honors differing perspectives on each debated issue, such as can be noticed in the works of respected variant Vedānta thinkers. In the end, all of this is for the sake of a best final position. The texts are pedagogically sophisticated, so as to open up for us a wide set of issues of learning. But they also, beyond pedagogy, present and explain doctrine (as a way of writing and learning that is attentive to what is true and real) and truth (as the intended end point of communal study, opening into communal values). Even Mīmāṃsā ritual reasoning can be said to be doctrinal in a certain way, but its heir, the "Later Mīmāṃsā" better known as the Vedānta, very markedly moves from exegesis and meditative practice to assertions about the way the world really is and how knowledge of it radically changes how we live and understand our lives.

The *Sentences* is also voluminous, two hefty volumes in the Latin, four in the English translation. It too is still a kind of summary that makes it easier for students to find their way into the Catholic tradition. Indeed, Lombard himself indicates this when he expresses his intent to save readers the trouble of finding for themselves the texts pertinent to each topic. His arrangement of topics is clear; his choice of a few passages (*sententiae*) to support key points is judicious; he shows us a reasoning that is respectful of tradition and willing to listen; he does not claim to have the last word on any topic. Such virtues make the *Sentences* ideal for inclusion in this book-length meditation on tradition, its transmission and reception.

After reflecting in chapter 2 on learning that leads us into the truth of traditions, in chapter 3 I return to the instructive role of texts introduced in this first chapter, to further reinforce my reading of the *Garland* by the study of Canisius's *Catechism,* followed by further study of the *Garland.* I have already said enough for now about these two texts and can only add that I follow this convoluted path—from instruction (introduced in this chapter), to doctrine (in chapter 2), and back to instruction (in chapter 3) because I found that instruction and doctrine each precedes and follows the other. Instruction is a prerequisite for the learning and teaching of doctrine, while doctrine provides the frame in which instruction takes shape. Nevertheless, some readers may wish to move from this chapter to chapter 3 and only thereafter take up the matter of doctrine introduced in the intervening chapter.

Chapter 5 (I turn to chapter 4 in a moment) pushes matters further, by asking whether readers can actually come to participate in the reality that they learn in the reading. Slow learning that is instructive and open to truth in its doctrinal form, explained with respect to two traditions, might seem more than enough for one volume, but traditions are not content with instruction and doctrine: they seek also a change in the life of readers, their shift from spectators to participants in the reality of what is read. Participation follows upon instruction and doctrine. Chapter 5 is dedicated to that issue of participation, by the study of a third and final pair of texts.

To highlight the matter of participation, I have once again drawn on childhood memories, by turning to the Catholic tradition of the rosary: the fifteen mysteries and accessory prayers that cover the entirety of the faith in short form; the compacting of the elements of faith into a prayer of Mary that is to be recited, preferably aloud and ideally with other devout Catholics; the fingering of beads; and all this for an affirmation of the faith by one's own heartfelt and often public testimony. Given the nature of the rosary—the same few prayers many times over—I found it would be more useful to reread the praying of the rosary though a text that seeks to inspire its readers to that prayer: the *Admirable Secret of the Most Holy Rosary* (*Le Secret Admirable du Très Saint Rosaire*, French) by Louis Grignion de Montfort (1673–1716). This is a practical work—instructive, homiletic—that above all encourages praying the rosary. It does so in part by arguing intensely that the rosary contains in itself everything essential to Catholicism in doctrine and practice. Montfort seeks to move beyond getting the readers to understand. He wants to touch the heart and conscience of the readers, so as to get them to take up the rosary and pray in a way that is all the more intense because the *Admirable Secret* has disclosed the great depths of the prayer. Reading Monfort's text leaves readers with a particular question: Why don't I follow his advice and pray the rosary each day?

I grew up in New York, and to my knowledge no one in my circle knew anything about Tamil Śrīvaiṣṇava Hinduism, an ancient and living branch of south Indian Hinduism that has flourished for over one thousand years. But it has its place in my store of memories, since I have been studying it for decades, nearly as long as I have studied Mīmāṃsā. It is also a most fascinating religion. It sees itself as heir not only to the great Sanskrit tradition that includes Mīmāṃsā and Vedānta, but also to the vernacular Tamil tradition of the poet saints known as the *āḻvārs* (those "immersed" in God). More often than not, we find that the Tamil writings are more affective and emotionally intense, appealing to the heart, asking the listeners (readers) to get involved in what they are studying. Interested once again in how traditions summarize and distill the mysteries of the faith, here too I looked to works meant to summarize but also impart the mystical power of Śaṭakōpaṉ's *Holy Word* (*Tiruvāymoḻi*), considered the most important of the sacred works of the tradition.

I have found in Śrīvaiṣṇavism my sixth case, a passionate Hindu text of devotion that prizes participation as core to its very meaning and message: the *One Hundred Linked Verses on the Holy Word of Mouth* (*Tiruvāymoḻi Nūṟṟāntāti,* Tamil) by Maṇavāḷamāmuni (1370–1450). Its form is admirably intense, as it reduces the 100 songs and 1,102 verses of the *Holy Word* to 100 verses that imitate the style of the *Holy Word,* probably the most important scripture of Śrīvaiṣṇavism, in order to delve into its deepest meanings, while yet preserving the performative element—it is to be sung with a vulnerable heart and mind, so as to be drawn into the *Holy Word* itself, to which it defers as the real destination.

The Odd Sextet

After first stumbling upon the *Garland* and its hidden treasures, I had then various reasons for selecting the ensuing five texts:

The Garland of Jaimini's Reasons
The Collection of Right Perspectives on Our Position
The Sentences Articulated in Four Books
The Greater Catechism
The Admirable Secret of the Most Holy Rosary
One Hundred Linked Verses on the Holy Word of Mouth

With instruction, doctrine, and participation in mind, I chose texts that I have found able to represent ably the pertinent strengths of their traditions, and with the goal of succinct presentation of the essentials. By the *Garland* and the *Catechism,* we are instructed; through the *Perspectives* and the *Sentences,* we learn doctrine; immersed in the *Admirable Secret* and the *Linked Verses,* we become participants. By the fact of their presence individually and together, they instruct, teach, and invite, and in different ways. Read together, the six foster the difficult work of learning deeply in a tradition, and then across the boundaries of traditions. They refine one another, even as contraries that, upon reading, force us to go back and reread what we thought we had already finished with.

Reading the Hindu and Christian Classics is therefore a departure from the kind of comparative theological learning I have undertaken on occasion in the past, as in my *Hindu God, Christian God: How Reason Helps Break Down the Boundaries between Religions.* This current book moves forward more slowly, clearing a path that must remain ill-defined because of my refusal to allow theory to predict before or apart from reading the route to be taken or destination reached. It offers a set of stepping stones in a dark, slippery space: each text is near enough to the ones before it and after it that readers can move along, a step at a time, without stopping, even if always in balance. At a disadvantage, we are also prevented from leaving the texts behind for the sake of shared themes readily found in all of them. And so: while I refer to comparative theology only rarely in these pages, the entirety of *Reading the Hindu and Christian Classics* may be taken to be an assertion of the fundamentals of comparative theology. This occurs not by way of a disquisition on its presuppositions or some theology of religions, but by enacting the work of reading texts that best underlies such projects. Not all comparative theological work needs to be textual, but even if one turns to ritual practice, or images, or even religious experience, there will be no quick way around the same unrushed and slow process of learning that is attentive to instruction, doctrine, and participation, positioned in one way or another.

I insist that my list of six books makes eminent sense to me. But I will not be shocked if readers still think, "What an odd list! Surely they don't belong together!" The larger differences—in language, culture, genre, doctrine, purpose—may be apparent already to those familiar with Hinduism and Christianity in more general terms. Many smaller and actually more interesting differences among them will arise and become clear as we study the six texts, traversing their rough surfaces.

But commonality has not been the goal, nor reaching a conclusion that one can readily take away by peeking at just the last few pages of this book. Rather, my point has been to collect six good cases for study, each instructive in itself, and yet cumulatively providing greater illumination for *readers* who stick with the work of slow learning. Such readers will have to strain their mind in understanding the complexities and subtleties of the case—before then moving on to another case, and another. The roughness of the comparisons provides the footholds by which we find our way forward, case by case, in the pages of this patient act of study.

Improbable companions, taken together they find their own distinctive chemistry. Such is the chemistry at the heart of this book, the constitution of a nearly infinite canon of texts, where religious readers can read, reflect, meditate, write, and teach—over and again, just one or two at a time, for the sake of an expanding matrix of insights that open into religious truths and enable willing readers to participate in what they read. All of this will best occur in the course of the reading itself, but in each chapter's concluding pages and at the book's end I take time to reflect on where I think we are in the work we have undertaken together, author and readers.

As I completed the final version of this book, all six texts were continually in my mind, everywhere exerting themselves. Two traditions of instruction hold their central place in my memory, thinking ritually and attending to catechesis. These keep affecting how I think, read, teach. Because I have studied medieval classics of doctrinal theology (and not because I have a better theory, as if I were a theological pluralist), I now hold two strong traditions of truth in my mind at the same time. Because

I have read two great devotional works of synthesis and intense focus, I feel strongly the tug (though not necessarily in different directions) of two invitations to participate, a Catholic call to praying the rosary and a Śrīvaiṣṇava call to share passionate songs evocative of still more passionate songs. This learning bears its own spiritual as well as intellectual cost; the "slow" in "slowing learning" can be primarily a form of intellectual discipline, but it bears also a contemplative dimension, insight through and in deep reading, by which without haste and without hesitation we also cross over to another, near tradition, perhaps unable really ever to find our way back again.

For all of this to work, readers must cultivate a certain indifference to what they might ordinarily want to know first. Our texts are not directly interested in or illuminative of what we would consider ordinary human experiences and human meanings, such as are so evident to us each day. Today we are also tempted to think of the scriptures and the great texts of traditions as "just books," just one frame of reference in a much larger world. But our authors—and I agree with them here—thought that scripture and tradition encompass and structure reality even as we experience it. To study the great texts carefully is not to leave the world behind, as if to hide in the library. It is rather to reenvision the world within the frame of what we read, the world from, in, through the book.

Reading Then, Reading Now, Reading All

It is worth saying a bit more now on this most important point, given the laudable but sometimes exaggerated tendency of many today to get outside of texts, into "the real world." Philipp Rosemann's exploration of medieval Christian learning practices shows us the way.[24] He notes particularly the extraordinarily patient and prolonged dedication to study and the conviction that patient reading was a way to gain insight into the world itself.[25] Behind this commitment, he shows, was also an understanding of the singleness of reality, the world, things, and the words about them, cohering in a way that is not entirely other than, or competing with, emerging scientific views of the world. There are not separate truths inside and outside texts, nor are texts places of refuge for those fleeing the harder realities of any given era. Rather, indeed, study shapes the world in which any and all kinds of knowledge might be received:

> Tell me how you read, and I shall tell you who you are. In the medieval monastery, following the recommendations of St. Benedict's Rule, reading was one of the principal activities. First of all, the day of the monks was of course structured by the rhythm of the liturgy, in which the rec-

> itation of the *Psalms* was central. Yet even outside the chapel—and, as Dom Leclercq notes, in some monasteries there was little life outside the chapel, for the liturgy occupied almost the whole day—the monks read or listened to readings in the refectory, as well as during hours of study and meditation. This *lectio divina,*[26] "divine" reading or reading as part of a greater quest for God, not only pervaded most aspects of the lives of the monks; it was also of a different quality than the kind of reading to which we have come to be accustomed.[27]

In that milieu, "the author is therefore less a controlling, mastering 'subject' than a being 'subjected' to the text that *lectio divina* has inscribed in his mind and body." Instructed by study, authors and readers, teachers and disciples, all learned to learn differently, refraining from "imposing a more 'logical' structure upon (the world)" such as might be derived in obedience to an a priori consideration of the divine, the human, the world, etc. The best readers were those who deferred to the text, because it is "the Word of God, and the texture of reality; it cannot be manipulated at will. The monk attempts to copy the book of Scripture, first in his own body and soul, and then in the books that he himself eventually produces. Hence, in the monastic culture of the Middle Ages, writing is an extension of reading. . . . Moreover, this writing, which is always a rereading, is an ethical, even religious activity."[28] From there, such readers might move at liberty in worlds literally and metaphorically removed from the contemplative spaces of study, but without the pretense of neutrality in the face of other lineages of learning. Wherever we learn, the study we have done shapes our dispositions in those new sites.

But Rosemann is no romantic. He is candid about the decline of the monastic model of study, which could no longer handle early modernity's explosion of new knowledge. We too need honestly to review and assess the resources now available to us, to see how and when the latest technologies both aid and distract us from the careful study we require for an interreligious literacy that is deep and not just broad. We need to recognize the medieval roots of our modern uncertainties as well as of many enduring values:

> The masters of High Scholasticism (who had to deal with many more pagan texts than their monastic counterparts) read their sources less intimately, less holistically. In their new reading techniques, with their increased sense of privacy and "mastery" over the text, we can discern the seeds of many of the dualisms of modernity: the text versus the real, the individual versus the community, the body versus the soul. The seeds are sown, but their full development is as yet far away.[29]

In new eras of faster and more efficient learning, faced with a burgeoning array of new texts and therefore new, diverse questions, many found slow learning to be inadequate, indeed too slow:

> Not only did they have to give lectures and hold their own disputations on a wide variety of subjects; in doing so, they also had to confront the task of comparing the new Greek, Islamic, and Jewish sources in a systematic way with the Christian heritage, weighing up their merits and demerits, and finally harmonizing the diverse material in some way. This is, of course, what the *quaestio* structure was meant to facilitate. The bottom line is that, as a result of the university culture, reading had to become quicker (that is to say, silent) and more efficient, more systematic.[30]

This quicker, efficient, systematic reading was prone, in the wrong hands (let us say), to skipping over the in-depth study of the older texts; summaries, distillations, and more pointed questions and debate styles keep knowledge focused, digestible, but also replace the classic texts, excuse readers from reading the texts, and also deprive them of the many benefits of (re)learning the tradition in a traditional way.

Now, of course, I can hardly complain about efforts to compact and streamline study, for two obvious reasons. First, my six texts are themselves all instances of efforts to distill tradition to a compact and manageable form. Mādhava, Canisius, Dīkṣita, Lombard, Montfort, and Manavāḷamāmuni were all innovators, facilitators of quicker and more efficient learning. While we cannot get behind this new and revised learning, such as I have been valuing highly in these pages, we can think anew about what we are doing when we read summary texts of this kind. Rather than treating them as replacements for their respective older traditions, we need to see them as wonderfully focused entrées into the classics on which they draw. They are gateways, portals, not ends in themselves.

Second, *Reading the Hindu and Christian Classics* itself would make no sense as a book of some length, were its only point to urge readers to go back and read the six great texts of which I write as such great length. The originals are available, and reasonable substitutes for them can be recommended (see below); it would take but a page or so to give readers the necessary bibliographical information. Like some writers of old, I too am in the position of calling old texts to the attention of new readers. I too seek to make the case for a slower mode of study, traditional yet now multitraditional too. I too have sought to facilitate this old-new form of study by my own summaries, distillations, apt cases, and apt quotations, all for the sake of commending my book as a portal of sorts, a gateway, back into the greater literatures of our increasingly interwoven pasts.

If we are mindful of the constructive role that every instance of new writing plays, we can be more confident about what we are and are not doing. It was a losing cause for a fifteenth-century scholar to lament the invention of the printing press as a death blow to true learning, and we cannot merely retreat to the familiar forms even of mid-twentieth-century reading practices. Today we can gather texts ever more quickly, acquire and employ resources helpful in the reading of texts, and, by fast search engines, etc., familiarize ourselves broadly with the great texts and their relevant contexts. The point is not to forego these advances but to use new technologies and to welcome the new ways of learning they make possible, even as seeds of a new dawning and global human consciousness, yet without unreflectively leaving behind the religious communities to which we belong. Of course, "I" cannot do this; religious communities in every tradition, working respectfully with scholars of every kind, need to build this exemplary library and, more importantly, work hard to provide students and younger scholars with opportunities and reasons for study that looks both back and forward at the same time.

Seeking the Right Readers: A Most Democratic Elitism

Certainly, these six texts would not be the first choices of most Catholics or most Hindus. They are difficult: serious, meticulous, subtle, and in some case more than a bit boring, too. Daunting, they need to be read over and again. Even if, as summations of their traditions, they greatly reward the effort we put into reading them individually and then together, they are not reference works, in which to look up this or that point. Nor are they in the class of revelatory texts, which are often most appealing, even if our six authors are at least students in lineages that reach back "to the beginning." But we can see in them, in process, the path from revelation and from the intense and deep learning of revelation to careful and elegantly stated instances of instruction, lucid articulations of doctrine, and intense appeals for participation. Reading them takes work, and as a kind of messenger for such texts, *Reading the Hindu and Christian Classics* is likewise for those willing to read slowly and patiently, for the sake of long-term results. It is not merely words that praise slow reading, but an instance of that slow reading in practice.

Second, this book is elite in the sense that it will attract readers who self-select, because they share my recognition that so much needs to be learned, and they recognize that becoming the kind of person able to do such reading often requires a reordering of values and time commitments. Aware of the urgency of the underlying issues—the need for both great depth and audacious breadth in learning—such readers are willing, and with patience become able, to enter upon the slow learning that is a singular way forward.[31]

Third, it is elite in the sense that it is also selective, marked by its omissions as well as its choices. Much is excluded for practical reasons that cannot, in the long term, be overlooked. My texts are by privileged male authors, respected figures who, within their communities, held places of honor. Hearing them, a worthy venture, means however that other voices are missing, the voices of men and particularly women left silent and ignored in the eras when these texts were written. I cannot deny the limits of this project in this regard. But while the texts stand within certain narrowed confines, and in other books need supplement, we can and will still read them according to our more diverse interests. There are many new angles that persistent and committed contemporary readers bring to old texts, and these new vantage points will necessarily disrupt the relatively enclosed worlds our authors imagined.

In these pages I wish to honor the six great books I take up for study, commending them for slow reading, patiently extended for as long a time as necessary. But by its comparative angle, by a persistent interreligious reading that none of our authors would have anticipated or welcomed, I also hem them in, reading them as they have never been read before, now as shelved in an incipient interreligious and theological library. I honor both the Hindu and Christian theological traditions greatly in this book, but neither by itself has the final word. I will be glad if committed readers bring still other unsettling perspectives to bear on these texts—for instance, by drawing in other, quite different texts in the same traditions, or noticing alternative views, perhaps silenced in these traditions, that go against what our texts set forth as true, instructive, and worthy of readers' participation.

Substitutions

Kind readers may appreciate the preceding exegesis and defense of elite, select learning. They may concede that these texts are indeed worthwhile. But they may also complain that they still require far too much time or take up space on a small library shelf that other books too deserve. But this book allows for substitutions, even invites them. My hope also is to inspire readers to do as I have done, in five ways: first, to search the bookshelf and the library for some long-cherished and still unread classic, simply read it and see where that reading leads; second, to be willing to be instructed by what we read, even if it means deferring for a time the urgent questions of our day; third, to encounter the truth of what we read, our modern presuppositions and habits challenged by venerable truths that are still true; fourth, to imagine at least what it means to undergo a conversion of life, so as to come to participate in the reality that the texts confess; and fifth, in the spirit of this book, to read in one's home tradition, but also, because of that learning, in at least one other as well. In chapter 6, I suggest some possibilities from elsewhere in the Christian and Hindu traditions that are simpler and easier starting points in what can turn out to be a lifelong habit of slow and deep learning.

How Wittgenstein Teaches Us to Read Slowly

I turn finally to chapter 4, skipped over in the just concluded review of the book's plan. This chapter serves as an interlude dedicated not to any of my six texts, but to reflection on how Ludwig Wittgenstein (1889–1951) wrote his *Philosophical Investigations.* I do not make this chapter-length detour because my project claims in an important manner to be "Wittgensteinian" or an instance of "slow reading after Wittgenstein." Nor do I consider the *Investigations* to be a great religious text. Two more modest reasons inspire this pause and reflection placed between the third and fifth chapters.

First (and to say what I hope will make more sense a hundred pages from now) the *Investigations* has always struck me as resonant with the interpretive particularity and minimalism of Mādhava's *Garland.* Wittgenstein is not a Mīmāṃsā thinker, but he interestingly (under)writes like one. Both Mādhava and Wittgenstein show little interest in historical arguments and retrievals; proceed by particular cases; rarely generalize, lest readers be tempted to skip over further cases; group cases according to resemblances, extensions, and exceptions that, if the roughness is put up with, turn out to inculcate also skill in traversing them; engage readers beginning to end and then dare those readers to start over again. After all, the *Investigations,* seemingly and fortunately impossible to summarize, benefits us only when we put aside ordinary philosophical expectations and settle down to read it slowly, page by page.

Second, I have always considered Wittgenstein to be an ally in comparative study, even if I have rarely referred to him in my writing.[32] His way of proceeding usefully illumines what I am doing in chapters 2 and 3, particularly with respect to the pedagogical value of the slow pace of writing he imposes upon us so that we have no alternative but to read him. He avoids the kind of speculation that prefers large and abstract ideas and that keeps its distance from specific cases and the problems particularity provokes.

Much of our (interreligious) worry and confusion dissipates if we put aside large questions arising from outside the practice of interreligious learning and instead keep at the work of study, paying attention to what we learn step by step from the religions around us. Wittgenstein stays with the particular; lavishes attention on minute and seemingly trivial examples; accumulates a storehouse of such examples; distracts us by changing the subject, just when everything seems running smoothly; writes so as to insure that meaning becomes accessible only to those who read slowly. In a way that Mādhava would understand (other variables aside!), Wittgenstein patiently and persistently puts aside large and seemingly irresolvable questions—on how language relates to reality, for instance—because he believes that attention to what we actually say and do supplies us with all we need to know. In a similar way, the readings that make up the following chapters rarely address directly matters related to interreligious dialogue or the project of learning from another tradition. But every page is an example of how this learning proceeds with this particular combination of texts.

TWO

Words of Truth

Reading and Writing Doctrine (Twice Over)

More than Instruction: From Catechesis to Doctrine

When religious people read slowly and deeply in their own tradition, thinking alertly but with an openness to the mysteries of faith, they are formed, even transformed, by that learning. They find a balance between tradition and the present moment, scriptural words and new words freshly written, the individual path alongside a freely chosen submission to an older and more encompassing wisdom. Such dispositions learned with respect to a home tradition recommend that such persons act similarly in reading another tradition with a similar intellectual openness and reverence for the faith of its authors and the wisdom they have appropriated.

Here too slow learning is key. As great religious texts instruct, they make claims on readers by communicating the truth of the tradition in clear, unencumbered terms. Readers within a community and from outside it who are willing to read slowly and properly are led deeper into a body of truths that has been passed down over the centuries, reasserted with clarity and in keeping with authoritative scriptural and traditional sources restated in accord with the needs of changing times.[1] The pedagogical concerns introduced already in chapter 1 (and to which we return in chapter 3) remind us that truth needs to be taught properly, so that it can be understood and appropriated by communities and individuals, with due deference to the authority of teachers as key to learning, even if today no teacher ought to want or expect unreflective, blind assent. All of this is to insure that the encounter with truth, in the words of doctrines, is not unduly reduced to what seems true to readers in the current moment. This chapter then is about learning truth through study, through the slow and intelligent learning of doctrine, guided by a master in a first and then in a second tradition.

To say that we learn the truth by study is not as myopic as might seem. Rather, I am thinking of truth as it comes to us in deep dependence on certain texts that we read: truth manifest inside texts, but not cut off from the world or reduced to words about words, as if merely an unending row of interpretations. Properly written doctrines lead us along word's narrow path, into truths greater than what can be said about them. Using words, not abandoning them, they guide us into mystery, heard now in its doctrinal form according to a long tradition of learning. Speaking of truth—and writing it—stands in a middle position between rigid formulations and insights undisciplined by a tradition's grammar. Truth in its doctrinal form offers a place for slow, gradual apprehension through prolonged study. By such study, students learn to see the world in a particular way, use words about it in the right way, and affirm that view and that usage to be correct and true.

It is true, of course, that we should not make too much of words, deafly reducing the mystery of God to the words we speak regarding it. Traditions would rot from within were their truths to depend on the abilities of theologians to write of doctrines persuasively or hierarchs to insure their vitality in living communities. But we would hardly be better off were we to decide that words are optional with respect to our encounter with truth—as if silence not only enhances (as it surely does) the work of study here and now but replaces it altogether (as it surely does not, exceptions notwithstanding). Finding the right balance—an attentive and respectful reading that is both patient and humble—is at the heart of the slow reading process I have in mind, and it concludes in truth.

The texts that are most intellectually and spiritually alive are those able to direct our attention to truth, without themselves becoming obstacles. The theological texts most worth reading are therefore those written with both seriousness and humility regarding the limits of language. This learning cannot be rushed, since reflection and appropriation are necessary components of its practice. It is a lifetime in the making, and indeed it depends on the many lives of those willing to take it up over the generations.[2]

Learning Doctrine across Religious Borders

If the learning of doctrine is conceived of as a matter of study, slow reading, then that learning of the truth of my own tradition is not contrary to learning the truth of another tradition. We have not a clash of truths, but the several truths being learned more deeply, often alongside one another. As we make our way along the path of thinking-words-doctrine-truth in the tradition to which we belong, we learn better how to travel so as to make other such journeys as well. We begin more clearly to see another tradition in a closer approximation to its fullness and then to ponder the new situation, in which we remember and understand doctrine in two traditions at once. My goals here are practical. I do not wish to make a theoretical point about truth, nor to speculate on notions of two-truths, the distinction of the noumenon and phenomena, various forms of theological pluralism, etc., but only to stress once again a practical one about what we *do,* as we learn properly.[3] By study, we submit to the power of the truth in texts, learning how the truth has been accessible to those who study and come to understand claims of truth over centuries and millennia. Only later, after we have begun to learn doctrine several times over—as in this chapter, in a Hindu text and a Christian text—and in the proper way, will we become able to face up to doctrinal conflicts in a mature way where intimacy in learning is at the fore, not posturing from a distance. *The* truth is a still larger concern, of course, for entire communities; but concern for that truth cannot be so important as to thwart the learning that must take place first.

Reading Brahman, Reading Creation

But enough of preliminaries. We must return now to our primary task, the actual reading of specific texts. For this, I turn to two great teaching/doctrinal texts, Appayya Dīkṣita's sixteenth-century *Collection of Right Perspectives on Our Position* (*Siddhāntaleśasaṃgraha,* henceforth *Perspectives*)[4] and Peter Lombard's eleventh-century *Sentences Articulated in Four Books* (*Sententiae in Quattuor Libris Distinctae,* henceforth *Sentences*).

Appayya Dīkṣita (1520–1593) was a South Indian from near Kanchipuram (not far from today's Chennai). Though devotionally a Śaiva, he was expert across a wide range of disciplines and wrote commentaries and analyses with respect to several schools of thought, including Mīmāṃsā, Vedānta, and Vaiṣṇavism. The *Perspectives,* as is announced by its title, draws together various authorities whose positions count as "portions" (*leśa*) of the Advaita overall true position (*siddhānta*). Peter Lombard (1100–1160), a Roman Catholic theologian, was a longtime scholar and teacher in Paris who became the bishop of Paris for a brief time at the end of his life. In addition to writing the *Sentences,* he wrote commentaries on the Psalms and some of the letters of St. Paul.

Both authors are exemplary in the work of balancing reading with the recognition of and assent to truth, in continuity with tradition, achieved in the instance of the careful learning of individual readers. Both Dīkṣita and Lombard attend to truth in accord with the language of scripture and tradition, and not as above or beyond words.

Vedānta: The Complexity of a Very Simple Truth

We have already seen in chapter 1 some of the possibilities and limitations regarding generalization and doctrinalization in Mīmāṃsā, overall and with respect to select cases in I.1 and III.5. It would be possible, with some great effort, to extrapolate Mīmāṃsā and Vedic sacrificial doctrines from the practices operative in the *Garland,* but the result would be rather "artificial, since the mainstream of Mīmāṃsā thinking, grounded in the 907 cases found in the *Sūtras,* declines to pursue philosophical issues for their own sake and shows little interest even in a philosophy of sacrifice or theology of the transactions with deities. Turning to Dīkṣita's text, I look instead into the kindred school of Vedānta, which is rightly also known as the "Later Mīmāṃsā" (Uttara Mīmāṃsā) because it brings the hermeneutical principles operative in Mīmāṃsā to bear in the interpretation of the Upaniṣads. These are the later Vedic texts that draw out and emphasize the inner mysteries of self (*ātman*), the ultimate reality (*brahman*), and the practices of text-grounded meditation that leads to a higher realization of self as the ultimate reality, or inseparably interior to it. From this recognition, there follows liberation from the body and this world. They are focused, not on sacrificial practice, but rather on the identity and nature of the performer who is liberated from conventional ways of viewing the world and thus too reimagined in relation to much deeper and broader cosmic and divine realities.

More specifically still, I look into the rich and difficult Nondualist (Advaita) Vedānta school (henceforth Advaita), which defends a radical identification of self (*ātman*) and ultimate reality (*brahman*). Reality is one without a second, as the Chāndogya Upaniṣad teaches in its sixth chapter (VI.2.1) Advaita is most famously connected with the Vedānta teacher Śaṅkara and is enriched by a wealth of commentaries over the centuries after him and thus too by distillations of Vedānta teachings by scholars such as Dīkṣita.

Systematic in its intentions, and thus like Mīmāṃsā, Vedānta seeks to systematize, articulate, and defend an underlying unity to the Upaniṣadic teachings related to self, *brahman,* and world. In the background of all Vedānta theology lie the *Brahma Sūtras* of Bādarāyaṇa. Like Jaimini's *Mīmāṃsā Sūtras* introduced in chapter 1, these *Sūtras* presume a prior oral teaching tradition. They distill those teachings in accord with problematic issues arising in the tradition and, by doing so, facilitate further teaching of the whole of Vedānta mapped according to the plan of the *Sūtras.* The *Brahma Sūtras* open with four brief, programmatic, and rather dense statements (clarified a bit my parenthetical comments):

1. Now, then, the desire to know *brahman* (The topic of the whole inquiry)
2. That whence the birth, etc., of the world (A definition of *brahman*)
3. Because it is the source of the instructive scriptures[5] (The source of right knowledge)
4. It (can be known there) because of harmony. (The rule of inquiry)

Once it is established that *brahman* can be inquired into by way of a study of the Upaniṣads as text and meditative practice, the serious work of Vedānta proceeds by a network of topics arising in the ensuing four books:[6]

> (In the first book),[7] i. cases where there are clear indications of harmony (among all pertinent texts); ii. cases where, though there is a lack of clarity, (harmony can be) gleaned from the object of meditation; iii. cases where what is to be considered is the object of knowledge; and iv. cases where words alone are to be considered. Thus the order in the chapters.
>
> In the second book: i. non-contradiction by tradition or reason; ii. the faultiness of other views; iii. the noncontradictedness of the revelation regarding things (to be enjoyed) and the enjoyer; and iv. noncontradictedness among texts and indications.
>
> In the third book: i. cessation; ii. clarification of the meaning of the words *thou* and *that*, the reality of conscious beings and of the highest reality;[8] iii. the collecting of qualities (from multiple Upaniṣads for the sake of a single meditation); iv. the performance of the subsidiaries external to meditative knowledge, etc.
>
> In the fourth book: i. liberation of the living; ii. the northern path of ascent; iii. the attainment of *brahman*, and iv. the world of *brahman*.
>
> Thus the summary of the content of all the chapters.[9]

The *Sūtras*, understated as they are, stimulated and indeed required interpretations that were passed down in teaching traditions, orally and then in written commentaries that grew and complexified, as every set of further questions generated still more.[10]

Reading Vedānta Doctrine with Appayya Dīkṣita

Works of synthesis were required. There are many teaching texts in the Vedānta schools, manuals that synthesize teachings and present them in as economical a fashion as possible. If we stay just in the Advaita lineage, several come to mind immediately: Dharmarājādhvarīndra's *Preliminary*

Rules of Vedānta (*Vedāntaparibhāṣa*), highlighting interpretive rules; aiming as complete prose synthesis, the *Collection of Objects of True Knowledge in the Vivaraṇa* (*Vivaraṇaprameyasaṃgraha*) attributed to Mādhava, known later in his career by his monastic name, Vidyāraṇya; for the sake of epistemology and its metaphysical implications, the *Discrimination of the Seer and the Seen* (*Dṛgdṛśyaviveka*) often attributed to Bhāratītīrtha; and, by major theme, the *Fifteen Topics* (*Pañcadaśī*), in part at least by Vidyāraṇya; Bhāratītīrtha's *Garland of Vyāsa's Reasons* (*Vaiyāsikanyāyamālā*), in the same form as Mādhava's *Garland,* works through the sum total of cases argued in the *Brahma Sūtras* (often attributed to the prolific and mythic Vyāsa).[11] Each of these manuals has its merits, and with any of them one might begin to learn the doctrines of Advaita.

But given my interest in the quest for the irenic and authoritative summation of tradition with attention to its truth—and with an eye toward Lombard's *Sentences,* later in this chapter—in the end I settled on Dīkṣita's *Perspectives.* I found it to be a most apt text for study here because it elaborates doctrinal claims with the matrix of scripture, tradition, and reason; and it also convenes, by its lucid and inclusive style, a conversation of likeminded scholars who, though at times disagreeing with one another, respect and ponder the same truth that has come down to them. With a mix of complexity and simplicity, it draws us into a famously demanding—because it is counterintuitive—view of the world, radical nondualism: all is one. This formidable text—an introduction that runs hundreds of pages—shows us Advaita theology thinking aloud about itself, as it were. Dīkṣita takes up the larger issues debated in his tradition and surveys the range of differing respected positions, on the premise that all of them make a worthy contribution to Vedāṇta doctrine.

In his English preface to the Sanskrit edition of the *Perspectives,* S. R. Krishnamurti Sastri comments on the essential and great value of the *Perspectives:*

> The *Śāstra-siddhānta-leśa-saṃgraha,* a comprehensive and scholarly work of Śrī Appayya Dīkṣita, is a popular Advaita text. It is at once a digest and a source book of Advaita Vedānta. One should read Śrī Dīkṣita's *Śāstra-siddhānta* to appreciate the luxuriant variety of views, both profound and subtle, which have been expounded by Advaitins, who closely followed Śaṅkara, in vindication of the central teaching of Advaita. Śrī Appayya Dīkṣita's *Śāstra-siddhānta-leśa-saṃgraha* makes a comprehensive survey of the doctrinal interpretations and arguments as formulated by post-Śaṅkara Advaitins.

Although its title concedes its partial nature, the *Perspectives* is a successful summation that shows the breadth and diversity inherent in Advaita, as S. R. Krishnamurti Sastri suggests in his English-language preface to the Sanksrit edition:

> Though this work, as indicated by the title, is characterized as a *saṃgraha,* an epitome, (but) which (in this case) refers not to the whole, but only to a part or fragment (*leśa*) of the various views relating to the final position (*siddhānta*) of non-duality as taught by Scripture, it is much more than a compendium of the different view-points within the compass of Advaita. It is invaluable as it helps us, by a careful analysis of the issues involved, to distinguish one standpoint from another. The order of topics taken up for discussion and the sequence in which the different views on each topic are presented in this book testify to the range and depth of scholarship of Śrī Appayya.[12]

The importance of the *Perspectives* is attested to also by N. Ramesan. He places the *Perspectives* first among the Advaita works of Dīkṣita in terms of the right order of study and then comments on its importance: "This work is a very elaborate and original treatise written by Śrī Appayya Dīkṣita wherein he has gathered and brought together in one place, all different dialectical thinking belonging to the *advaitic* cult." Accordingly, "traditional scholars and students of *Vedānta* have a rule that they would start reading the *Bhāṣya*[13] only after they finish the *Siddhānta Leśa Saṃgraha.*"[14] These encouraging words affirm my intuition that the *Perspectives* is a very good place indeed to start learning Vedānta slowly and carefully.

Here is a detailed overview of key sections of the text, an overview that I have drawn from the table of contents in the Sanskrit edition of the *Perspectives* and in turn summarized in my own words. I follow the Sanskrit table of contents in giving fuller detail regarding the first book.[15]

FIRST BOOK:

> 1 *The injunction to study;*
>
> 2 *The definition of Brahman* with respect to birth, continuation, and dissolution;

Brahman, Lord, Individual Self:

> 3 Whether *brahman,* the undivided material and efficient cause, is the twofold cause in its pure form, or only in its form as Lord, or only in its form as individual self;

On *māyā* and ignorance (*avidyā/ajñāna*),[16] Cosmic and Individual Ignorance:

4 *māyā* as material cause; 5 the proper natures of the Lord and individual self; 6 whether the individual self is one or many; 7 if individual ignorance is multiple, questions regarding the oneness and manyness of the material expanse made by it;

Characteristics of *Brahman:*

8 That *brahman* is an agent; 9 that *brahman* is the all-knower; the nature of the world known by *brahman;* 10 description of conditions in accord with karma; 11–13 a closer examination of certain scripturally based technical terms

The States of Individual Ignorance:

14 The beginning or beginninglessness of ignorance in its various states; 15 that ignorance in those states is beginningless; 16 the restriction, "knowledge in general ends ignorance"; 17 the correction, "*direct* knowledge in general ends ignorance";

Consciousness as Witness:

18 The proper nature of the witness-consciousness; 19 whether the witness-consciousness is concealed; 20 the unconcealing of the bliss of the witness; 21 the plausibility of remembering the manifestations of the pure witness;

The Movements of Error:

22 The overcoming of the concealment that obscures reality, and the mental movement taking the form "this" as the cause for particular errors; 23 whether mental movements with respect to error are one or many; the purpose of the arising of erroneous movements of the mind.

SECOND BOOK:

In general: scriptural authority; perception in relation to scriptural authority; the contested compatibility of scriptural evidence and phenomenal evidence regarding nonduality and duality; the nonduality of *brahman* and the individual self; the nonplurality of individual selves.

THIRD BOOK:

The roles of knowledge and action in the attainment of *brahman.*

FOURTH BOOK:

> The removal of the remnants of ignorance, and the path to the liberation of each individual self and of all selves.

This is a daunting list indeed, and as such is only an outline of the detailed and subtle topics considered from multiple angles in the *Perspectives.* Dīkṣita has selected for consideration topics that are still open to debate in his time or, if largely resolved, worth relitigating for the sake of deeper learning of Advaita. Throughout, he takes seriously differences arising among respected Advaita theologians who were largely in agreement on other issues. These are differences arising inside this religious-intellectual community and not divisive of it. They point to multiple possibilities at least seemingly at issue in the Upaniṣadic texts, and that could not or should not be swiftly dismissed.

By working through each section of the *Perspectives* in turn, students are being taught to reflect on the individual truths of the tradition. The Upaniṣads, the scriptural sources, are presumably well known, at least in their relevant portions; and students will have learned already some well-known tenets of Advaita, at least in general terms. Here students focus on points where there is disagreement among the learned teachers who are still within the tradition and who hold views that merit attention rather than dismissal. The larger truth of Advaita can be taken as settled, but here Dīkṣita leads his readers through a variety of wise views that, even in their differences, help make manifest the truth as a whole. Sastri rightly observes that "every one of the views mentioned and discussed here has been championed by one or more Advaita theologians of great repute; and all of them have been formulated in consonance with the central thesis of Advaita, viz., that *brahman* is real, that the *jīva* in its essential nature is non-different from *brahman,* and that the world of plurality is illusory. It is open to anyone to prefer any particular view which is appealing and tenable to him according to his taste and judgement."[17]

Students are taught also how to see the individual truths in a sequence, each prepared for and preparing the way for others. Sastri notes too how Dīkṣita arranges the positions under consideration, each possessed of implications that prepare the way for the positions considered next and later:

> Śrī Dīkṣita does not always follow the chronological order in the presentation of the divergent views on each problem. The sequence of views that are presented here is more logical than chronological. The views are so arranged that there is a smooth transition from the one to the other. The

last point sheds light on the subtle inner workings of Dīkṣita's pedagogical writing, as he leads his students and readers through the complexity of Vedānta positions, each new topic in some way prepared for by the preceding, each earlier topic preparing the ground for those which follow.[18]

This is in itself a strong argument for reading the *Perspectives* in the way it was intended, start to finish, rather than as if it were a reference volume into which one can dip here and there for insights into topics of interest. The architectonic of the whole is instructive, and the several perspectives (the *leśa*) mean much more when read in the order given. The *Perspectives* is ideally a text to be read slowly, worked through, page by page, over as long a time as it takes to learn the whole of it: perhaps a year or two. Reading it beginning to end leads students through all the best positions on each topic, so that they appreciate all those views, even those that in the end are considered less persuasive.

In his own introduction, Dīkṣita locates himself in a dynamic, vital lineage of teachers that reaches back to Śaṅkara, the great nondualist commentator, and beyond him into the revelatory truth of the Upaniṣads. He uses the familiar and religiously evocative image of the sacred river arising at the feet of Kṛṣṇa (Śauri) and then dividing into many streams, all of which flow vitally insofar as they remain connected to the source:[19]

The sacred word, intent solely on the nonduality of *brahman,* ends all births.
It is victorious, arising from the auspicious lotus mouth of the revered Śaṅkara,
Like the river arising at the feet of Śauri and then dividing in many parts,
It first reached the great teachers whose views then divided a thousand ways.

Recognizing this differentiation of one truth into a plurality of perspectives on that truth fosters the coherence of tradition:

The ancients were intent on proving the oneness of the self and had no patience with worldly intents.
They put forth manifold paths, whereby differences in the true position took shape.
I gather them here in summary form, for the sake of the purification of mind,
Elaborating them according to the explanations of my father.

Dīkṣita sees himself as no innovator, but as simply one person in a longer lineage. He received from his father and the generations before him wise teachings that he then explained anew for his own readers.

Among them, I elaborate simply and by consensus those positions in need of explanation.
For this purpose, I write without extensive elaboration.[20]

Like Mādhava in his *Garland,* Dīkṣita sees his *Perspectives* as in fact simple and spare, saying just what needs to be said on pertinent topics. This is the case although it is a rather large book indeed. One measure: it is about three hundred pages long in its English translation. He is not giving an overview of Vedānta, but rather investing his energy just where it is needed, holding together points of consensus and difference in his tradition. His hope is that not only will dedicated readers learn truly to understand doctrines key to Vedānta in light of scripture and the best thinking of the best teachers, but also that such students will become an active part of tradition, receiving it, living by it, and passing it along.

Can Learning Be Commanded? An Initial Test

We saw in chapter 1 that the *Mīmāṃsā Sūtras* and consequently the *Garland* open with a consideration of *dharma.* As we have just seen, the *Brahma Sūtras* too begins by justifying the possibility of an inquiry, by study, into the mystery of *brahman.* There is a topic for investigation, *brahman.* Although it is the supreme, incomprehensible reality, it is neither impossible nor fruitless to undertake the work of close reading, since reason on the words of scripture—reasoning about what we learn from scripture—aids us in knowing *brahman* by way of disciplined, focused words in keeping with tradition.

The first section of the *Perspectives* looks deeper into the kind of learning appropriate to the task. It poses apt questions in a manner resonant with Mīmāṃsā's ritual manner of thinking, always in the background: does it do any good to command Vedānta's transformative knowledge? can a person be commanded to understand, or to be transformed through study? or can one at best merely give advice on the value of learning, and let the student, alone or with a willing teacher, decide the best way forward?

The text that occasions the debate is from the *Bṛhadāraṇyaka Upaniṣad:* "The Self, my dear, should be seen, should be heard, should be inquired into, should be deeply meditated on, Maitreyī. By seeing the self, hearing the self, by inquiring into the self, by discerning knowledge, all this is known." The announcement of the desire to study (the *jijñāsā* of the *Sūtras* I.1.1) is taken to imply this rich and deepening learning process. It is now further specified by a particular injunction, "One should study one's assigned portion (of the Vedas)," Mīmāṃsā's *svādhyāyo 'dhetavyaḥ*

("Personal study must be undertaken"), which we considered in chapter 1. What is the force of "must" here? Dīkṣita lists a number of opinions, which I now recount by summarizing the series of positions as stated in the Sanskrit table of contents to the Sanskrit edition of the work.[21]

First, simply and literally, "One should study" offers valuable information:

> 1 This is an injunction of a way of knowing that would not otherwise be known. This is the view according to the *Explanation of Clear Meanings* (*Prakaṭārtha-Vivaraṇa*).

But what is the method that is unknown, that needs to be found out? It is hard to detect which way of learning is unknown here, except perhaps what is the content of the portion assigned to any given student as his or her *svādhyāya*. So what could be enjoined? The next six views treat the injunction as ruling out familiar alternatives here judged to be inappropriate:

> 2a The injunction narrows the learning to a focus on *brahman* without qualities.
>
> 2b It rules out learning from other Vedānta schools.
>
> 2c It rules out ways of learning other than learning from the guru.
>
> 2d It rules out learning from books in languages other than Sanskrit.
>
> 2e It rules out learning from related books, such as epics, texts of mythic narrative (*purāṇas*), traditional texts (*smṛti*), etc. This is the *Vivaraṇa* view.
>
> 2f It rules out relying on yoga to learn the truth of *brahman* directly.

Or, it is a positive indication of the need for learning of a particular kind, which various schools identify in various ways:

> 3 The command restricts learning to study that is accompanied by thinking and meditating. This is the view of some in the *Vivaraṇa* school.
>
> 4 Lesser ways, appropriate to learning lesser things, are ruled out, since nothing but direct knowledge of self is the goal. Others hold this view.
>
> 5 It is a learning that, if accompanied by thinking and meditating, removes obstacles that cloud the underlying consciousness. Still others hold this view.
>
> 6 This is a knowledge that remains indirect and therefore inadequate to *brahman*, unless accompanied by thinking and meditating. Those

> following the teaching of (Sarvajñātman's) *Summary of the Vedānta* (*Saṃkṣepaśārīraka*) hold this view.

Yet another alternative finds at issue here the ruling out of any learning that, because it obviously serves a good purpose in ordinary life, need not be enjoined, and can be left to common sense:

> 7 Acts of ordinary learning unrelated to knowing the self and realizing *brahman* are ruled out, since these need not be enjoined. Those following the *Vārtika* hold this view.

Dīkṣita considers all of these views in turn, recounting each position and reasons for it. He is respectful of the premises of each regarding ways of learning that are relevant or not to knowledge of *brahman,* what is wise or unwise to say to students about yoga and about the vernaculars, etc. Throughout, his point is that there is no reason for an injunction on matters where common sense might suffice: one does not need a guru to learn grammar or Sanskrit or how to read a book. One can in fact learn much by private study of the Upaniṣads, from Sanskrit scriptures other than the Upaniṣads, from vernacular texts, and from personal experience. Even if yoga does not, according to Vedānta, give the required knowledge of the self, it is not prohibited by the Upaniṣad. Such can be apt ways of learning that in themselves are not contrary to the Upaniṣads. There is no need for a special injunction to rule them out.

The table of contents then states the eighth and final position at greater length, twelve full lines in the Sanskrit. Here is my summary of it:

> 8 That the self is nothing, but *brahman* can be learned by a careful study of the great Upaniṣadic sayings, learned according to the rules of Mīmāṃsā. Injunctions to know the self by studying such texts are commendatory statements that encourage the importance of this learning, yet without literally enjoining it. So there is no independent injunction of learning here. This view is in accord with the opinion of Vācaspati Miśra.

Since Dīkṣita does not stop here, we can surmise that this too is not his own position.

As he sees the matter, the remaining (and favored) view is that proper study is study done by a proper student with a proper teacher, and that this is what the Upaniṣad stipulates when it says, "It must be heard"—heard, that is, right from the teacher's mouth. The Upaniṣadic method is not entirely different from how people ordinarily learn, but here the intimacy of face-to-face discourse with a proper teacher is reinforced. What we have then is simply an injunction to learn directly from the teacher, regardless of whether other methods of learning are otherwise effective or not. Dīkṣita explains:

> Since there is no injunction regarding inquiry itself (since learning happens in many ways), what is enjoined is the approach to a guru for the sake of knowledge. When an obvious interpretation (of this sort) is possible, the assumption of a non-obvious interpretation is not fitting. So the point is that this inquiry culminates in knowledge, only when that knowledge is gained by way of reflection on Vedānta such as depends on the word of the guru. For that reason reflection accomplished by one's own effort is ruled out as not the appropriate subject for a command.

He reemphasizes the point:

> Granting that there is no injunction regarding proper ways to study, what is enjoined is the need to approach a guru for that study, The injunction cannot merely have to do with learning the letters of the words, which cannot be the point of an injunction. The injunction rather stipulates the manner of study: reciting in the manner first recited by the guru by his own mouth. This does not assert the exclusion of the study of written texts, etc. It is rather a restriction that makes known that learning by study with the guru is what is fruitful.[22]

The rule is strict, since most of the ways of study available to most of us—by reading, in translation, etc.—are put aside, not condemned but judged irrelevant with respect to the higher goals of Vedānta. Dīkṣita thus defends a quite traditional frame for Vedāntic learning: with a traditional teacher. In doing so, he narrows the body of students to the few people who have proper brahmin teachers because they have been deemed worthy by teachers who can be very selective about who they teach. Yet he is also offering a minimalist interpretation of the very strict injunction, since he acknowledges and does not denigrate all those other ways of study. This, I suggest, is the further point that Vedānta theologians today need to consider: What about all those other ways of learning Vedānta, particularly in a world where gurus are few and potential disciples widely scattered?

Dīkṣita concludes the entire discussion of the injunction to learn this way:

> Thus, because there can be no injunction of hearing (as simple learning), it is study of the portion of the Veda related to *brahman* that is the topic of the injunction to study (in this specific way, with the teacher), just as (in Mīmāṃsā) the proper study of the portion of the Veda related to ritual performance was enjoined.

Brahman *as (Not) Lord and (Not) Self*

Once this restriction is in place, further questions within the realm of Vedānta learning can be considered, and precisely by those who have become insiders because they have studied with teachers who allowed them to be their students. Dīkṣita is now able to think as honestly and incisively as possible about the issues arising within the strictures of tradition.

Let us turn to just a few examples of that teaching, as we read a bit further into the *Perspectives*. Mindful of the pitfalls hampering even the beginnings of study, we might now commit ourselves to the study of the whole of it, page by page, and readers who can do so will benefit greatly. Traditional students reading with traditional teachings will not need a book like this for the sake of that study, though here they would learn many things traditional learning cannot teach them. The rest of us will fall short of what the Vedānta tradition considers the normative manner of study and thus remain unable to achieve its fruits, but as with all our six texts, we find our way as we can, for the sake of some traditional fruits and some entirely new.

Specifically, we will examine how the *Perspectives* explores the self-lord-*brahman* relationship in the first book, in two sections entitled "Reflection on whether *brahman,* the undivided material and efficient cause, is such only in its pure form, or also by taking on the form of the lord, or also in the form of the individual self" (Book I, Section 3) and, "An inquiry into the proper forms of the lord and individual self" (Book I, Section 5).[23] And then we will double our learning by studying the doctrine of creation in the *Sentences,* in order to see how Peter Lombard thinks about the relation of the divine and the human. We begin to learn two doctrinal systems together, holding their truths next to one another, not because we think that to do so is a good idea, but simply because we must do so, because we have studied both together.

In Book I:3, Dīkṣita considers seven different views of the relation of *brahman,* the lord (*īśvara*), and the individual self (*jīva*). Each view is an attempt to make necessary distinctions without endangering the principle of nonduality or entirely ruling out basic conventions of ordinary speech. "Lord" and "individual self" are to be understood as utterly non-different from *brahman,* but in a way that does not empty the two words of all meaning. A further complication, which contributes to both the problem and its solution, is repeated references to a cosmic material reality (*mūla prakṛti; māyā*). In a nondualist frame this can only be *brahman* "outside" itself as the world's underlying material cause: neither a separate reality nor merely matter evolving by its own rules. Here too I turn to the Sanskrit table of contents to give an overview of the seven positions:[24]

1. An exposition according to the view of those adhering to the *Summary of the Vedānta:* since, at *Brahma Sūtras* I.1.2, pure *brahman* alone is the referent of this statement[25] and thus indicated as primary, then it follows that to *brahman* alone can the material causality of the world be attributed.

2. A second view, though not contrary to that of the *Summary of the Vedānta,* is that of those belonging to the *Vivaraṇa* school: *brahman*-consciousness alone is the material cause, but it takes the form of a lord who has the qualities of omniscience, etc. As such, it is distinguished as a reflection (of *brahman*) and in the form of a conditioning factor (*upādhi*) of *māyā.*[26]

3. The exposition of the view of those arguing difference between *māyā* (cosmic reality of *brahman* outside itself) and the ignorance (of the individual): the lord alone is the material cause of the evolution of the cosmic elements, the air, etc., which are transformations of *māyā.* But both the lord and the individual self are the material cause of the inner faculty, etc., because they have entered inside those. Lord and self are thus the substrate of the subtle elements that are transformations of the individual self's ignorance. But these are in turn founded in the cosmic elements that are transformations of the lord's *māyā.* This is an elaboration in the *Short Commentary* (*Ṭīkā*)[27] on the stated position. It refines the consensus, grounded in revelation and tradition, that *māyā* and ignorance are different (in a certain manner only).

4. The exposition of the view of those who say there is a (clear) difference between *māyā* and ignorance. They say that the lord is the material cause of the evolution of the air, etc., which are transformations of *māyā,* but that the individual self alone is the material cause of the inner faculty, etc., which are transformations of ignorance.

5. The exposition of the view of those who say that there is no difference between *māyā* and ignorance: the lord is the material cause of the evolution of the air, etc., but the individual self alone is taken to be the material cause of the inner faculty. This is due to the view that those faculties constitute the individual self.[28]

6. A specification of the view of still others who say that *brahman* alone is the material cause of the entirety of the ordinary evolved world, while the individual self is the material cause of merely apparent transformations that occur in sleep, etc.

7. A specification of the view of those propounding the "to perceive is to create" (*dṛṣṭi = sṛṣṭi*) doctrine. They hold that the entire cosmic evolu-

> tion is merely apparent. In fact, the individual self alone is the material cause of the evolution of all that is seen, the air, etc., and of the lord too, just as it is the material cause of transformations in sleep.

The mystery is a great one: How can there be a world filled with diverse beings when *brahman* alone exists? How to speak of that diversity without introducing, intentionally or not, differences into the utterly simple reality of *brahman?* There are various strategies for dealing with the limitations of words: silence; the apophatic path; or, as here, an intelligent and nuanced use of words, such as aims to say just enough and nothing more. These positions make good use of "*brahman*," "lord," "individual self," "ignorance," "*māyā*," "conditioning factor," "sleep," etc. Dīkṣita has gathered differing more or less radical technical theological positions that for good reason were held by one or another nondualist theologian and his successors. They use the same terms over and again but with different nuances, seeking the simplest way to speak of unity and diversity that is in accord with scripture, in agreement with Advaita doctrine, and compatible with reason. Here too, Dīkṣita respects those who have tried out various configurations of the key components that are in play: *brahman;* the lord, consciousness personified as a cosmic figure; the individual self, consciousness personified as a person in the world; *māyā,* the cosmic creative power of *brahman* as if it were outside itself, and *avidyā,* the individual's ignorance. All these factor into the several calculations of an ordered but dependent cosmos, of the individual's own world, and even as events that occur only in the consciousness of a dreaming individual. To save time, we might be tempted to generalize about Vedānta's view of the world in relation to *brahman,* but if we do, we will have fallen short of the actual deliberations that count as Vedānta theology. We may not have time to read all the sources Dīkṣita has in mind, but his text is the short course that leads us into the complexities, alert now to the need to avoid oversimplifications of the apophatic or kataphatic kind. Advaita comes down to us in various forms, of course, but this complexity demands the attention of those who would seek to study it (from inside or outside Advaita schools of learning), and simplistic vocabulary is of no help here.

To get a feel for Dīkṣita's own writing, we can look at his exposition of the second view listed above, that of the *Vivaraṇa* school:

> In distinction from the school of *The Summary of the Vedānta,* which held that *brahman* is directly the cause of the world, the matter is explained by the followers of the *Vivaraṇa* school in the following way: We have the scriptural text, "He who knows all (*sarvajña*), who knows everything (*sarvavit*), whose austerity is of the form of knowledge—from him proceed this *brahman* (the Veda), name, form, and food (i.e.,

> the earth)" (*Muṇḍaka Upaniṣad* I.1.9). By this text, we know that the underlying material cause is only that form of *brahman* which is the lord (*īśvara*) who is defined as knowing all, etc., and who is distinguished by his relation to *māyā*. In the *Commentary* (*Bhāṣya*) on *Brahma Sūtras* I.1.20 and I.2.1, it is said that this (*brahman*) is the self of all, and for this reason it is the material cause of all. This too is declared in scriptural texts such as "That alone is the recited verse (*ṛg*), the sung verse (*sāman*), the recited verse (*uktha*), the whispered verse (*yajus*): all these are *brahman,*" (*Chāndogya Upaniṣad* 1.7.5) and "containing all actions, all desires, all odors, all tastes (all this, without speech, without concern; this is my self within the heart, this is *brahman.*)" (*Chāndogya Upaniṣad* 3.14.4): Thus the distinction of (*brahman* as) lord from (*brahman* as) individual self.[29]

In this dense little passage we are informed of the views of this important school, though, since it is listed second, we will do well to read back and forth between it and the former view. The *Muṇḍaka* and *Chāndogya* Upaniṣads are quoted, and the reference is made to the *Brahma Sūtras,* and to Śaṅkara's commentary thereon. Readers are invited to ponder those authorities too, studying the scriptures and the interpretations of them for the sake of a deeper understanding of this particular explanation of the truth of Advaita: *brahman* reflected in the form of a lord—superior personal deity—who is possessed of various perfections, and who undertakes the world of creating the world. Since the individual self cannot make these claims, it is necessarily distinguished from the lord and from *brahman* in the form of lord.

Dīkṣita then returns to the *Summary of the Vedānta* school that had been considered first. To do so, he entertains a further objection that, although to be refuted, affords him the chance to clarify further how it is that *brahman* alone is the material cause of all:

> Objection: If intelligence as such, not distinguished by individual self or lord, is the material cause of all, then it cannot also serve as the characteristic mark that distinguishes the lord from the individual self.
>
> Response: The *Summary of the Vedānta* rejects the underlying material causality of that intelligence, distinguished as stated, only in order to refute material causality characterized (solely) as (an independent) *māyā*. But the intent is not to reject the notion that the material causality of (*brahman* as) intelligence takes the derivative form of lord (even if not as the individual self).[30]

There is no room here for blanket affirmations or rejections. The danger of duality—an independent *māyā*—must be ruled out, but without depriving Vedānta of the advantages that the twilight reality of *māyā*—it is *brahman,* it is not *brahman*—affords in negotiating the space between a diversified world and its utterly simple source, *brahman.* He therefore can conclude with an appeal to authority, and to the right reading of reality:

> Near the end of the first chapter of the *Brahma Sūtras* (at I.1. 20), it is said that the material causality of the world pertains to *brahman* because texts indicate this. But attributing causality to a lord (as distinct from *brahman*) can still indicate the undivided intelligence implied by it, just as a bough indicates the moon (even if the moon is beyond it). So *brahman* alone is still marked as that which is to be known.[31]

What we learn from Dīkṣita's exposition of all seven views is considerable. First, *brahman* alone is the cause of the world. Second, scriptural texts such as the *Muṇḍaka Upaniṣad* warrant the use of lord-specific language when indicating this active role of *brahman.* Third, this scriptural usage identifies superior features of the lord's consciousness, but does not thereby warrant extending the same features to some or all individual selves. Fourth, claims about a lord as world maker can be justified as useful and in keeping with scripture, but are not to be taken as proving also that there is a lord who is truly different from *brahman.* Fifth, Dīkṣita is showing his readers how to think within the bounds of what scripture allows. More radically different scenarios—e.g., theistic or Buddhist or purely materialist—never come up, since the conversation stays in-house, within the frame of selected scriptures and traditional readings, vocabulary, and topics.

Above we saw Sastri's claim that "the views are so arranged that there is a smooth transition from the one to the other." If so, then here we see a downgrading of both "lord" and "individual self," so as to protect the doctrine of nonduality, but without making it entirely impossible to speak of them both. The first views, 1–4, accept the provisional reality of the world and explain it in terms of the real and distinct roles of "lord" and "individual self." Dīkṣita declines to dispute these views fundamentally, since they intend to leave intact the sole causal role of *brahman,* even while admitting as provisionally useful certain statements about the lord and the individual self.

The Enduring Meaningfulness of "Lord" and "Self"—Even When There Is Only Brahman

If a robust commitment to the doctrine that there is in reality only *brahman,* one without a second, still leaves room for a continuing discourse about "lord" and "individual self," the door is opened then to further questions about the difference between these two dependent forms of consciousness. Words such as "lord" and "self" need not be banished, but their use must be further clarified, lest we equate them or inadvertently introduce a dualism of lords and selves. Accordingly, Section 5, "An inquiry into the proper forms of the lord and individual self," seeks a viable language of difference between lord and individual self. Here too Dīkṣita is very compact indeed, aiming to highlight major nuances but without explaining all related matters and secondary points. The Sanskrit table of contents divides Section 5 into an exposition of ten different positions:[32]

1. Both the individual self and the lord are reflections (of *brahman*). The lord is a reflection of consciousness in *māyā,* and the *individual self* its reflection in ignorance. The difference between ignorance and *māyā* is that of a portion (ignorance) in relation to that to which the portion belongs (*māyā*). Ignorance is nothing but a potent portion of the concealing and projective powers of *māyā.* This is the analysis according to the author of the *Explanation of Clear Meanings.*

2. *Māyā,* the fundamental material reality, is primarily pure being (*sattva*),[33] while ignorance is that being as if soiled. Granting this stipulation of difference between *māyā* and ignorance, it can be said that the lord is the reflection of *māyā,* and the individual self the reflection of ignorance. This is the position expressed in the *Discernment of the Real* (*Tattvaviveka*) by Śrī Vidyāraṇyaswāmi.

3. It is sometimes said that the fundamental material reality is just *māyā* acting specially by its projective power, as it takes on the conditioning factor of being lord. But when it acts specially by its concealing power, it is then ignorance and takes on the conditioning factor of being an individual self. Thus the difference between individual self and lord.

4. The lord is the reflection of (*brahman* as) consciousness in ignorance, and the individual self is the reflection of that same (*brahman* as) consciousness in the inner organ. Thus the view of the *Summary of the Vedānta.*

5. After stipulating that consciousness has a fourfold differentiation (*brahman,* lord, individual self, inner organ), one can say that the lord is pure consciousness reflected in nonknowing (*ajñāna*), colored by the lingering effect of the consciousness in all living beings that depends on *brahman.* The individual self is that same consciousness reflected rather in the inner organ. This is the view of the "Varied Light" (*Citradīpā*),[34] and an explication of the meaning of the statement, "I am *brahman.*"

6. The view expressed in the *Brahmānanda* commentary applies to the individual self what the *Citradīpā* had said regarding the lord. This explanation is elaborated in the *Short Commentary* on the *Traditional Verses on Māṇḍukya Upaniṣad.*[35]

7. Assuming that consciousness has three forms, then there are three forms of the individual self: the real, the everyday, and the apparent. This exposition accords with the *Discrimination of the Seer and the Seen* by Śrī Vidyāraṇyaswāmi.

8. The lord is not a kind of reflection, nor is pure *brahman* what is reflected. But the individual self is the reflection of the lord in the mirror of ignorance. Pure consciousness pertains to both. This exposition is in keeping with the *Vivaraṇa.*

9. The individual self is distinguished by the inner organ; the lord is not distinguished by that, but is distinguished simply by ignorance. Such is the view of those following Vācaspati.

10. The individual self is neither a reflection nor distinguished (by the inner organ). Rather, it is only unmodified *brahman,* characterized by being, consciousness, and bliss; but only by its own ignorance does *brahman* appear as the individual self. This is the account of those following (Sureśvara's) Verses (*Vārtika*).[36]

The language of "reflection" (*pratibimba*) and that which is "reflected" (*bimba*) is employed to suggest how distinctions can be recognizable and articulable, even if not substantial. A reflection has no substantive reality apart from that which it reflects, and yet it can be meaningfully spoken about. All these positions are striving for a way to speak of difference, such that the words "lord" and "self" and "creation," etc., are meaningfully and distinctly used, but without falling into undesired metaphysical claims that would assert fundamental pluralities. All the positions share this intention, and Dīkṣita believes that students will benefit from working through them all.

Here the actual text of the *Perspectives* is certainly tough going, covering nearly forty pages, with the largest sections afforded to the eighth and ninth views. And yet, given the vast amount of commentarial material in the background, his exposition is still an admirable summary that is most useful to the beginner in the serious study of Vedānta.

The tenth and last position may be closest to Dīkṣita's own view even if, by his teaching style, it can be appreciated only after study of the preceding nine items. Dīkṣita's own comment opens with an analogy:

> Others[37] say, the individual self is neither a reflection nor is it a distinction. Rather, the self is like the son of Kuntī who appears to be the son of Rādhā. "Individual self" exists due to ignorance of the unmodified *brahman* itself.[38]

Dīkṣita is alluding to a familiar story from the *Mahābhārata,* the great epic: Karṇa, an ill-fated hero, is the son of Kuntī but for complicated reasons grew up away from home and throughout his childhood thought himself to be the son of Rādhā. When he learns his true identity, he does not change; only the mistaken identity is removed. So, too, the self does not change when it recognizes itself and discards false views of itself. He elaborates:

> This is explained in the *Commentary on the Bṛhadāraṇyaka* (II.1.20) by the example of the king's son raised in a clan of hunters: "*Brahman* alone, by its own ignorance, wanders in *saṃsāra;* by its own knowledge, it is liberated." So too in the *Vārtika* (commentary on the passage), "When the son of the king regains his memory, his condition as hunter ceases. Thus too, due to the statements, 'You are that' (*Chāndogya Upaniṣad* 6), etc., the ignorant self (lets go of its limited sense of self)." Because *brahman,* by its own ignorance, takes on the being of an individual self, and conjures the evolved form of everything, so too the lord, with characteristics such as being the "knower of all," etc., is conjured by the individual self, just as deities are perceived in dreams.[39]

Like the "to perceive is to create" position that concluded Section 3 considered earlier, this last position is radical: the illusion of plurality has to be *brahman*'s own illusion, since there is nowhere else to place it: where else could ignorance reside, according to a radical nondualist worldview? Yet because this more radical view aims to remain located firmly in tradition, it is not interpreted as a condemnation of all other views.

Practically speaking, everything, on the divine, cosmic, and individual levels, depends on the awakening of the self from its individual and cosmic misapprehensions. But since in that awakening one realizes that this is only *brahman* knowing itself, in fact it is mysteriously *brahman* that was misled and *brahman* that comes to self-realization. The position is a tricky one indeed, and many questions remain, as can be expected with so deep a mystery. Yet it too is grounded in tradition, drawing on the *Chāndogya Upaniṣad,* Śaṅkara's *Commentary on the Bṛhadāraṇyaka,* and Sureśvara's *Vārtika on Śaṅkara's Commentary on the Bṛhadāraṇyaka.*[40] The mystery is overwhelming, but this does not mean that its expression in words is haphazard or unreliable.

By the process of working through the ten views, readers come to a more refined view of Vedānta doctrine, with a clearer understanding of what Vedānta, proceeding by analysis grounded in the close study of the scriptures and with due deference to prior teachers, asserts to be true about *brahman,* the lord, the individual self, and the world. If readers are willing to trust the words of scripture and the methods of scriptural interpretation, then learning the truth is possible. There is much to be learned, of course. When the best scholars starts to read such a text, even they will have to stay there for a long time. But there is nothing mystical about the method of the *Perspectives;* through Dīkṣita's hard-won words, students read our ways into the deepest insights of Vedānta, caught between the utter simplicity of truth and the very ordinary complexity of words. Reality is one; *brahman* alone is the cause of all; there are no separate lords and selves; yet distinctions among all such terms turn out to be useful, if taken seriously as the wisdom of tradition, but not taken too seriously. Reading and then thinking all these points in English of course makes the matter still more complicated, but there is no reason to think it is not still worth pursuing. It just takes time, much time, and indeed, a much deeper course of study than I am undertaking here.

As we study the *Perspectives* carefully, we begin to think in accord with the truth of Vedānta and in a mature manner. Even if we, children of the twentieth and twenty-first centuries, find new questions to pose, if we have been reading and learning well, we will still be thinking the truth of Vedānta in accord with Vedānta tradition, and not as modern free agents who move quickly but rarely dwell quietly at home. Stereotypes and generalizations about Vedānta—"monism," "the world as illusion," "the individual as a mistake," or even merely "Śaṅkara's school of Vedānta"—dissipate. We find ourselves learning a truth in doctrine that takes most seriously the differences among words; and we realize that most of us, most of the time, will learn Vedānta only by the study of a text such as the *Perspectives.*

After the *Perspectives*

In the preceding pages we have considered just three passages in the *Perspectives,* such as pertain to the nature of study, *brahman* in relation to the conscious beings known as lord and individual self, and the differences between lord and individual self. Learning such distinctions has been facilitated by Dīkṣita's determination to state large and complex questions in a clear and relatively simple form, suitable for beginners yet satisfying to experts. Dīkṣita never merely states doctrines. Rather, with clarity he leads his readers through the manifold subtleties of scripture and learned opinions about scripture's meanings. Persevering readers are rewarded with a subtler vocabulary that facilitates speech about radical nonduality in a way intelligible in a diverse world of experience, in a world where words must still work, yet without absolutizing what can be only a temporary pluralism. As we study, the Advaita doctrine of "the Self, one without a second" works its way into our minds in a concrete display of its meanings, and without erasing the terminology of "lord," "individual self," *māyā,* etc. The core truth of Vedānta is no longer just a matter of what has been revealed. It is now equipped with a theological vocabulary, and the truth is heard in a vital manner, within a learned and demanding intellectual community still able to debate issues of importance.

Dīkṣita makes clear at the end of the *Perspectives* that this intense and erudite work has extended tradition not just notionally, but in a more personal sense. He speaks of his father and of himself:

> Śrī Raṅgarājamakhin, wise guru and *adhvaryu* priest at the prescribed Viśvajit sacrifice, son of one who performed the revered *sarvatomukha* and *mahāvrata* rites, took refuge with lord Śiva who wears the moon as his crest—and born of his flesh, there is one known as Appa Dīkṣita.

Indebted to the tradition of his family, grounded in scripture and in devotion to Śiva, having studied a variety of productive and kindred Vedānta views, he locates himself in that great tradition:

> And he, after studying all the systems now made clear by a portion of expert perspectives faultlessly explained, and in keeping with tradition grounded in scripture, he has composed this accessible collection of small differences within our doctrine.

He closes by asking again for kind correction from the tradition and for its sake:

> If there is anything regarding the courses of our teachings written incorrectly by me and spoiled with error, may generous people of a good disposition toward true tradition and entirely free of doubts be compassionate in correcting me.[41]

By slowly reading the *Perspectives,* for a start venturing to understand just several portions of its ideas, we begin to be informed by and formed in the teachings of Vedānta. Patient study, hard thinking, honest questions (ideally in the presence of a good teacher) gradually make one an insider, albeit imperfectly so. Committed to slow learning, willing to learn from tradition, and open to correction, students read their way into this continuing tradition of Vedānta and thus become able to glimpse its truth. Further study makes this apprehension clearer, more deeply rooted.

Learning Christian Doctrine with Peter Lombard

Creeds, so fundamental to Christian theology, are paradigmatic statements of the faith, brief and easily memorizable. They say just enough to mark the parameters within which Christians speak of the truths of the faith, and to rule out ways of speaking that lead to confusions and oversimplifications. Creeds encode the faith but leave unspoken many ramifications and concerns implicit in what is stated, which theologians over the centuries must draw to the surface and explain. There are, of course, many, many instances of brief and succinct doctrinal texts in the Christian tradition that we might read alongside the *Perspectives.* Throughout the history of Christian theology, many have sought to write Christian doctrine in a succinct and ostensibly introductory form: from the premodern era, Augustine's *On Christian Doctrine,* Anselm's *Why God Become Human,* Thomas Aquinas's *Summa of Theology* (a very large introduction, indeed), and Bonaventure's *Ascent of the Mind to God,* come to mind as texts with which one might profitably begin.

But I was looking for a doctrinal text more closely analogous to the *Perspectives:* introductory (even if arduous), balancing scriptural fidelity and reasoned consistency; reverent toward doctrine and committed to truth, yet also showing the way to think through the truth by exploring alternative views on its meaning; indebted to tradition even while making discriminating choices in the use of traditional sources and opinions. For this purpose, I turn now to Peter Lombard's *Sentences.* This great text was one of the most influential books of the Christian Middle Ages. In the *Sentences* we find a highly respected theologian and teacher at work, teaching his students how to read and think theologically. Lombard is articulating truth in its doctrinal form, clearing the way for Christian readers to learn to think through and understand the mysteries of the faith. Though less often read in the past century, it has enjoyed a new burst of attention with the publication of Giulio Silano's excellent translation.

Reasoning amid Scripture, Tradition, and in the Face of Mystery

In his introduction to the *Sentences,* Lombard highlights the great balancing act that marks proper study: reading diligently pursued; reason honestly exercised and always at the service of revelation and tradition, and for the community; work dependent on the grace of God. As he puts it, "With diligent investigation, we have pondered over and over again the contents of the Old and New Law; by God's prevenient grace, it has become clear to us that the study of the sacred page is principally concerned with things or with signs."[42] In a way that a Vedānta theologian would approve, Lombard announces his intention to clear away error, so as to enter upon the depths of truth:

> Burning with that zeal (for the house of God), we have striven to protect with the bucklers of David's tower (*Song of Songs* 4.4) "our faith against the errors of carnal and brutish men" (Augustine, *De Trinitate* III, prologue); or rather, we wish to show that is already so protected. We have also attempted to reveal the hidden depths of theological investigations and to convey an understanding of the Church's sacraments, with whatever little intelligence is ours.[43]

Though an individual accomplishment, this study is for the sake of the community:

> (We do this) because we were not able rightfully to resist the desires of our brethren devoted to study, who begged us to assist their praiseworthy studies in Christ with our tongue and pen; the love of Christ is the driver of these two yoked together in us" (Augustine, *De Trinitate* III. Prologue);[44]

and occurs within a tradition:

> Wishing to cast down the assembly of [wicked] people, which is hateful to God, and to stop their mouths, so that they might not be able to spread the poison of their malice to others, and in order to put the light of truth on the lamp-stand (*Matthew* 5.15), we have, with God's aid, put together with much labor and sweat a volume from the witnesses of truth established for all eternity (*Psalm* 118.152), and divided it in four books. Here you will find the precedents and teachings of our ancestors. Here, by the sincere profession of the Lord's faith, we have denounced the falsehood of a poisonous doctrine.

Also like Dīkṣita, Lombard refuses to place himself in the center of things:

> Embracing an approach to showing the truth without incurring the danger of professing impiety, we have pursued a moderate middle course between the two. And if in some places our voice has rung out a little loudly, it has not transgressed the bounds set by our forefathers. (*Proverbs* 22.28)[45]

As a result, the *Sentences* too tells us almost nothing about its author—except by way of every word he writes. Like Dīkṣita, Lombard is hidden everywhere in his book. He is selective, of course, and makes judgments, but he does not see himself as in a position to judge tradition, rather dwelling within it. Insightful yes, erudite yes; but loud, no.[46]

Lombard's modest working presupposition, Silano points out, is that "all that one needs to engage in what is coming to be called theology has been culled from the previous thousand years and more of Christian reflection and has been made available in one place."[47] Like Mādhava and Dīkṣita, Lombard finds virtue in a *lack* of novelty. For this he offers this passage from Augustine:

> And so this work should seem superfluous neither to the lazy, nor to the very learned, since it is necessary to many who are not lazy and to many who are not learned and, among these, even to myself. In this brief volume, we have brought together the sentences of the Fathers and the testimonies apposite to them, so that one who seeks them shall find it unnecessary to rifle through numerous books, when this brief collection effortlessly offers him what he seeks.[48]

The *Sentences* exemplifies a studious lack of originality and a refusal to privilege novelty over the work of preserving tradition in all its richness. Theologians must still do their work, seeking a right balance between "the necessary piety and respect for what has gone before" and a conviction about "the necessity for freedom and the dignity of the questioner in the present."[49]

Like Dīkṣita, Lombard is patiently inclusive and respectful of diversity even, perhaps especially, regarding matters of the greatest importance. The truth is one, but good people try to teach it doctrinally in various ways, as Rosemann explains clearly: "Thus, there is no one theory in the *Sentences* on such a question as the image and likeness of God in the human. Even in cases where Peter Lombard has a clearly stated preference (as with the interpretation of the hexaemeron), he is loath to dismiss alternative accounts altogether. The *Book of Sentences,* then, often remains precisely this: a book, a collection of "sentences," that is, of authoritative opinions."[50]

Still early in his opening discussion of the Trinity in Book One, Lombard exhorts his readers to the humble and collegial learning that is needed regarding such great mysteries:

> Therefore, this highest and most excellent of topics is to be approached with modesty and fear. We must extend a most attentive and devout hearing when investigating the unity of the Trinity, namely of Father and Son and Holy Spirit, because in no other matter is error more dangerous, inquiry so charged with effort, or discovery more fruitful. And so let each person who hears and reads what is said concerning the ineffable and inaccessible light of the Godhead see to it that he imitates and keeps what the venerable teacher Augustine says concerning himself in *On the Trinity,* Book 1: "In case of doubt, I will not be loath to ask; in

case of error, I will not be ashamed to learn. And so let whoever hears or reads these things, if he shares my certainty, continue on with me, if he shares my hesitation, continue to search with me; if he acknowledges his error, return to me; if he notes an error of mine, call me back. In this way, we can enter together upon the path of love, moving toward him of whom it is said: '*Seek his face always.* (*Psalm* 104.4)'" (*De Trinitate* I.2–3 n7)[51]

Modesty, fear, attentive and devout hearing, the intention to learn from and be reformed by what one reads, humility, and a willingness to be corrected: such qualities are valuable in any inquiry into truth, and, Lombard tells us, particularly in the face of the greater mysteries of God. Dīkṣita put the matter in other words, of course, but he would recognize the kindred nature of Lombard's demeanor and ethos. And even if Dīkṣita's commitment to the guru-discipline mode of traditional learning has no exact parallel in Lombard, surely the latter would appreciate the need for prerequisites, proper instruction, and moral formation as prerequisites to thinking through the higher mysteries of the faith.

The virtues Lombard highlights are essential to the slow learning at the heart of this book. We learn to respect scripture and tradition, to reason honestly and attentively, but also to stand humbly in the face of the mystery inscribed in the very texts we read, of God but also, with Dīkṣita, the mystery of *brahman,* of the human condition. Slow learning may ill fit the modern university, not just because we race along by a much faster, economics-driven pace of life, but because such learning, in religious scholarship, entails new and possibly unsettling thinking on the truth we study and the truth of ourselves.

The *Sentences* as a Transitional Text

The *Sentences* is a transitional text, between the monastery and the university, between the traditions of contemplative reading and dedicated, lifelong study characteristic of the earlier Middle Ages, and the emerging quest of the "high" Middle Ages for a more systematic ordering of truths that highlights the coherence of the faith, even in contrast to the irregularity and roughness of scripture and earlier tradition. (Mīmāṃsā and Vedānta too are not immune to the tendency to neaten up the scriptures.) Lombard's style leaves exposed the workings of its learning. We see clearly the movements back and forth between a simpler reading of scripture and citing of tradition, reason at work within tradition, and so too the effort to put doctrines in good order.

Rosemann thinks this transitional nature is a virtue of the *Sentences.* He observes that one can find the *Sentences* inadequate if measured by later scholastic masterworks, but in his view there is a more constructive way to appreciate what Lombard is up to:

> Peter Lombard wanted to keep theology closer to its roots in Scripture and in reasoning from authority, without however taking the side of "traditionalists" like Hugh of St. Victor. In his summary of the *Sentences* at the beginning of book 3, we have noticed his reference to the "irrefragable witness of the Saints," as well as his stated desire to follow "the model of certain authorities." . . . This is a programmatic statement, not a mere *captatio benevolentiae* to please his readers. The preface contains very similar remarks on a volume compiled "from witnesses to truth that are founded in eternity," a volume entirely made up of "the teachings of the Fathers," in which the author's voice makes itself heard but rarely [52]

This methodological modesty and commitment to continuity—rather than a statement of a new, superior, final position—is a key measure of the success of the *Sentences.* As Rosemann further observes,

> it is precisely the positive character of Peter Lombard's theology that ensured its continued success over the centuries. Had Peter forced the theological material 'into any one, preemptive, philosophical mold,' subsequent generations would have found it difficult to use his collection of authorities as the basis for their own reflections. The fact that the coherence of the *Book of Sentences* is real, but not rigid, afforded it the malleability necessary to make it a classic.[53]

For this reason, it is endlessly generative of commentary, as new readers and teachers are continually provoked to new learning.

At the end of *Peter Lombard,* Rosemann similarly reiterates that lack of perfect system and finality in the *Sentences* may actually be for the good:

> some of the weaknesses of the Lombard's *chef d'oeuvre* might turn out to be hidden strengths. We have spoken of Peter Lombard's frequent hesitations, as well as his tendency to declare himself unable to solve crucial theological problems. *Horum autem quod verius sit, non est humani iudicii definire,* "it is not up to human judgment to decide which of these (positions) is more true"—how often have we encountered sentences such as this one in our discussion of Peter's theology! But is such an attitude of humility not, in fact, extremely appropriate with respect to the deepest mysteries of human existence: the nature of God, sin, and salvation?

The application to our times follows directly:

> In our postmodern age, we have grown weary and suspicious of those pretending to offer us seamless systems of "absolute knowledge." Much of contemporary philosophy is nothing but an attempt to deconstruct such proud rationalism, in order to rediscover the mystery of existence beneath the tightly woven structures of knowledge that have enabled us to master our world ever more efficiently. But mastery at what price! Peter Lombard's humility, his hesitations, and perhaps even his inconsistencies are important and attractive reminders of the radical finitude of human thought and existence.[54]

It is easy to extend this insight interreligiously too, in favor of resistance to the desire to neaten up the world of many religions by a simple and flat assertion of one-truth only that, unless informed by serious study, comes across merely as stingy, or by an all-encompassing relativism that may inadvertently diminish every firm and passionate tradition. Most admirably too, Lombard shows us that humility in the face of mystery is not at all the same as letting go of the mysteries of the faith.[55]

Doctrine in the *Sentences*

The four books of the *Sentences* treat the mysteries of the faith, Trinity, Creation, Incarnation, and Signs:[56]

Book I: The Mystery of the Trinity

- 1 Things and signs
- 2 Biblical testimony to the Trinity
- 3 The Trinity's traces in creatures
- 4–9 The Father and the Son
- 10–18 The Holy Spirit
- 19–28 The relations and distinctions within the Trinity
- 29–30 Time and eternity
- 31–34 The properties of the persons, as properties of God
- 35–41 God's knowledge, in God and in relation to things
- 42–48 God's power and God's will

Book II: On Creation

- 1 The fact of the one beginning of the world, in God's creative act
- 2–11 On the creation of the angels, the nature of angels
- 12–15 The days of creation

16–18 Creation of the human, male and female
19–20 State of humans before sin
21–23 Temptation, sin, and the fall
24–29 Free will and grace
30–33 The transmission of sin
34–37 Sin and evil
38–44 Will, intention, sin

Book III: On the Incarnation of the Word

1 Why the Son became incarnate
2–3 Incarnation in the whole of human being, soul and flesh
4 The role of the Holy Spirit
5–8 The Incarnation in relation to divine nature
9–17 The nature of Christ's humanity
18–22 The manner of Christ's redeeming us by his death; the nature of his death
23 Christ's faith, hope, and charity
24–25 Faith
26 Hope
27–32 Charity
33 The four principal virtues
34–36 The seven gifts of the Spirit
37 The ten commandments
38–39 Lying and perjury
40 The letter and spirit, Law and Gospel

Book IV: On the Doctrine of Signs

1–2 Sacraments
3–6 Baptism
7 Confirmation
8–13 The Eucharist
14–22 Penance and remission of sins
23 Extreme unction
24–25 Ordination
26–42 Marriage, and the laws of marriage
43–44 On the resurrection of the saved and the damned

45–50 Judgment, reward and punishment, the final destiny of the good and bad

Within each distinction or group of distinctions, Lombard unfolds the topic at hand in a straightforward manner, and without much in the way of preamble or justification. The topics are familiar, already recognized as important and deserving of careful study. His intent is to consider each doctrine from several angles, opening it to new thinking without abandoning the truth that is at stake. Tradition provides the repertoire of such angles and avenues of approach.

At every point, Lombard pays close attention to biblical evidence, though he does not engage in thorough commentary on full chapters of biblical texts. He cites authorities (*sententiae*), apt passages from highly respected theologians that clarify and lend authority to a given position and often settle an issue at stake. His selections also save students the considerable trouble of reading "everything" and painstakingly tracking down all the right sources on their own. Contemporary views too are cited but, as in the *Perspectives,* are left anonymous—"some say," "they say," "there is an opinion," etc. This gives him flexibility in noticing and perhaps disagreeing with such views without full exposition. Lombard's disposition, no matter what the topic, is to respect the authority of those he cites and to learn their ideas. He favors certain conclusions but does not exclude alternative views that stand within the bounds of tradition: consensus, not an exclusory rendering of truth, is the goal. He too opens spaces where, on occasion, more than one acceptable view can be entertained. Cited authorities are prompts to thinking, not substitutes for it.

Reading Christian Doctrine with Lombard

As with my treatment of Mādhava and Dīkṣita, the following short readings are simply cases, starting points for the sustained and complete study to be done by those who would read their way into the Christian tradition in this way. My examples come from Book II, Distinction II.4–6, on the creation of angels and humans, and Distinctions XVI–XVIII, on the creation of Adam and Eve. Each topic is studied in the context of *Genesis* 1–2. Within the frame of this book, my hope is that these selections—so few from so much—will show what is possible and at stake in reading Lombard's book as a school for learning Christian doctrine. They will also resonate, even if inexactly and to an extent dissonantly (depending whence one reads and how one thinks about doctrine), with the passages from the *Perspectives* on the *brahman*-lord-human relationship. We will, by chapter's end, be observing how religious intellectuals in two traditions have thought about the intelligent beings and the forms in which that intelligence can be embodied. If we learn properly and remember what Lombard read, just as we needed to be alert to Dīkṣita's sources, this achieved double set of "sentences" cumulatively helps us engage still more richly in comparative learning, in fidelity to each tradition, first of all one's own, but without ignoring the multiplicity of traditions that intellectually and spiritually must command our respect today.

On the Creation of Intelligent Beings

In the first part of Book II Lombard investigates the doctrine of creation in accord with the *Genesis* account, read according to key questions debated in his era. First, he notes God's creative act and then, turning to his direct interest, the fact of two kinds of created beings, as his own distinction and chapter titles show:

> Distinction I The fact of the one beginning of the world, in God's creative act
>
> Distinction II On the creation of the two kinds of rational beings, angels and humans

In Distinction I.4–5, Lombard covers an array of basic points about individual conscious beings:[57]

> Chapter 4: 1. Why the rational creature was made. 2. How the rational creature is distinguished (as angels and humans). 3. Why the human or the angel was created. 4. For what is the rational creature created? 5. A very brief response to the question of why or for what the rational creature has been made. 6. As the human was made to serve God, so the world, to serve the human. 7. How all things are ours.
>
> Chapter 5: 1. How it is sometimes said in scripture that the human was made in reparation for the fall of the angels.
>
> Chapter 6: 1. Why the soul was united to the body. 2. First cause (because God willed it). 3. Second cause (that in the human God might show the blessed union of God and spirit (body notwithstanding). 4. (As an example of the future fellowship of God with rational beings.) 5. Third cause (that by serving God even while embodied, humans would deserve greater glory). 6. After the mystery of the Trinity, we must three the threefold creature, and first the worthier one, that is, the angelic.

Lombard treats these questions with a deliberateness that tolerates some instructive repetition along the way. In chapter 4, for instance, the questions multiply: "Why the rational creature was made," "Why the human or the angel was created," and "For what is the rational creature created?" The goal is a slower, more reflective consideration of key issues from multiple angles, each disclosing a fresh insight into the truths considered. Consider the first sections of chapter 4:

> 1. *Why the rational creature was made.* No one can be a sharer in his blessedness, which is had so much more fully the more it is understood, except through intelligence. And so God made the rational creature, which might understand the highest good, and love it by understanding it, and possess it by loving it, and enjoy it by possessing it.
>
> 2. *How the rational creature is distinguished (as angels and humans).* And God distinguished it in the following way, so that part would remain in its purity and not be united to a body, namely the angels; part would be joined to the body, namely souls. For the rational creature was distinguished into the incorporeal and the corporeal; and the incorporeal is called angel, but the corporeal is called the human, who consists of a rational soul and flesh. And so the condition of the rational creature had God's goodness as its first cause.

Lombard then reaffirms the point that right distinctions among created beings are grounded in God's own goodness. Here he calls Augustine as a witness:

> 3. *Why the human or the angel was created.* And so if it is asked why the human or angel is created, it can be briefly answered: because of God's goodness. Hence Augustine, in the book *On Christian Doctrine:* "Because God is good, we are; and insofar as we, we are good." (*de Doctrina Christiana* 1.32.25)

By its nature, this sovereign goodness is mutual, indeed flowing toward the created: everything belongs to God, yet it is created beings who benefit from this fundamental manifestation of divine goodness:

> 4. *For what is the rational creature created?* And if it is asked for what is the rational creature created, answer: to praise God, to serve him, to enjoy him. By these things, the creature profits, not God. For God, who is perfect and filled with the highest goodness, can be neither increased nor diminished. And so God's making of the rational creatures is to be referred to the Creator's goodness and to the creature's utility.

Lombard then repeats the point, in order to highlight the balance of goodness and utility:

> 5. *A very brief answer to the question of why or for what the rational creature has been made.* And so, when it is asked why or for what the rational

creature has been made, it may be answered more briefly: because of God's goodness and for its own utility. For it is useful for it to serve God and enjoy him. And so the angel or human is said to have been made for God; not because the creator, God and most highly blessed, needed the service of another, since he does not need our goods (*Psalm* 15.2); but so that the creature might serve and enjoy him, to serve whom is to reign (Gregory, *Liber sacramentorum,* Collect for the Mass for Peace). For in this it is the servant who benefits, and not the one who is served.

The final two paragraphs of chapter 4 beautifully extend the teaching in a still more comprehensive vision that looks also to the wider community of nonrational beings:

6. *As the human was made to serve God, so the world, to serve the human.* And just as the human was made for God, that is, to serve him, so the world was made for the human, namely to serve him. And the human was placed in the middle, so that he might serve and be served; that he might take from both and all might redound to the good of the human: both the obedience which he received and that which he extends. For God willed to be served by the human in such a way that it would not be God, but the servant human, who would benefit by that service; and he willed that the world serve the human, and by that too the human might benefit.

7. *How all things are ours* And so all was a good for the human, both what was made for him, and that for which he was made (Augustine). For, as the Apostle says, "all things are ours" (I *Corinthians* 3.22), namely the higher, the equal, and the lower ones. The things superior to us are ours to be enjoyed, as God the Trinity; the equal ones are for the sharing of life with them, namely the angels, who, although they are now superior to us, in future will be our equals. Even now, they are ours because they are ours to use just as the possessions of lords are said to be their servants', not by right of ownership, but because they are theirs to use. And the angels themselves, in some passages of Scripture (*Hebrews* 1.14; *Psalm* 90.11–12), are said to serve us when they are sent to minister for our sake.[58]

Teaching this passage today, we would want to ask still further questions: What is the duty of the human toward other living beings? How are animals, for instance, to benefit from their service to the human? How are the goods rightfully belonging to animals and plants to be taken into account? This correlate consideration would be quite apt in a dialogue with Hindu theological traditions, providing an opportunity for a richer consideration of the other living beings (*jīvas*) also possessed of spirit and some degrees of intelligence, with bodies in many ways like human bodies. Although we can hardly scold Lombard for not answering questions he did not ask, there is benefit in our raising new questions *after* immersion in a classic such as the *Sentences,* if we have read it closely enough that it has liberated us from a preoccupation with the questions of our own era.

In God's Image and Likeness

Lombard then embarks on a thorough study of angelic beings:

> Distinctions III–IV On the formal and moral nature of the created angels
>
> Distinctions V–VII On the good and evil choices of the angels
>
> Distinction VIII On the corporeality of angels, and the relation of the angelic and divine to bodies
>
> Distinctions IX–XI On distinctions among angels, their relation to humans, and their own fate regarding final judgment

We cannot study these distinctions here, but it certainly would be profitable to do so, so as to learn from Lombard about these spiritual beings and also, again with the help of Hindu intellectuals, to think more broadly about living and intelligent beings other than the human. Then, after a briefer account of the first days of creation (Distinctions XII–XV) Lombard turns finally to the creation of the human:

> Distinctions XVI–XVIII On the creation of the human, male and female, in the image and likeness of God.

These distinctions take up the *Genesis* account of the creation of the human in *Genesis* 1 and 2. Distinction II already explained the basic matter of God's goodness and put in place the right order of sentient and insentient beings. More now is said on the human, in light of the doctrine of creation, and as an early sector in the longer narrative of sin and fall in Book II, which in Book III opens into the drama of Incarnation and Redemption.

Distinction XVI focuses specifically on the *Genesis* 1.26 statement that the human is created in the image and likeness of God:

> Chapter 1: On the creation of the human, in which is to be considered why the human was created and how he was established: these two were treated above; also, what the human was like when he was made and how he fell, and finally how the human was restored: these are to be discussed.

> Chapter 2: How "Let us make the human in our image and likeness" is to be understood.

Lombard then seeks out the deeper meanings implied by the two words:

> Chapter 3: 1. That "image" (*imago*) and "likeness" (*similitudo*) here is taken differently by different people: by some as uncreated, by others as created; and the uncreated one either as the essence of the Trinity, or as the Son and Holy Spirit. 2. The opinion of those who helped that the Son is to be taken here by the terms image and likeness. 3. The opinion of those who said that image (refers to) the son and likeness to the Holy Spirit. 4. He does not approve the view of these latter, but he teaches that the image and likeness of God is to be sought and considered in the human, and that image and likeness is understood to be created. 5. In what things is the image and likeness considered. 6. That both the image itself and that in whom it is called the image of God.
>
> Chapter 4: 1. Why the human is said to be an "image" and "in the image," but the Son is said to be "image" but not "in the image." 2. That he may be said to have been made in the likeness of God in respect to the body.

"Image," "likeness," "in the image:" Lombard, like Dīkṣita or any theologian who studied scripture and tradition slowly and attentively, cares for the proper use of word. He is alert to subtle difference communicated by words that are not, he assumes, needlessly repetitious. Although truth is not merely a matter of words, it is refracted in the inevitable entanglements of human speech, small distinctions serving as clues to greater realities. Reverence for scripture and tradition is not a bland generality, but a program for study, for taking every word seriously. As Lombard thinks through the differences among words, he is exemplifying for his students a manner of skilled usage, respectful of text, according to tradition, and aware of the great truths at issue. He confirms the consensus of tradition in XVI.3, paragraph 5:

> 5. *In what things is the image and likeness considered.* And so the human was made in the image and likeness of God in respect to his mind, by which he excels irrational creatures; in his image, however, according to memory, intelligence, and love; in his likeness, according to innocence and justice, which are naturally in the rational mind.

That different readers interpret the words of *Genesis* differently complicates matters, but even from other opinions something can be learned:

> Or image is considered in the knowledge of truth, his likeness in the love of virtue; or image in all other things, likeness in the essence, because

> it is immortal and indivisible. Hence Augustine, in the book *On the Quantity of the Soul:* "The soul was made like God, because God made it immortal and indestructible." And so image pertains to form, likeness to nature. Hence the human was made, in respect to his soul, in the image and likeness, not of Father or Son or Holy Spirit, but of the whole Trinity.[59]

This last observation does not replace the preceding. Harmonies of mind, memory, intelligence, and love sit nicely next to consideration of truth and virtue, matters of essence and plurality. There is no need, Lombard is telling us, to settle things definitively.

The two paragraphs of XVI.4 further refine the commonality and difference between Christ and other humans. The Son and other humans are all the children of God, though in different ways:

> 1. *Why the human is said to be an "image" and "in the image," but the Son is said to be "image," but not "in the image."* And so the human is said to be both image and in the image; the Son, however, is image, but not in the image, because he was born, not created, equal and in no way unlike. The human was created by God, not begotten; he is not equal by parity, but approaches God by some likeness. Hence Augustine, in *On the Trinity,* Book 7:
>
>> "We read in *Genesis:* 'Let us make the human in our image and likeness.' (*Genesis* 1.26) It said, 'let us make' and 'our' in the plural, and it is not fitting for this to be taken other than of relations, so that Father, Son, and Holy Spirit be understood to make the human in the image of the Father, Son, and Holy Spirit, that the human might subsist as image of God. But because that image was not made entirely equal, as not being born from him, but created by him, so the human is an image in such a way that he is in the image because he is not made equal by parity, but approached by some likeness. The Son, however, is image, but not in the image, because he is equal to the Father. Therefore, the human is said to be 'in the image' because of the unequal likeness; and 'our', so that the human be understood to be the image of the Trinity, and not equal to the Trinity, as the Son is equal to the Father." (*On the Trinity* 7.6.13)
>
> See, it has been shown in what respect the human is like God, namely in respect to the soul.[60]

That the bulk of this explanation is a long quotation from Augustine is typical of Lombard. He does not hesitate to yield the floor to an eloquent authority when that voice will be most eloquent on the issue at hand.

Though he is not asking his readers actually to open *On the Trinity* and study the cited words in context, the specificity of his reference leaves the door open to that further study as well. The second paragraph draws in a quotation from Bede, a poetic fancy that shows what God had in mind even in making bodies:

> 2. *That he may be said to have been made in the like of God in respect to the body—Bede.* But also, "in the body, he has some property which indicates this, because his stature is erect, so that the body suits the rational soul, because it is erect toward heaven." (Bede, *Four Books on the Beginning of Genesis* 1.26).[61]

It is as if Lombard remembers here the wise words of Bede and cannot resist citing them in order to get his students to imagine in a more immediate way what the mystery of image and likeness is all about. "But also:" there is no reason to exclude further insights that enrich our understanding of the mystery of human creation. Most readers of *Reading the Hindu and Christian Classics* will be more familiar with the words of *Genesis* than with the Upaniṣadic vocabulary Dīkṣita is handing; but even the most well-read Christian can benefit from the reminder that there are also more and deeper truths latent in scripture.

Eve, and Adam

In Distinction XVIII Lombard turns to the creation of woman:

> Chapter 1: 1. On the formation of woman. 2. Why he created the man first, and afterwards from the man, the woman, and not both simultaneously. 3. Another reason why all humans come from one.
>
> Chapter 2: Why she is formed from his side and not from some other part of his body.
>
> Chapter 3: 1. Why the rib was withdrawn from him sleeping, and not waking. 2. On the mystery of this deed.
>
> Chapter 4: 1. Why was she made from a rib, multiplied in itself without the addition of any extrinsic thing, through the power of God, just as the five loaves were in themselves multiplied. 2. That although this work was completed with angelic help, however the angels were not creators.
>
> Chapter 5: 1. Whether the woman was made according to superior or according to inferior causes superior and inferior causes, that is, whether seminal reason arranged it that she be so made, or only that she be able to be so made, but the cause that she be so made was in God alone. 2. He discusses the causes of things more broadly: that the causes which are in

God are properly called primordial, and why they are spoken of in the plural. 3. That not of all things that are made are the causes in creatures. 4. That even the causes which are in creatures are nevertheless called primordial, although improperly, and why they are so called. Another reason why they are primordial.

Chapter 6: 1. A useful distinction among the causes of things, namely that some are in God and in creatures, and some are in God only. 2. Why they are said to be made naturally or not. 3. On the twofold work of providence.

Chapter 7: 1. On the soul of the woman, which is not from the soul of the man, as some have thought, saying that souls are *ex traduce.* The opinion of others who think that all souls were created simultaneously from the beginning. 2. The *sententia* of the Catholic Church. 3. Here are erased two false opinions and the *sententia* of the Church is confirmed. The authority of Gennadius. 4. (The view of Jerome.)

Lombard works his way through this series of questions, prompted surely by his own interest, but intent upon lifting up true and deep currents of tradition that merit special attention and that had, in fact, already been topics of discussion. Here too some points are phrased so as to leave room for a second or third voice: "It is also usual to ask" (4.1), "It is also fitting to know" (4.2), "Some have believed . . . others have held" (7.1). He wants to understand the texts properly, but he is always also noting down a variety of opinions, for the record and sometimes for occasional commendation. He gives no sense that discussion is to be closed off by his own judgments. This perhaps is why the *Sentences* were so widely taught and commented on in the Middle Ages: the readers are induced to take up the learning themselves.

By extension, I suggest, the mix of deep learning, good reading practices, and an enduring commitment to truth all serve us very well when we venture then to read in another tradition. Students who have learned the *Sentences* will be better able to read the *Perspectives* than those who have never read slowly in their own traditions.

Here is Distinction XVIII.1 in full:

1. *On the formation of woman.* And in the same paradise, God formed a woman from the substance of the man. After the planting of paradise and the placing of man in it, and after all the animals had been brought before him and had been designated by their names, Scripture adds: "God cast Adam into a deep sleep and, as he slept, took one of his ribs and formed it into a woman." (*Genesis* 2.21–22)

> 2. *Why he first created man, and afterwards the woman from the man, and not both at once.* Here we must attend to why he did not create man and woman at the same time, as with the angels, but first created the man, and afterwards the woman from the man. For this reason: namely that there should be one beginning of humankind, so that the devil's pride should be confounded in this and the lowliness of human nature be raised by its likeness to God.[62]

Lombard closes with a still more lovely reason:

> 3. *Another reason why all humans come from one.* God also willed all human beings to be from the one man so that, recognizing that they are all from one, they might love each other as if one.[63]

In XVIII.2, he explains how it is fitting that Eve come from Adam's side:

> Since she was made neither to dominate, nor to serve the man, but as his partner, she had to be produced neither from his head, nor from his feet, but from his side, so that he would know that she was to be placed beside himself whom he had learned had been taken from his side.[64]

Here at least, Lombard does not give the man priority over the woman; rather, he stresses their connectedness, arising from one source by the specific intention of God, each created by God directly. He treats Eve with no less respect than Adam.[65]

Today we expect sensitivity to gender equality and mutual respect and insist on reading scripture by that standard and judging tradition accordingly. We do not need Lombard for this, any more than we need to find in the *Perspectives* indications that contribute to social justice. But it is instructive to see how Lombard's patient and meticulous reading enables him, without fanfare, to affirm the equality of man and woman as fundamental to creation itself. Reading the great texts of the past can at times surprise us with the reminder that we are not so far ahead of them after all.

XVIII.3 and XVIII.4.1 elaborate the truths just stated with a series of striking spiritual insights surely intended to get students to see in particular ways the mystery radiant within what they are studying:

> 1. *Why the rib was withdrawn from him sleeping, and not waking.* It was also not without cause that the rib was taken from the man while asleep rather than while awake, the rib from which the woman was made in order to be of help to man in generation. This was done so that it might be demonstrated that he was undergoing no punishment by this, and at the same time a wonderful work of divine power was shown, a power

which opened the side of the sleeping man, and yet did not arouse him from the repose of sleep.

2. *On the mystery of this deed.* In this work, the sacrament of Christ and his Church is also prefigured. For just as the woman was formed from the side of the sleeping man, so the Church was formed from the sacraments which flowed from the side of Christ sleeping on the cross, namely blood and water, by which we are redeemed from punishment and washed clean of our faults.[66]

The mystery is there, for those who take the time to read.

In XVIII.4.1, Lombard add a further lovely insight. The rib suffices for the making of the woman, not because she is merely a derivative piece of the man, but so that we can contemplate how her creation is a sign like the multiplication of the loaves and fishes:

1. That by God's power, she was made from that rib, without the addition of anything extrinsic, just as the five loaves of bread were multiplied from themselves. It is also usual to ask whether the woman was made from that rib, without the addition of anything extrinsic. This did not please some people. But if God added anything extrinsic in making the body of the woman, then the addition would be greater than the rib itself; and so the woman should rather be said to have been made from that from which she had received the greater part of her substance than from the rib. So it remains that the body of the woman be said to have been made by divine power from the substance of that rib alone, without any extrinsic addition, by that very same miracle by which Jesus would later multiple the five loaves of bread with a heavenly blessing, and the five thousand men were filled.[67]

This is a lovely insight, and to argue it, the critical edition tells us, Lombard has woven together two sources from his own time—the *Summa sententiarum* (III.3) and Hugh of St. Victor's *de Sacramentis* (I.6.36). He seamlessly makes their words his own as he states his insight.

At Distinction XVIII.6.3, Lombard is aware once more of pointing to mysteries beyond his capacity, and here too he lets Augustine take the lead in testifying to God's action in the beginning and at the fulfillment of every being:

3. *On the two-fold work of Providence.* "Therefore, God has, hidden in himself, the causes of some future things which he did not place in created things; and he does not fulfil them by the same work of providence by which natures exist so that they might be, but by that by which he governs as he willed the things which he has made as he has willed.

> Hence the causes of all things which were made miraculously, not by the natural motion of things, in order to signify grace, have been hidden in God; one of these was that woman was made from the side of the sleeping man."[68]

The most careful reading and the sharpest thinking still do not drag mystery into the light of day as if by strip mining. But by study readers can be guided in thinking more properly through words that imperfectly yet effectively communicate the mystery to those who take the time to read them carefully and at length. In the end, though, the truth can still be asserted and contrary views ruled out:

> *The sentence of the Catholic Church.* But the Catholic Church teaches neither that souls were made simultaneously, nor from one another, but that they are infused into bodies which have been inseminated and formed through coition, and that they are created at the moment of their infusion.[69]

Tradition, authority, and assertions of truth, all within the Church, go hand in hand with a humility in the face of mystery. The cultivation of these dispositions, through the reading of so famous and well-read a book, is a good reason why the *Sentences* are still worth reading.

Reading Truth with Lombard

Earlier in this chapter I commended Dīkṣita for his explicit references to the various schools within the Advaita, naming texts and identifying positions. Lombard too is to be commended. Lombard's *sententiae* (authorities) rival the many *leśa*s (perspectives) introduced by Dīkṣita as he draws again and again on sources old and recent. The critical edition of the *Sentences* alerts us to the complexity beneath the surface of the cited text and any passages in the four books, by noting first of all the rich set of scriptural authorities cited and traditional sources on which he regularly draws. To illustrate this, we can return to Book II, I.4, "why the rational creature was made," examined earlier in this chapter.

In Lombard's exposition, various scriptural and traditional sources are explicitly cited or implied, from books of the Hebrew Bible and New Testament and from the Venerable Bede, St. Gregory, St. Augustine, and several medieval collections of authorities closer to his time. These authorities are adduced to confirm a point, and yet more practically so as to provide the collection in a single place of apt scriptural and theological passages appropriate for further study. Readers' education in the words, ideas, and sentiments of Christian tradition is deepened, while they are also being taught to cultivate a mind and heart disposed to respect and accept authorities.

Second, less visible, especially to those of us not already deeply steeped in writings contemporary to the *Sentences,* are the words of relatively contemporary theologians Lombard incorporates into his own writing, drawing their voices into his own. As Rosemann puts it,

> [Lombard] was well acquainted with the works of the principal theologians of his day, which again served him as sources both of older quotations and of contemporary teachings. In this context, we must mention, on the one hand, Hugh of St. Victor's *De sacramentis christianae fidei* and the Victorine *Summa sententiarum,* and, on the other hand, two works by Peter Abelard, the *Theologia "Scholarium"* and *Sic et non.*[70]

There are so many implicit sources that, as Joseph de Ghellinck puts it, "one of the great strengths of the *Sentences* is to have gathered together, into one complex mosaic, all the influential theological opinions of its time."[71] Indeed, Rosemann adds, "To us, it must seem strange, and very unscholarly, that so many of Peter's quotations were not garnered from original works, but simply repeated second- or thirdhand from some other source. Ce 'plagiaire,' Father de Ghellinck jokingly called Peter Lombard."[72]

Of course, Ghellinck was no despiser of Lombard, quite the opposite, and Rosemann offers a wise caution that may be applied nicely to Dīkṣita too:

> But let us be careful not to project the conventions and methods of contemporary scholarship onto another age, which had totally different conceptions of literary propriety and little regard for the "originality" that we so prize. More remarkable than Peter Lombard's reliance upon derivative quotations is the large number of authoritative works that he did, in fact, read in the original."[73]

Lombard's text inscribes a select library, well-chosen sources, annotated for specific insights on specific topics. Reading the *Sentences* is also to be reading Lombard's tradition with him. Not only do the writings of medieval authors such as Dīkṣita and Lombard have a history—how could they not?—but more importantly each of these authors, in their impressive summations, is recollecting and giving fresh voice to older and contemporary conversations that expanded greatly the import of the doctrines each examined from various perspectives.

Lombard, like other great theologians, is offering deeper and clearer insight into Christian thinking, as he makes distinctions, raises questions, and writes from and for the truth of the faith. By his observations on the views of venerable authorities and of contemporary figures, and by a gentle forward movement toward a satisfactory and satisfying final view, Lombard opens up the articles of the Catholic faith: God alone created the human; each soul is created by God in alignment with the physical act of conception; the soul thus has a beginning; it is not divine, but once created, is undying; the human is meaningfully distinguished from angels, who have a meaning role to play in a hierarchy of created beings that is not merely focused on the human; Eve, created from a rib from Adam's side, is not derivative of Adam, but his equal and partner. Along the way, the truth of the faith is being more deeply inscribed in the minds of diligent readers. Of course, other dispositions and virtues are required to render this reading fruitful, but a very good place to begin is with the sustained and patient work of reading.

Holding Together the Doctrines of Two Traditions

Both Dīkṣita and Lombard write with the conviction that words can effectively help us see true and false positions and note the better positions even among those that are not false. Difference is appreciated, within bounds, as a teacher that guides us in how to read and appreciate words properly. The *Perspectives* and *Sentences* are perfect texts for slow learning.

I conclude this chapter then by thinking for a moment about what we are up to when we read Dīkṣita and Lombard *together, in the same chapter,* without casting one as merely a prelude to the other, or using them both simply as comparative methodologies or to shed light on a select doctrine. We have seen that the *Sentences* and *Perspectives* are both deeply grounded in their learning cultures, each drawing readers more deeply into its tradition. Read together, they cooperate in drawing readers into two cultures of learning, two communities attesting to and investigating truth in its doctrinal form. Readers hold two truths, not because they have a theory in this regard, but because they has read slowly and carefully and forgotten as little as possible of what they have read.

As best we can, we become educated in doctrines discussed by generations of teachers, now compactly put before us in the words of Dīkṣita and Lombard. If we retain what we have read, our minds are flooded with technical terms: *brahman,* lord, individual self, *māyā,* ignorance; God, creation, angels and humans, image, similitude, service, enjoyment, benefit. Multiple scriptural narratives and commonsense analogies will come to the fore: the false and true identities of Karṇa, the bough that, though not the moon and far from it, adequately points us to it; the fittingness of Eve's creation from Adam's rib; why it was that Adam slept as God kindly took out that rib. These richly detailed and articulated accounts of creation and nonduality quietly marginalize generalities about "creation," "emanation," "the one and the many," etc. We may be pleased, or alarmed, to realize that these words, in whatever language, have a life of their own, work within us, and survive the temptation to flatten differences ("all of it is true") and the temptation to say nothing at all about truth and truths ("it's all hermeneutics").

Venturing to read, we may have thought we knew these traditions well enough already. But now we realize that we have hardly begun to learn. We are becoming aware of the Vivaraṇa school and Vācaspati's school, the *Summary of the Vedānta* and the *Varied Light.* We have begun to read passages from Augustine and Bede and John of Damascus, and perhaps for the first time we have become curious about the *Summary of Traditional Views* (*Summa Sententiarum*) and *On the Sacraments* (*De Sacramentis*). The inquisitive mind finds here treasures to explore, and yet at every point the prospects for truth become clearer and more imposing. We may have been reading just two great books, but page by page, the doctrinal vistas opened before us turn out to be both vast and very close up, wonderfully educative for those willing to do the undramatic, often unnoticed work of reading in two doctrinal traditions at once. As we read in both traditions, it turns out, also in a rather undramatic way, that the learning the truth by way of two courses in doctrine is certainly possible—because with the two books open, we find ourselves already holding two doctrinal truths together in our educated memories.

We must be clear on what is and is not at stake. *Readers* are not faced with incompatible truths between which they must choose, or in reaction to which they must opt for a truth higher than the doctrines taught in the books. *Readers* have no need at this point to ponder whether truth is one or many, or whether it might be the case that words must fail to tell us of the higher reality. Rather, by careful study *readers* simply begin to know two truths twice over, in some depth though never enough depth.

At this point the right question is no longer, "Is it possible to affirm both nondualist Vedānta and theistic Christian doctrines about the world?" nor "Is the world radically 'one without a second' or truly created by the Triune God?"—but instead, "How do readers who has been instructed in two streams of doctrines and thus brought into the presence of truth twice over thereafter continue therefore to think in a way that holds those truths next to one another, yet without theorizing a higher truth that makes the two into one?" Baldly stated, the competing truths may be incompatible—the nondualist versus the monotheistic—but for careful and patient readers, compatibility and incompatibility give way to myriad small points of similarity and difference, with respect to the objects and the subjects of the learning, all of which points can be savored and reflected on by those who want to know the truth.

This double learning may disturb those who read in only one tradition (and perhaps without even caring much about other traditions), and who wish for an end to such learning by a firm judgment regarding what is true or false. Saying that this takes time, and cannot be rushed, may seem rather shifty. Others may be annoyed because careful and patient readers do not concede that reading requires one to admit that pluralistic theologies have won the day. But serious readers need to be patient and not indulge in assertions that are hasty and do no good. It may take a very long time—in this century or the next or one after that?—until enduring habits of interreligious learning find their place in the new scholasticism wherein issues of truth can be confronted with both eyes open.

From Doctrine (Back) to Instruction

There is much that can and needs be done, by careful and patient labor, if we are to hold multiple truths next to one another, recognized, observed together, neither blended nor nullified. Our minds are often unruly. We crave simplifications, or generalizations. We are in a hurry and want to get to the conclusion right now. We are tempted to (over)simplify complex religious truths, so as to not have to live our lives as readers who negotiate two (and perhaps then still other) sophisticated doctrinal heritages at once. If we have read well, we can resist such distractions and dwell with two (or more) truths, read and understood together. But in order to deflate the expectation that we have quickly moved on to the higher things, we need also to be reminded that our education has barely begun, and we have much to learn even at a basic level. Chapter 3 therefore circles back to instruction. Those who have learned doctrine have to find ways to communicate it to beginners, yet without disappointing those already well versed in the teachings: instruction both precedes and follows the learning of truth in its doctrinal form. So, as we took note of the theme of instruction in chapter 1 with particular attention to the *Garland,* now we must return to the theme of instruction, first in a great catechetical text of Christian tradition and then again in the *Garland.*

THREE

Words of Instruction

Informed by the Faith

Instruction of course takes many forms, and it is important not to conflate various approaches to the truths and values to be taught and the ways by which they are to be learned. As I explain in chapter 1, my almost accidental decision to study the *Garland* was for me a learning opportunity with great implications. I was soon confronted with the prospect of so very much to learn, but not enough time even in one life. The *Garland* is on the surface not an exciting text at all, but my close reading of it turned out to both enhance and sorely test my enthusiasm for study. This wonderfully instructive text, I found, can captivate even modern readers if they are willing to read slowly and patiently. It can draw even novice readers into an understanding of the sacrificial-legal reasoning unfolding by a series of cases concisely argued. Even when the details of sacrificial practice could not be clear for those among of us—almost all of us—who are not expert in Vedic ritual practice, the reasoning about such details remained accessible. But such learning is hard work, and its path mundane, unsensational, hardly open to debate: slow reading, patiently working our way through the bulk at least of the *Garland*'s 907 cases. If readers learn from the vocabulary, order, and practice of Mādhava's Mīmāṃsā tradition, they learn a great deal about Hindu ritual reasoning, but also about how case reasoning works, and how such cases lead to rich insights heavy on particulars and light on generalization. There is value in digesting traditional wisdom of this sort as deeply as possible, slowly and painstakingly. Such learning has to take place first, before making decisions about the truth of traditions, and certainly well before the further work—inevitable today—of deconstructing our traditions and of embarking on disciplined interreligious learning (though I am hoping to show that this latter enterprise is quite compatible with the old-fashioned study of one's own tradition). And it is also, once again, a pathway into interreligious learning of a particular and grounded sort.

The Catechetical Turn

It is fair to insist that priority be given to learning one's own tradition in this detailed manner. This is appropriate and also a practical consideration. If we do not have a good hold on the vocabularies and rules of a home tradition, then a similarly shallow study of another tradition, or study of another tradition without due knowledge of our own, risks making a muddle of both. Interreligious learners may have to be more cautious and rather more patient than those who anticipate a lifetime of studying just their own tradition. The trick is to go deeper into one's own tradition, even while at the same time beginning to be instructed in the vocabulary, practices, and logic of another. This is the course of catechesis, and so now we return more richly and deeply to catechetical learning.

At the start of this book I mention that as a child I learned my catechism in the way common to 1950s Catholics, by memorizing short answers to short questions. Most American children do not learn that way any longer, for many reasons, including a good concern for better pedagogies better suited to the questions children actually have, and for the sake of more integral and unitive ways of learning. But the decline of ordered and disciplined catechesis is due also to a loss of care for or confidence in the idea that truths can be stated in a simple fashion. In retrospect, I can see that it was good to memorize so much detail, even if I knew even as a child that there was always more to learn than such questions and answers could accommodate.

This is not the place, nor I the scholar, to offer an adequate history of catechisms. But it is important at least to stress the formative as well as intellectual value of catechetical learning.[1] Following in the footsteps of Martin Luther, the great pioneer in the use of the catechetical style, Protestant and then also Catholic reformers found in the catechism a vehicle not just of right answers, but also right questions, and then too of the reformation of dispositions necessary to the living the Christian life. Instruction necessarily intended also the formation in a way of life in accord with the faith and stated the sacramental participations expected of the well-informed believer. As in Luther's pioneering *Small Catechism,* such texts habitually took the form of commentary on Church creeds and familiar prayers, particularly the Ten Commandments;[2] the Apostles' Creed;[3] the Lord's Prayer (Our Father) as taught by Jesus in the *Gospel according to Matthew.*[4] Linking the teachings to familiar prayers and scriptural passages confirms the view that there is depth and meaning in both the prayers and the rules. When teachings are linked to the prayers, meanings go deeper and are carried forward mnemonically and as woven into daily piety: prayers are said, truths are affirmed.[5]

To say a little more on catechisms, I must be very selective, turning now to the *Catechism* of Peter Canisius (1521–1597). He was a Jesuit scholar, teacher, and pastor, who devoted much energy to formulating and teaching the Catholic version of the faith, over against Protestant constructions of the same. His *Greater Catechism* (henceforth *Catechism*) offers a complete and coherent religious universe, complex yet integral. That it was rewritten in larger and smaller forms aimed at different audiences makes it all the more interesting, and studying all the forms of his teachings—as expansions and contractions of one another—makes good sense. For my example, however, I draw on simply his *Catechism* in its post-Tridentine form[6] and, as illustrations, several of its teachings on the truth of the faith and the truth of the human.

Thereafter I return to the *Garland* for a second look, taking up a series of cases that more deeply illustrate its teaching, even catechetical bent, in communicating a particular view of the human as a "Vedic human being." By this route our sense of catechesis will be stretched a bit. The *Garland,* though fitting nicely into a question-answer format, deals with topics rather different from those we find in a catechism, and what is learned inculcates a different kind of learning. While a catechism stresses content, aiming at a detailed and integral presentation of the faith, the *Garland* stresses a way of reasoning that unties knots and disposes of doubts regarding sacrificial texts and practice, dealing far less with anything approaching doctrinal content. But common to both the *Garland* and the *Catechism* is the work of study, the deep appropriation and internalization of what has been learned, even memorized. In both contexts, readers are given over to an ordering of topic and rendering of vocabulary that cause them to submit to tradition.

As we read in both, we learn twice over, and by the chapter's end, we will have twice over allowed ourselves to be instructed, simply by the careful and patient work of reading. As in each instructive tradition by itself, we will become able to observe how we are to think and speak of and by a more learned faith, informed and transformed in a double learning that prepares us for still further learning.

Peter Canisius's *Catechism*

So let us see what we learn from the *Catechism* of Canisius. As already mentioned, a striking feature of Canisius's catechetical writing is that it appeared in three forms: Greater, Smaller, and Smallest: the pre-Tridentine *Catechismus Maior: Summa Doctrinae Christianae* (1555–1565);

the post-Tridentine version of the same (1566–1592); *Catechismus Minor seu Parvus Catechismus Catholicorum* (1559–1597); *Catechismus Minimus: Summa Doctrinae Christianae per Quaestiones Tradita et ad Captum Rudiorum Accommodata* (1556–1568),[7] and even an illustrated still simpler version, adorned with images provided by Christoffel Plantijn, an influential Renaissance humanist, book printer, and publisher.

Jean-Claude Dhotel notes that the *Catechismus Maior* (henceforth *Catechism*) served as a compendium of theology most useful to the priests who teach, while the smaller catechisms served as aids for memory for the priests as teachers and for the people able to read them. In a sense, each simpler catechism is a distillation of the more complex, compressing it still more thoroughly to more essential and fundamental forms. Dhotel summarizes the interplay, pedagogical and conceptual, between the larger and smaller forms:

> If the *Summary* (*Greater Catechism*) was written for youth eager enough to use their imaginations, but also already able to comprehend concepts, then it corresponds well to the attention of its listeners. But the *Smaller Catechism* is only a summary of the *Greater,* and the *Smallest Catechism* appears as a reduction of the *Smaller.* Doctrine is more and more concentrated and thus less and less assimilable. If these abridgements were only an aid to memory such as presupposes knowledge of the principal text, such concentrated versions would be justified.[8]

The several versions of the *Catechism* are therefore mutually dependent and referential. The community of the Church as a whole, even if not many individual readers, moves back and forth constantly between the larger and small compendia of the faith.[9]

The *Catechism* functions as an expert entrée into the intellectual and moral substance of the Christian faith, more or less detailed and nuanced, depending on which version one reads: an intelligent rendering concisely of the full essence of tradition, the essential (and perhaps only) things one needs to know, or simply an enhanced awareness of the richness of tradition that accompanies even the simple recitation of the Lord's Prayer, Creed, etc. In this largest form, the *Catechism* is of course hardly a teaching tool for ordinary instruction. Canisius's answers to succinct questions are at times rather elaborate, and they bear with them marginal annotations indicating authorities from the Bible and Church fathers, pertinent to any given point that is being made.[10]

Whichever his intended audience, Canisius's goal was never primarily a rebuttal of the Protestants. Rather, he intended a convincing presentation of the faith amply supported by the wisdom of the Bible and Tradition. The best defense and promotion of the faith was a constructive presentation of it that would facilitate an intellectually and spiritually responsible commitment to faith as well as the living of a just life.[11] It is this integration that made the *Catechism* clearly *the* text to be studied.[12]

The *Catechism* proceeds as commentary on brief statements and prayers such as the Apostles' Creed, the Lord's Prayer, and (in this Catholic text) the Hail Mary,[13] and the Ten Commandments. Thus the first three parts of the *Catechism:*

I. On Faith and the Creed (*De fide et symboli fidei*) (22 questions)
II. On Hope and the Lord's Prayer, with the Angelic Salutation (*De spe et oratione dominica cum angelica salutatione*) (19 questions)
III. Charity and the Ten Commandments, and the Commandments of the Church[14] (*De Charitate et de Decalogo, et de praeceptis ecclesiae*); *decalogi* (20 questions on the Ten Commandments, and 19 questions on the commandments of the Church)

The final sections turn to practice and ethics, and these are in parts so comprehensive as to read like appended treatises:

IV. The Sacraments (*De Sacramentis*): Baptism, Confirmation, Eucharist, Penance, Extreme Unction, Orders, and Matrimony
V. Christian justice, with special attention to the sins that obstruct the just life (*De Iustitia Christiana et de peccatis*).[15]

Under each heading, Canisius states succinctly the teaching of the Catholic Church. He links his exposition to each article of the Creed, or word of the Lord's Prayer, and so forth, and then undergirds them with very numerous quotations. The post-Tridentine *Catechism* is over one hundred pages long, to which are added seven pages on the fall of Adam and Eve and the justification of the human. Later, Pierre Busee published an edition of the same, containing in full all the passages noted only marginally by Canisius. The work then attained a still weightier form,[16] over fourteen hundred pages: as with the three volumes of Mādhava's *Garland* with its auto-commentary, summations that ambition full adequacy to their traditions often end up being very large indeed.

To Be a Christian

We now look at several passages in the *Catechism,* so as to be able to see close up what reading it and learning from it are like: the opening questions; several portions of the exposition of the Creed, particularly the meaning of "conceived by the Holy Spirit;" portions of the Lord's Prayer; the sacrament of Penance; and finally, the teaching on sin.

Canisius does not open his *Catechism* with a formal introduction, but his first question sets the tone. Thrice he calls attention to doctrine and defines community in conformity with that doctrine:

> *Who is to be called a Christian?*
>
> Those who profess the salutary doctrine of Jesus Christ, true God and human, in his Church. The true Christian is one who damns and detests all those cults and sects, which are outside the doctrine of Christ and outside the Church, wherever found among the nations, that is, Jews, Gentiles, Muslims, and heretics.[17] This person is one who firmly submits to this teaching (*doctrina*) of Christ.[18]

We are reminded here that the *Catechism,* however pastoral its disposition, still draws sharp boundaries that exclude dangerous outsiders. The competing views are rarely adverted to and never adequately represented since, Canisius might say, his work serves a purpose inside the Church community. We find something of an analogue in Mādhava's *Garland.* While its immediate arguments are only with scholars of Vedic text and sacrifice who care similarly about the details, his great silence on alternative views on sacrifice, Hindu or Buddhist, makes it clear that at least during the time of instruction—or the whole life following up it—unfriendly competing views have no bearing on the right instruction that is at issue.[19]

The second question allows for the stating of fundamentals operative in any summation of the faith:

> *By what summation can Christian doctrine be encompassed?*
>
> Surely, that a Christian should know and observe those things that pertain to wisdom and to justice. Wisdom, as Augustine showed, pertains to the theological virtues, faith, hope, and charity, which are founded in the divine and which, when cultivated purely and greatly in this life, render humans blessed and divine. Justice resolves into two parts, turning away from evil and the doing of the good.

When these are in place cognitively and morally, all else follows:

> Out of these fonts of wisdom and of justice it is not difficult to drink other things, which conform to the Christian institution and discipline.

Canisius next (in question 3) emphasizes the primacy of faith as the gateway to encountering and calling upon God and then (in question 4) finally explains what he means by faith:

> Faith is the gift of God and light, by which the illumined human person firmly assents to and adheres to those things revealed by the divinity and proposed to us by the Church, that they might be believed.

Key beliefs inform that disposition to accept the following:

> These things are of this kind: that God is three and one, that the world was created from nothing, that God was made human, and endured death for our sake, that Mary was both a virgin and mother of God, that all the dead will be restored to life, that the human person is "reborn by water and the Spirit" (John 3.5), and that the whole Christ is contained in the Eucharist. Other mysteries of this sort in our religion are to be honored, revealed by the divinity though not to be comprehended by the human senses, but to an extent apprehended in faith.

These, in turn, require faith if they are to be understood, and faith comprehends the whole of life, as aptly cited authorities show: "it is most proper to faith that it 'take into captivity all understanding, as subservient to Christ' (*II Corinthians* 10.5), 'for whom nothing is difficult' (*Luke* 1.37) and 'no word impossible' (*Jeremiah* 32.17). This faith is the light of the soul, the doorway to life, the foundation of eternal salvation."

Like Lombard, Canisius amply supports his every question and answer with ample marginal references. Regarding the first question just cited, he adduces passages that speak to the name "Christian" and what it means before God and within the Church community. *Acts* 11 and *I Peter* 4 are cited, followed by passages from Athanasius, Cyprian, Ignatius, Augustine, and Tertullian. Similarly, when discussing the nature of the gift of faith under the fourth question in the *Catechism,* he cites *Ephesians, Hebrews, I John, Genesis, Romans, Luke, I Corinthians, John, Ecclesiasticus,* and *II Corinthians,* plus passages from Basil and Augustine, and from the Councils of Ephesus, Constance, Florence, and Trent. Every text leads to other texts, and in principle at least the whole of the tradition is gradually rendered useable by the readers. It turns out to be a vast archive, selected largely from sources respected by Protestants as well as Catholics.

Learning the Creed

After introducing the twelve articles of the Creed in the fifth and sixth questions, Canisius uses the seventh to ground the entire teaching—and thus the life and practice of the Christian too—in the Trinitarian reality of God:

> *What especially do the words of the Creed intend?*
>
> They surely intend that we should have knowledge, understood succinctly, of God and those things of God that are necessary to each person for living well and blessedly. The recognition and confession of the most holy Trinity holds the first and most important place, lest it be

> doubted in any way that God, than whom nothing greater or better or wiser can be thought, one and simple in essence, in his divine nature, is distinguished into three persons, one the Father, another the Son, and a third the Holy Spirit. Before all else, these are to be believed. The Father, who generates the Son from eternity, is the font and builder of all things; the Son, born from the Father in substance, is the redeemer of the world and savior; the Holy Spirit, who is called the Paraclete, is the administrator of the Church, Christ's faithful. Indeed, "these three are one" (*I John* 5.7), that is, the one, true, eternal, immeasurable, and incomprehensible God.

This great mystery also structures the Creed itself:

> The three notable parts of the Creed correspond beautifully to this most holy and undivided Trinity. The first part regarding creation, the second regarding redemption, and the third regarding sanctification.

From the truth of the Creed, rooted in the truth of God, there follow the truths of the faith, and their practical application as well. Canisius sees his *Catechism* as a consequent enactment of that simple faith, thus oriented to the practical considerations of its fourth and fifth parts, respectively, concerning the sacramental life of the Christian and the living of a just life.

Believing in the Father

Canisius leads his readers through the articles of the Creed one by one. Thus, in number 8 he takes up the first article, for the sake of a brief explanation buttressed with a few salient quotations from the Bible:

> *What does the first article of the Creed, "I believe in God the Father," mean?*
>
> It shows us first that God is one, and that the first person in the deity is the heavenly Father, eternal, supreme in power and majesty, for whom there is nothing that is impossible or difficult to do, and "who holds all power over life and death" (*Wisdom* 16.13). This very Father begets the Son from all eternity, and in this time of grace, adopts us as his children. Such is his power, that by word alone he produces all things visible and invisible from nothing, and then truly preserves what he has produced, governing it with the highest wisdom and good, he from whom all comes and to whom all returns. This "Father of lights, in whom there is no change," is also the "Father of mercies" and "God of all consolation" (*I Timothy* 4.10, 6.15f.; *Romans* 11.36; *James* 1.17; *II Corinthians* 1.3; *Acts* 14, 14–16).

The conclusion offers a comforting reassurance:

> Such he is, and so great, that all things above, on earth, and below immediately obey his command. By this leader and protector, even amid the greatest evils and dangers, we are kept unharmed and protected.

What we believe also protects us; what we believe erroneously harms us. Although the words are surely already familiar to most readers of the *Catechism,* here they are invited also to ponder the authorities adduced in support, to think about these matters a bit more deeply and at length, and to envision a life lived in accord with the truth of this first article of the Creed.

The second article (number 9) is similarly concise, yet packed with references:

> *What does the second article, "I believe in Jesus Christ," hold?*
>
> It shows in summary form the Second Person in divinity, "Jesus Christ, true God and true human" (*I John* 5.20), named Jesus, that is "savior of his people" (*Luke* 1.31 and 2.21, *Matthew* 1.21, *Isaiah* 9.6) and Christ, that is, "anointed by the Holy Spirit" (*Luke* 4.18, *Psalm* 44.8, *Psalm* 88.21, *Acts* 4.27, 10.38, *I Kings* 9.16, 10.1, 16.1, 3, 6, 13), and "full of all grace and truth" (*John* 1.14, 41, *Revelation* 17.14, 19.16), the messiah, king, our pontifex, who holds "primacy among all" and in whom there dwells corporally the complete fullness of divinity (*Colossians* 1.18, 2.9; *Ephesians* 1.3, 23).

Here too, the cited passages are all from the Bible. Bedrock sources count most, rather than further questions or views that might please some and offend others. Careful and patient readers learn to read around the text, instructed by each answer and also by the new avenues it opens.[20]

Conceived by the Holy Spirit

We cannot go through the entirety of Canisius's exposition of the Creed here, and so the third article (number 10) will be our final example:

> *What does the third article—"conceived by the Holy Spirit"—propose as requiring belief?*
>
> It testifies that the same Lord, who was begotten from eternity from God the Father without mother (*Micah* 5; *John* 1; *John* 1.16; *Isaiah* 53; *John* 6.40, 46, 51), for our sake descended from the heavens and assumed a human nature (*Galatians* 4.8; *Romans* 1.25; *Matthew* 1.18–23; *Luke* 1.26 ff..; *Luke* 2.1 ff..; *Isaiah* 7.14; *Jeremiah* 31.22), by which he was temporally conceived in Nazareth and "under Caesar Augustus was born in

> Bethlehem" without a father and from the intact Virgin, the power of the Holy Spirit working within her so that—as exceeds all wonder—the Word became flesh and God became human (*Council of Ephesus,* canon 13), and Mary was at once the mother of God yet still a virgin (*Luke* 1.31, 2.4–20; Jerome, *Against Helvidius;* Ambrose, *Letter 81 to Syricius; Ezekiel* 44.2).

This fact is of the greatest significance, since it charts the future destiny of the human:

> This temporal conception and generation of the Son of God contained the beginnings of human well-being and redemption (*John* 3.5; *I Peter* 2.1–3, 21; *I Peter* 3; *Hebrews* 2.2–4; *Hebrews* 7.25; *Titus* 3.50, and is the form of our rebirth. We, the accursed children of Adam, "conceived of an impure seed" (*Job* 14.4, *Ephesians* 2.3–5; *Romans* 6.3–4; *Romans* 8.1 ff..) and the "children of wrath" might be purified, and might from the carnal become the spiritual (*Romans* 8.4, 12–17), and clearly made "children of God" in Christ, to whom "the eternal Father wished the chosen to be conformed." This was so that "he might" in a certain way, says Paul, "be the first-born among many brothers and sisters" (*Romans* 8.29).

Canisius is not arguing these points, nor even inquiring into the truths of the faith as did Lombard. He is simply stating them as clearly as he can, drawing in an array of supporting texts that enhance readers' understanding of the truths at issue. Students can learn, and learn more deeply, as they choose. But at every point much more is at stake than the rote memorization often applied to catechisms.

Interestingly, after explaining "suffered under Pontius Pilate" (number 11) Canisius inserts a useful side question regarding the sign of the cross: "What use and fruit lies in this, that we form the cross of Christ with our fingers and mark our forehead with it?" (number 12) He responds amply, with six points: we are prompted to gratitude at all God has done for us in this great mystery; we remember that our true and holy glory and our salvation are anchored in the cross of Christ; we are reminded that we have nothing in common with Jews and pagans,[21] but rather confess against them the Lord Jesus and this crucifix; we are reminded to be patient in suffering and to seek God's glory by the way of the cross; by the cross we are strengthened against Satan and all the enemies of our salvation; and we are reminded that we conquer by this sign of the cross. As a result, "We do not hesitate to say, 'In the name of the Father, and of the Son, and of the Holy Spirit.'"[22] The point is well made, that even a popular and probably rote practice is actually rich in layers of religious significance.

Unfortunately, we see again a sharp edge to Canisius's interpretation that today most of us cannot countenance, the cross as a kind of weapon to be used against Jews and pagans, and surely must prune his practical wisdom in light of practical concerns that hold our attention today.

How Much Knowledge Is Enough?

Canisius's exposition of the Creed concludes in the twenty-second paragraph with a practical question:

> *Is it enough for the Christian to believe just those things that the Creed includes?*

His response fills out a very Catholic attitude toward the articles of the faith and their place in a long tradition and living community that swells beyond just the Creed itself:

> First and foremost, the things handed down in the Apostles' Creed must be believed and openly professed by everyone. These are made more explicit in the collation that is the creed of the fathers, ascribed to Athanasius. Second, the Christian must believe whatever is included in the divine, canonical scriptures. It is forbidden to see as legitimate books of scripture others than those identified by the judgment and authority of the Church. Third, those things pertain too, such as are of necessity deduced in part from the articles of the creed and in part from scripture, as from divine fonts. Fourth, those things must be held as sacrosanct and with most firm faith, which the Holy Spirit has revealed to us as to be believed and has pronounced through the Church, commended to us as written or by the voice of living tradition. Concerning these, more will be said later. Orthodox faith has to do with all these things; without them, the heretics in vain promise grace and salvation in Christ for themselves and others.

That Canisius keeps mapping the whole of the faith professed by Christians is once more evident here. The paragraph cited above is supported by twenty marginal authorities, drawn from the Councils of Nicaea and Chalcedon, Toledo and Trent, and from theologians such as Irenaeus, Cyril of Alexandria, Augustine, Jerome, and Leo the Great. Readers able to follow the clues might well then be drawn beyond the straightforward answer much deeper into the tradition of the Church: instruction is clear and simple, but it is also a beginning and opening, not meant to seal things off. The Creed is a whole, and part of a larger, older, living whole; its parts cannot be broken asunder. It marks out a way of life that is both an affirmation of a salutary path and a rejection of the many alternatives.

Reading the *Catechism* teaching of the Creed thus leads reflective readers deep into matters of faith. We may think we know all this, but a slow and attentive reading of Canisius's text turns out to be quite instructive. This does not mean that we need to praise it without reservations. There are gaps, the exclusion of other Christian views, and a host of historical and critical considerations that might cause even Catholic readers to revise or push back against one or another of Canisius's answers. Of course, too, new and different concerns matter to Catholic Christians today, regarding the fullness and deficiencies of Church teaching and, indeed, regarding how individuals are best to be instructed so as to achieve a mature faith. But all such further questions and criticisms work better, I am suggesting, if we have *first* studied the *Catechism.* Its instruction deepens and shakes up what we know now and take for granted now, thus affording us a greater depth in what we took for granted—and thus a firmer foundation on which to do what Canisius did not anticipate: learn from other faiths as well.

On the Deep Meanings of Prayer: The Case of the Lord's Prayer

Canisius's exposition of the Lord's Prayer takes the same form, aiming at thorough exposition, yet with an eye toward moral implications. He is mindful here that the words of this prayer will have been already prayed regularly by readers instructed by any of his catechisms. The practical effect then—understanding more deeply what one has already been doing—might be less novel, yet all the more effective. Headed by "Our Father who art in heaven," the Lord's Prayer is explained in accord with its seven petitions: 1. hallowed be thy name, 2. may thy kingdom come, 3. may your will be done, as in heaven also on earth, 4. give us this day our daily bread, and 5. forgive us our debts as we forgive those indebted to us, and 6. do not lead us into temptation, but 7. deliver us from evil. Each petition is explained in a paragraph. After opening questions on hope—the general theological virtue illustrated by the prayer—and regarding the wording of the Lord's Prayer, the lead question follows:

> *What things are taken up in summary form in the Lord's Prayer?*
>
> Seven petitions are proposed in it, to which all species of all prayers can and ought to be referred: either for the sake of asking for goods, or for destroying sins, or averting evils—regarding whichever we implore divine help. In the first three petitions, we ask serially for those things that properly pertain to eternity. In the remaining four, for the temporal things that are necessary to us if we are to seek the eternal.

Canisius then explains the words "Our Father who art in heaven":

What does the beginning of the prayer, "Our Father who art in heaven," intend?

> It is a preface, to render us mindful of the highest benefit by which God, the Father, that eternal majesty who reigns most blissfully in the heavens, "received us in grace, and because of Christ his Son, through the Holy Spirit adopted us as among his children and heirs of the heavenly kingdom (*I Peter* 3.22).

This opening moment of recollection is essential for the intellectual and affective dimensions of what follows:

> The memory of such great benefits not only arouses our attention, but also exhorts God's children to love the Father in return and to obey him, and no less, it increases in them confidence in praying and beseeching.

Canisius next summarizes the prayerful and practical benefit latent in this first petition:

What is the meaning of the first petition, "Hallowed be thy name"?

> We ask that in us and in some way in all others there be ever promoted and increased whatever is to the glory of our highest and best Father. Most importantly, that the confession of the true faith, with hope and charity, and at the same time the holy conversation of the Christian life might exercise their light and force in us, that all who see us might likewise "glorify God" (*Matthew* 5.16).

The witness of a Christian fully alive is the most convincing confession of faith, hope, and charity altogether; as the three virtues are taught—and made the subject of this catechetical conversation—they become a way of life, filled with light and power, all for the glory of God.

After similarly pointed expositions of each petition of the prayer, the concluding question again emphasizes how one finds in the prayer a guide to the spiritual and moral life, what is to be sought out and what is to be avoided:

How then to summarize the Lord's Prayer?

> It contains not only the perfect formula for praying and seeking after what is good, but also of deprecating and fleeing evils of all sorts. Among the goods, first must be that the heavenly Father be glorified by all, always and everywhere; next, that we be made participants in his kingdom, and that those means be provided to us by which we can easily reach the kingdom of God: As for the soul, that we conform to the divine will, and as for the body, that we have necessary food. There is added in the second part, up to the prayer's end, those prayers that

> express the disposition to deprecate evils, that by the grace of God and by virtue those things that are corruptive of all goods be entirely removed, and the mass of other evils be tempered, since by their own power we cannot achieve the things needed for salvation. Included here are various temptations in this world that induce calamities in the present or future life.

Thus the moral force of catechetical instruction: inform and shape the mind and vocabulary of readers, teach them to pray, and by sustained prayer reform their lives in the living out of their Christian vocation. All of this takes time, of course, slowness in reading now as a spiritual and moral necessity.

Practical Matters: On Penance

The *Catechism* is everywhere practical, but in its latter parts Canisius focuses all the more on how one is to live the Christian life in which one is instructed. Knowing and living the faith are inseparable; as in Mīmāṃsā's ritually informed universe, noticing distinctions enables one to negotiate the complications of the moral life with great agility. The answers to the questions in the latter part of the *Catechism* point to applications, to be lived out in ordinary life: no longer faith or hope, but charity, related to the Ten Commandments (Part III), the sacraments (Part IV), and justice (Part V).

By way of example, let us first look briefly at the sacrament of penance in Part IV, as a matter of sacramental and moral teaching. As always, Canisius sets out his teaching in steps, each question drawing students deeper into the theology and its moral implications: 1. What is the sacrament of penance? 2. Of what use is the sacrament of penance? 3. When is this sacrament properly received, and when does it work effectively? 4. What is contrition? 5. Is confession necessary? 6. How do the fathers write about penance? 7. What more should be thought about satisfaction? 8. Some other views of the fathers regarding satisfaction. 9. Is there a place for satisfaction even after death? 10. How is the sacrament of penance commended, and what is its dignity?

Both the sacrament and the concept of satisfaction for sin are of course sensitive matters in the Reformation era. Accordingly Canisius makes all the greater effort to ground the practice itself in scripture and tradition. When he asserts the necessity of confession to a priest (n. 5), he confirms his position by abundant testimonies of the fathers, drawing on Basil, Cyprian, Augustine, and Leo the Great (n. 6). The Catholic position on satisfaction for sin (n. 7) prompts an added section composed of many further Patristic citations (n. 8), citing Cyprian, Augustine, Jerome, and

Ambrose. In explanation of postmortem satisfaction in Purgatory (n. 9), Canisius adds three long paragraphs filled with biblical references and still more citations from Augustine, Cyprian, Origen, Dionysius, and Clement. The complexities, no longer hidden, are explicit, and readers are invited to read them slowly and take them to heart. Not simply marginal notes, these are rather placed in the body of the text. We are now quite far from brief pairs of questions and answers. And yet Canisius still sees himself as summarizing a great tradition in a most succinct manner, highlighting what needs to be known, particularly by those who are teachers and in positions of leadership. The smaller catechisms will of course omit much of the detail, perhaps with the expectation that pastors and teachers will amplify the shorter answers as needed.

Canisius explains the preceding teaching on penance and satisfaction for sin more amply in Part V, in his extensive treatment of sin and virtue. The general heading is justice. First, we are given definitions of justice (n. 1) and sin (n. 2):

> *Which things pertain to Christian justice?*
>
> In sum, there are two things contained in these words: "Turn away from evil, and do good" (*Psalm* 36.27; 33.15; *I Peter* 3.11), and as Isaiah taught, "Cease from acting perversely, and learn to act well" (*Isaiah* 1.16). This is, as Paul admonished, to put off the old man in his actions, and put on the new man in justice and the sanctity of the truth. The first is placed in knowing and fleeing sins, because these things are most evil for mortals. But the latter occurs in the goods that must be sought and executed. That we excel in this office of justice, both ways, is promised and imparted to us by the grace of God through Jesus Christ, and is always necessary. By that going first and cooperating, there is effected in us what John affirms: who does justice, is just, such as God is just. He then adds: "Who does sin, is from the devil" (*I John* 3.7–8).
>
> *What is sin?*
>
> As Augustine testifies: "Sin is the will to retain and pursue what justice forbids, and from which it is free to abstain. And as he teaches elsewhere: Sin is what is said, or done, or desired, against the law of God" (*Concerning the Two Souls, Against the Manichees* 2; *On Genesis according to its Literal Meaning* 1). Ambrose truly said: "What is sin, if not duplicity regarding the divine law, and disobedience regarding the heavenly precepts?" (*On Paradise* 8).

The third section asks, "How many kinds of sin are there?" and then outlines, with scriptural authority and the nuances of a moralist, three kinds of sin, original, mortal, and venial. The remaining three questions further refine the matter: (n. 4) Why must sin be fled? (n. 5) Which is the path that leads one to fall into the pit of sin?[23] And, as a remedy, (n. 6) How are sins easily avoided?[24] By the end of the chapter, readers not only know much about sin, but also about the dangerous path leading to it and the crucial precautions that can save one from this sad end. If they learn well, they are informed, reformed, transformed with respect to the right way of doing things.

The other sacraments are treated in the same fashion, though not so thoroughly. At issue is not so much the practice of any of the sacraments—known from church, lived in practice—but the understanding of what is implicit in that practice. Here, as readers work through the *Catechism,* they learn the deeper import of familiar Catholic practices now disclosed in accord with scripture and tradition; by that instruction they will be, Canisius expects, drawn deeper into the sacramental life of the Church. Similarly, Mādhava assumed that many of his readers would have some familiarity with Vedic practice. His exposition too was not about how-to instruction, but rather about the deeper meanings implicit in the practice. By that understanding, his best readers learn to think properly, in accord with tradition.[25]

Reading the *Garland* (Again): Some Cases

By way of the *Catechism* or any such instructive text, we glimpse the deep learning in tradition made available to those with a mind and a heart for it. But it is also to firm up the practice of a slow reading that can become at least a double learning. This is because the point now is not to seek instruction in one's own faith tradition simply to abide there. It is also to acquire the habits of mind and heart that enable one to learn from other rich traditions, instructed by them in similar depth and with due attention, in regard to the tenets of their faith, the ways in which faith functions in traditions old and contemporary and in the revitalization of religious ways of life. In light of our texts of doctrine in chapter 2, and with a clearer idea, by way of Canisius's *Catechism,* of what "instruction in the faith" looks like, it is now time revisit the *Garland,* in light of the *Catechism.*[26]

As mentioned at the start of chapter 2, Mīmāṃsā reasoning as we find it practiced in the *Garland* does not privilege philosophical positions or the formulations of doctrine. Accordingly, neither does it lend itself to the acquisition of settled truths that can float free of the richly configured ritual contexts in which the deliberations occur. The point is to work one's way through problems deep within the Vedic world of text and practice, with much less attention to what might be said in theory about the world, God, gods, and the human, right action and the truth. As such, the *Garland's* instructive power, evident in what it says and what it leaves out, has a real force to it. Returning to it after the *Catechism* will help us sharpen our understanding of how we are comprehensively and in practice educated by detailed instructive texts that require the submission of the minds of the readers to what they are being taught moment by moment, case by case.

To show how Mīmāṃsā case reasoning extends locally grounded insights into the human condition without making general claims about human nature, I offer three sets of examples that bear ethical implications: four cases from III.4 on the limits on the generalization of ethical rules stated in a sacrificial context; four cases from VI.1 on eligibility to be a sacrificial performer, generously conceived, then contracted by added stipulations; and four cases from I.3 on the significance of customary behavior that, though lacking explicit Vedic warrant, is seen to be habitual to people steeped in Vedic tradition. These too are complex enough to resist easy summary, but Mādhava's drive to concision makes it possible for us to begin to learn them in brief. In them we will find some echoes consonant and dissonant, with doctrines and instructions we have been studying in the *Garland,* the *Perspectives,* and the *Sentences.*

Four Possibly Small Moral Dilemmas: Untruth, Yawning, Reviling, Consorting

My first cluster of cases is found in *Garland* III.4, a chapter in the long third book of the *Sūtras.* This book is dedicated to setting forth and balancing six norms for interpreting texts: literal meaning (*śruti*); inferred meaning (*anumāna*); the meaning of a full statement (*vākya*); textual and sacrificial context (*prakaraṇa*); position in text and sacrificial site (*sthāna*); the names of things (*samākhya*). Each norm is weaker than the one preceding it when it comes to deciphering a difficult text, since it is more complicated than those preceding it. By understanding their relative authority, one can line up properly all the accessories of a sacrifice, things, words, and actions. The cases in III.4 have to do with resolving small problems of ritual uncertainty—by as simple an exegetical move as possible. Right in the middle of III.4, we find four cases of ritual detail with potentially wider import: a prohibition of lying, a rule about yawning, a prohibition of insulting brahmins, and a prohibition of speaking to a woman during her period.

In case 4, the *Garland* weighs the reach of a prohibition against lying, as a transgression that might occur in the context of sacrificial performance, or as more broadly pertinent to life in general. Or is this prohibition not an ethical norm at all, but simply one more detail of good performance? Here is how Mādhava puts it:

> Is 'Let him not speak untruth' an enjoined character pertaining to the person generally speaking, or is it a character pertaining to the person just in the sacrificial context, or is it just mentioning a character already know to be pertinent to the sacrifice itself, or is it an injunction pertaining just to the sacrifice?
>
> Some say: Because it here speaks of non-truths as pertaining to the person, then so too their prohibition should pertain just to that person (and to all moral situations in which he finds himself.)

This is the obvious reading, as if to state "Thou shalt not lie" as a universal moral norm.

> Others say: But here it is simply a reference to what is already known, now merely recollected, since the force of the explicit text and its context both pertain to both the person and the sacrifice.

That is, the person is simply being reminded, as might be thought fitting during a sacred ritual, not to lie; but obligation in this regard would have to be found elsewhere, not in a ritual text. But the final decision holds to a still more narrow reading of the prohibition's scope:

> No. That the person should not speak untruth is here not reducible to the verb taken by itself (so as to be applicable wherever prohibitions of speaking are heard), but rather is relevant here in the sacrificial context, just as with Vedic fore-sacrifices (which matter only in context). The connection is narrower and therefore different from the general restrictive rule about not speaking non-truth. So, this is an injunction pertaining just to the sacrificial context.

Although "one should speak the truth" is a rightly generalized rule of universal pertinence, "one should not speak untruth" makes sufficiently good sense as a narrow restriction—no untruth speaking here and now. There is no reason to generalize, when the prohibition can be thought to serve a ritual purpose.

Case 5 has to do with a mantra that is to be recited should one yawn during a sacrifice. It asks in what circumstances this mantra is to be used—whether in the sacrifice alone or, as more universally pertinent to the human, whenever the person might yawn, anytime, anywhere:

> Is the rule about reciting a mantra after yawning a character of the person as such (taken universally), or of the sacrifice? Some say: The former, due to the clarity of the statement.

Here, too, the right reading is a conservative one:

> No, let it be the latter, since limitation to context is uncontradicted.

There is no reason for *not* reading the rule as specific to the sacrificial context. If so, that easier interpretation is to be preferred. Therefore, generalizations such as, "Every time someone yawns, he or she should recite this mantra," are unwarranted further steps.

Case 6 takes up a prohibition against reviling a brahmin. Here, too, at issue is the extent of the prohibition's applicability, whether it is context specific or of universal import: never revile a brahmin, or just don't do so during this sacrifice? One might expect that this rule, too, like the preceding case, will be context specific:

> Does the rule, "He should not revile the brahmin," pertain to the sacrifice or to the person? Some say: Because it is stated in the context of a fruitful sacrifice, it belongs just to that sacrifice, as did the previous yawning mantra.

But here the reverse is true: the mantra's applicability to the brahmin is taken to be universal:

> No. The fruitfulness of the prohibition can be explained as having to do with deterring vindictiveness (more generally). So this prohibition, because it pertains to the person as such, ought to be freed from any narrow context.

Mādhava here is reporting the decision of his tradition, more than a thousand years old in its Mīmāṃsā form, without any added justifications. That this prohibition applies usefully to the person in all instances is taken as known from tradition. We might be suspicious, since the outcome is to strengthen respect for brahmins, the very people who compose and then interpret such rules. But for the moment, students—then or now—need to put aside suspicions, in order to learn how this tradition adduces different kinds of arguments, as needed. Here, the appeal to established custom is decisive. Students are being trained to apply precedents properly and in accord with the traditional reading of them, rather than stepping back and considering "the human as such." The "reason" in such cases is by no means pure reason, but rather the lived wisdom of a particular tradition evident in these particular circumstances.

Case 7 considers what might be either a narrowly contextual or universally applicable prohibition against conversing with a woman during her menstrual period. Here there is no first opinion, but only an assertion, like the preceding, that this prohibition too is universal:

> "He should not speak to her while she is in soiled clothing" is like the preceding case, pertaining to the man (outside the sacrificial context too).

But here a reason is given:

> Indeed, speaking with her was never an option inside this sacrifice.

In his *Elaboration,* Mādhava indicates that he treats this as an obvious matter: a menstruating woman is for other reasons, not mentioned or contested here, already barred from the sacrificial context. An added prohibition specific to the sacrifice would be superfluous, since she is not there to be spoken to. Lest the rule be taken as useless—forbidding what cannot happen—it must be treated as universally pertinent. Here, too, we might contest the very notion of exclusion on the grounds of female "impurity," but here, too, Mādhava wants his students to pay attention more narrowly to the best reading of the situation as a whole, the economy of words, and further experience in broadening or narrowing the force of commands and prohibitions. It is this reasoning—thinking inside the box, so to speak—that contributes to the formation of persons able to read situations and understand how more broadly or narrowly governing rules are to be applied.

Consider how we have been instructed here: context specificity (regarding not telling falsehoods), lack of reason to transgress context (regarding yawning), the fruitfulness of a wider generalization (regarding not reviling brahmins), and a commonsense generalization of a (seemingly specific) prohibition to save its purposefulness (regarding discourse with women during their period). All four are argued in contexts rich in tradition and already long formed by habits of practice. All are adjudicated not by appealing to general moral norms, but through the interpretation of key texts, in accord with precedents, and in accord with the weight apportioned to explicit and implicit claims, injunction, commendation, and reference. A wider debate about what might be good for society simply does not take place, just as Canisius never stops to consider a Jewish or pagan opinion on some point he is making. Everything that matters is also a matter of context.

Generalization from context is ruled out in the first two cases but affirmed in the latter two. Nor is there any recognition that some cases are more important than others: an expiatory mantra connected with yawning just stands there alongside cases that attract our attention, pertaining to lying, the treatment of brahmins, and the treatment of women, all as first of all narrowly sacrificial matters. The best students, it would seem, are those who become able to review all four cases—and then nine hundred others—with equanimity, alert to every nuance and without being distracted by questions the tradition had never raised.

Narrowing the Path of Happiness through Sacrifice: Disability, Gender, Caste

Cases in VI.1 of the *Garland* shed further light on the human person as performer. At issue in VI.1 is eligibility to perform sacrifices. Mādhava starts with the tradition's postulation of a universal human desire for happiness (stipulated to be the final goal of sacrifice) but also various limitations that accrue due to physical factors (disability, gender discrimination), wealth (or lack thereof), and caste (as stipulating inclusion or exclusion). Human rights and capacities are at issue throughout, but here too we see restrictions that have more to do with sacrificial context than any larger reflection on the human.

The first case asks whether the performance of sacrifices is possible and even obligatory for all interested persons, or only for certain persons who are particularly eligible due to learning disciplined by the constraints of social and religious norms. Everyone desires happiness, signified by "heaven," but a command ("should sacrifice") targets a smaller group:

> Does every agent have eligibility for sacrifice, or not? Some say: Not every agent is eligible, because the text is explicit, so that it is evident from the verb ("He who is desirous of heaven *should sacrifice*") that there is an obligation to act (which must oblige certain people only). This rules out the relevance of the enjoyment of results as a factor.
>
> No. Fulfilling the obligation is to be read in accord with the explicit injunction ("*He who is desirous of heaven* should sacrifice.") What is to be brought about through sacrifice is heaven. Because this (goal) is for the person's sake and because it is connected to the action, all have eligibility.

If sacrifice is for the sake of heaven—stipulated to be a state of happiness rather than a place—then it follows that the performance of sacrifice is potentially for everyone, since all want to be happy. Were sacrifice only a duty, and heaven just a place, the action would take precedence over rewards and incentives; but as final cause, it takes precedence. Much of this case has to do with parsing "should sacrifice," in relation to the adjectival "desirous of heaven," with the decision that the latter governs the former. Accordingly, the scope of sacrifice includes everyone who wishes to be happy.

But that very wide scope, once established, is narrowed by further rulings. Case 2 examines whether certain required acts, such as gazing upon the melted butter that is then to be poured into the fire, are sufficiently important as to bar the participation of the blind, who are able to do most required acts, but not the gazing. Mādhava summarizes the case this way:

> Do the blind and others (with disabilities) have eligibility or not? Some say: Because they too desire heaven, they do. Measured against the importance of the primary sacrifice, subsidiary rites are to be done insofar as one is able.
>
> No. The injunctive force in statements such as, "Gaze upon the melted butter," is not about the person, but pertains rather to the sacrifice. Therefore, there is no eligibility for anyone lacking the capacity.

Human needs and wants can be compensated for if a human good, such as happiness, is the main issue. But when there is an important sacrificial detail at stake, accommodation of deficiencies is generally not allowed; what is important to the sacrifice will not always coincide with what is important for the person. Therefore, a person who cannot see and who cannot perform the mandated "gazing at the melted butter" cannot proceed with the sacrifice.

Cases 3–6 deal with the status of women as sacrificial performers. Underlying these cases is whether the command "He who is desirous of heaven should sacrifice" really intends "him" as gender specific, rather than merely as a marker inclusive of all performers, as "humans." Case 3 puts it this way:

> Are women eligible or not? Some say: No, because the injunction is marked by the male gender. With respect to the meaning of the root, gender is like number, not unintended.

Thus, a literal reading is proposed: if a text says "he" or "him," that is exactly what it means, just as one, or two, or three performers can be stipulated literally. But the final view overrules this generality, by indicating that in certain contexts, "she" is included because it is not explicitly excluded. Which contexts? Here, too, practice speaks: Mādhava seems to be assuming that "everyone knows" that she is present and does participate at certain points in certain sacrifices—which cannot be performed by a widower or bachelor. So it must be possible for her to be the person addressed by certain commands, even if the phrasing uses only the masculine:

> No. She does have eligibility, because the text in question[27] intentionally refers to her, as in the case when number is intended and consequently there is a point to the change in case ending, etc. Gender is not ascertained simply by the verbal form (which indicates the masculine).

Here too the *Garland* omits all that Mādhava judges not germane to the crux of the textual problems at hand—including discussions of gender more widely conceived and the rights of women more broadly defended. He leaves aside such points because his goal is more narrowly to communicate to his readers the importance of skill in reading and understanding texts if one is truly to understand right practice. Rules matter: sometimes the mention of male gender excludes, while in other cases, exclusion is not intended, and good readers knows when gender matters, and when it does not. Guided by tradition, such readers distinguish the one context from another; students reading the *Garland* learn the fine art of distinguishing such cases from one another. That is the training Mādhava has in mind.

There follow further specifications regarding what the Vedic texts allow female performers to do. Case 6 raises the issue of the learning of Sanskrit or more precisely the limits placed on the woman's role in the sacrifice due to her sanctioned lack of Sanskrit:

> Do the acts of approaching (the altar), etc., belong to the couple, or just to the man? Some say: They belong to the couple, because they are both sacrificers.
>
> No. Because he alone has knowledge, such acts are his alone.

That is all the verses say, but Mādhava's prose *Elaboration* explains that the woman cannot recite the Sanskrit because she lacks proper training in Sanskrit. But it gives no reason why she lacks this education. We may be annoyed at this, but the challenge is first of all to learn from what the text does tell us.

Case 7 considers the eligibility of śūdras, fourth-caste men, and here we find another narrowing of the chapter's opening assertion that everyone who is happy is eligible to sacrifice. Śūdras are barred from learning Sanskrit in the ritually sanctioned manner that we saw defended at the beginning of the *Perspectives.*[28] Here the first position is the more liberal, arguing that while knowledge of Sanskrit is required, no particular way of gaining it is stipulated:

> Can the śūdra be a sacrificer or not? Some say: By acquiring knowledge other than in the enjoined way, or by learning from the mouth of a teacher, he becomes knowledgeable about the sacrifice (and what needs to be recited, etc.), and so he can be a sacrificer.

Śūdras might learn the needed Sanskrit even if not allowed to study with an orthodox teacher. By other means—from a book, by another more generous teacher—they might have sufficient Sanskrit so as to be able to utter the words required during a sacrifice. But given the cautions that both the *Garland* and the *Perspectives* have regarding nontraditional learning (as we saw in chapters 1 and 2, respectively), it is no surprise that nonconventional learning is judged inadequate. The response, again the voice of tradition, once more relies on an unexplained prohibition:

> No. It is by those in the three religious classes knowing the Veda that injunctions regarding the sacrifice are fulfilled. But these injunctions do not anticipate that knowledge might belong to a person of the fourth caste. So how can a śūdra be a sacrificer?

Here the argument is still more obviously circular. The śūdra's knowledge does not count, because it has not been gained in the right way. Why? Because no one—no one among *us*—even imagined that he might have the requisite knowledge. The reason is clear, but so thick with tradition that when questioned, the response can only be a repetition: he cannot, because he cannot. Here, too, we may well raise many questions about such tradition-grounded exclusions, but again, such is not Mādhava's interest. His concern focuses on the task of learning to think properly by certain rules that pertain not to the innate qualities of persons but to the conventions of ritual identity. We may very well at some point reject what we have learned. But if we dismiss his view before learning it, we will miss the opportunity to learn deeply from a religious classic of another time and place, and indulge in learning only from people like ourselves.

Tolerance and Disapproval at the Edge of Tradition

Our final examples are from I.3. This chapter of the *Garland* (as in all the Mīmāṃsā texts back to Jaimini) assesses customs not explicitly legitimated by the Veda but implicitly sanctioned as part of the ordinary practice of people otherwise known to respect Vedic tradition. Customs without explicit Vedic grounding may be tolerated, and even seen as enhancing the sense of righteousness, if there is no direct contradiction of what is explicit in revelation. The general principle is worked out in the first case:

> Do traditional texts regarding eighth day rites, etc., have no authority with respect to *dharma,* or are they authoritative? Some say: Because they lack grounding in the Veda, they have no authority. They are irrelevant with respect to what concerns the Veda.
>
> No. Because they are passed down by those observant of Vedic practices, it can be postulated that such texts (and hence practices) are rooted in the Veda. By gathering together disparate insights, such texts have a purpose, and thus have authority.

Mādhava's *Elaboration* gives as examples practices such as the thread ceremony for twice-born boys and the duty of scriptural study carried out with an orthodox teacher, such as the *Perspectives* too had privileged. The "collection" of disparate good practices is not contrary to orthodoxy, and secondary, traditional texts serve the purpose of collating such practices.

Case 2 poses a counterexample. The traditional custom of covering the sacrificial post with a cloth thwarts the explicit Vedic command that at a certain point in the sacrifice the post be touched directly, not through a cloth:

> 2 Here there is a doubt: Is the traditional text, "The udumbara-wood post is to be entirely wrapped," authoritative or not? Some say: Yes, because this is like the eighth day rites just mentioned.
>
> No, because another text, "Let him sing, touching the udumbara-wood post," is explicitly Vedic and contrary (to any wrapping of the post), so one cannot infer Vedic grounding here. It therefore has no authority.

The *Elaboration* explains what we cannot know from the verses: this practice cannot be judged legitimate, because the sequence of actions is problematic. The covering is mentioned first, as occurring before the obligatory touching; implementing the commands as given would preclude touching the post first and wrapping it later on.

Case 3 shows that a lack of contradiction is not in itself sufficient grounds for approval. Ill motives such as greed may prompt the invention of a novel practice merely for personal gain—for example, the acquisition by the priest of a nice cloth:

> 3 Does the traditional text about "the acquisition of the oblation cloth related to the release offering" have authority or not? Some say: Because no revealed text is contradicted, it is authoritative, like the eighth day rites.
>
> No. When there is the possibility that the custom is rooted solely in greed, there can be no postulation of a scriptural source. Even if it lacks contradiction of the sort pertaining the wrapping of the post too, it still has no authority.

But how does one determine when greed is the likely motive? Here too Mādhava, like commentators before him, follows tradition and simply holds up the case of the gift of such a cloth as a cautionary tale that might shed light on other situations where lesser motives taint ostensibly neutral practices.

The fourth case discusses an action that seems intrusive because it apparently violates a sequence prescribed in the Veda:

> 4 Is the traditional text "Rinse (after a sneeze)" authoritative or not? Some say: Let it not be so, since a Vedic text, "After making the broom (then make the altar)," establishes an authorized sequence (regarding broom and altar) that would be interrupted by an added rinsing.
>
> No. "Rinse . . ." marks a purposeful action, while sequence is a character of those purposeful actions. Because a character depends on the thing having such characters, here there is no contradiction among the purposeful actions (but only in their sequence) and so (this added injunction regarding rinsing) has authority.

The sequence of acts is clear: first "make the broom," and then "make the altar." It is true that the insertion of a purification after sneezing disrupts the sequence, so that it is now: first "make the broom," then "recite the mantra for sneezing," and finally, "make the altar." Order is indeed disrupted. Nevertheless, individual acts that are purposeful have a place in a sacrifice, and this utility may overrules the concern about sequence. Here too there is a certain generosity on the part of the Mīmāṃsā scholar: even if it is "merely" traditional, the practice can be given its due space, if no harm is done.

Rethinking the Human

We have taken a short journey into the *Garland,* to learn from a catechesis aimed at preparing select students to think, act, and react in a certain learned and cultivated manner. In a very particular way, we have been rethinking the human through these cases. It is true that the cases do not address important and harder questions about universal values or human dignity that contemporary readers may expect from great religious texts. Even more uncomfortably, the cases seem over and again to leave no room for such questions, instead assigning the human a place as simply one factor in a larger sacrificial web of meanings and values. The right reading of practices is largely cast as a matter internal to the texts, as if independent of active human agency and immune to historical, contextual matters. Desires are treated, if at all, as instrumental to the performance of sacrifice or, in a few cases, as suspect because they draw into the sacrificial realm impure motives that distort right practice.

The *Garland* is therefore formative in a certain way. The cases form and re-form those students who work them through slowly, that they might with equanimity and a certain detachment look to the text and read it according to its internal rules. The education of even a small number of such fair-minded readers, no mean achievement, is the goal. But Mādhava gives an intriguing clue as to a larger significance in his introduction to the *Garland,* where he portrays Bukkaṇakṣāmpati, his royal patron, as embodying the rules of reasoning at work in each book of the *Sūtras:*

> Thus Śrī Bukkaṇakṣāmpati: Wise in authoritative reasoning (I), firmly resolute amidst differences (II), skilled in refined purposes (III), agile in adjustments (IX), accomplished in right order (V), skilled in right practice (IV), sublime in apt adjustments to the praise of all (VII–VIII), competent regarding the regular and adventitious (VI), ever free of obstacles (X), sovereign lord (XI), alert, skilled amid wise counsel (XII).[29]

Skill in reading sacrificial texts and performing sacrificial actions harmoniously mirror the skillful king's reading of his world and his wise practice in that world. The *Elaboration* notes that all these are virtues known also in the moral guidebooks for kings. The king lives what Mādhava teaches. Traditional virtues are played out in two realms of power. If so, we may also presume that dedication to intense study of the *Garland* informs the mind and shapes the practical life of students who learn to interpret the world, put things in order, adjust when necessary, put aside obstacles, and perform public and private duties in an assured, regular manner.

But there is no denying that learning this path is slow going, since the reader needs to work through the text, case by case, all 907 cases, until their practical wisdom fill one's mind. Its brilliance remains geared to the matrix of Vedic texts to be recited and obeyed, but the overflow into the rest of life is inevitable and, for Mādhava, welcome. The *Garland* does not anticipate readers such as ourselves, but, ironically, its splendid lucidity and rigor make it possible for any careful reader to start learning from Mādhava.

The *Catechism* and the *Garland:* Two Instructions for a More Intense Learning

What does this initial reading of the *Catechism* and the *Garland* tell us? A first insight, emphasized by the way I have intertwined these opening three chapters—instruction-doctrine-instruction—is that instruction and doctrine stand in a mutually dependent relationship. One must be instructed, if one is to be able to grasp doctrine; the articulation of doctrine is the foundation for proper instruction. Which comes first at a given moment—Shall I study doctrine? Shall I return again to my catechism?—depends on whether one is thinking about the relationship of traditional deposits of knowledge to one another, or about the requirements for learning. Doctrine as content precedes catechesis; catechesis as pedagogy precedes doctrine. As readers who choose now to take up such matters, we should not be distressed to find ourselves shifting back and forth, instructed at one moment, reading deep into the truth at another.

In any case, "instruction" and "catechesis" can now receive back something of their richer meaning as they are enacted in the humble work of slow, patient study. The *Garland* is not a how-to book for Vedic sacrifices nor a theological defense of the notion that sacrifice is a transaction between the divine and human. Rather, as its title suggests, in this garland we find a threaded circle of reasons that help readers detect the coherence deep in the Vedic texts and practices by means of skilled legal-religious reasoning. It presumes and subjects to scrutiny the rules and priorities at work in Vedic and Hindu tradition, as these had been honed and tested over many generations. It is deeply instructive in what it teaches and for what it leaves out, and so too in its limited and sacrifice-grounded view of being human. It makes available a view of the world unusual (to the modern West) and leads us page by page, step by step, in disclosing the significance of that world. This is advanced catechesis, teaching the grammar of an older Vedic corpus of words and deeds so that readers can think, speak, and act accordingly.

Canisius's *Catechism* is informative in the best possible sense—formative, transformative. His teachings are effective because Canisius is deeply rooted in his Catholic tradition and puts truths familiar from tradition together in a right order attuned to right understanding, intelligent prayer, and the cultivation of good moral habits. Faith, hope, and charity; counsels and commandments; wisdom and justice; sacraments and pieties: all fall into place even as they cohere in a complete Catholic life that is both holy and just.

By studying the *Garland,* readers are formed in accord with the rules of the Vedic dharma; by the *Catechism,* those readers are formed in accord with a particular version of the Christian salvific narrative of the world, the self, and God. The *Garland* forms students able to act virtuously and with discernment within the bounds of tradition's ethos.

Both Lombard and Dīkṣita hope that readers will be able to suspend during study other and further questions and for a time remain resolutely on the surface of things, able to learn from the *Garland* and the *Catechism,* within their settled margins. We are not medieval Hindus nor Reformation-era Catholics, but if we for a time suspend our larger questions we can learn deeply from instructive texts hitherto distant in time and space. The challenge is to assess the cost of accepting a body of knowledge ordered by particular questions and answers instead of impatiently putting those aside for the sake of favoring matters urgent in our day. Faith seeking understanding drives the learning process old and new, but in the moment (year, decade . . .) of slow learning, faith appears most notably in the forms and words of tradition. Modern readers, invested in slow and careful learning, slow down for a time at least and accept humbly the truth that has preceded this generation and will outlast it as well.

Still, we must admit, such instruction is always only a beginning, and the reading heads in unanticipated ways. My way of signaling that there is more to be done is by the simple fact of venturing in this chapter to begin to read the *Garland* and *Catechism* side by side, acquiring some skill in moving back and forth between them, preferring neither to the exclusion of the other. Both the *Catechism* and the *Garland* are to be taken very seriously, but now remembered in proximity to the other. By its questions and judgments, each instructive text prompts careful readers to remember and hold in place what both texts are up to: both honored again by careful reading, both unsettled by the presence of its instructive and entirely unanticipated other. The result is instruction well learned, doubled as a new instruction that leaves readers deep in their own tradition, yet also implicated in another as well. And yet, surely Mādhava nor Canisius would have been shocked at the very prospect of a double instruction.

If we can hold all this together, we can also add to it the singular work of chapter 2, the slow reading and appropriating and holding together of two traditions of truths in their doctrinal form. As there, here too we need to be readers who remember, who notice how the moral force of what is learned changes minds and hearts. After all this, patient readers become accomplished readers who have managed, in a rather simple and mundane way, page by page, to see the world and live in it as few people imagine possible (or worthwhile).

But there is still a bit more to be done. First, I return to the question of the kind of study done in this book: why not generalize, make my points without these prolonged detours into old texts? Can I not generalize according to this or that great theme? My self-defense in this regard will be the work of chapter 4, by way of a detour into how Ludwig Wittgenstein wrote his *Philosophical Investigations* and expected it to be read. After that, in chapter 5 we can turn with renewed energy to the third of our dispositions, the more daring and risky prospect of participation in what we read and take to heart.

FOUR

Reading with Wittgenstein

Resistant, Particular, and Poetic

We have thus far taken up as cases two texts of instruction and two of doctrine. If all has gone well, then by reading them slowly, we become able to hold all four in mind, surveying the paths for further reading they open to us, paths back into their sources, and forward into the new imaginative theological terrain awaiting those who venture to read them together. Instructed by what we read and learned from both Christian and Hindu sources, we come to see how Mādhava and Canisius, Dīkṣita and Lombard, all deeply rooted in their traditions, have structured what they see to be true, and how it is to be learned. Instruction illumines doctrine; doctrine is instructive. I have worked by way of examples, cases that provide substance to a slow religious reading that necessarily takes a very long time. If anything enduring is to be accomplished, the details must be thought through and not skipped over.

None of this has been easy going, and I am grateful to readers who have stayed with me thus far. In the reading that has led up to this book, I recognized over and again that there is little prospect of "mastering" the texts, so as to support a single thesis, or contribute neatly to a theory about religions or comparative study and then be done with the texts. I have rather traced a path through incongruencies and side matters—whole worlds of learning diverted into the notes, as it were—that make improbable a single smoothly crafted set of conclusions or a well-refined theory. Coherence arises *in* the work of reading, not after it by the acquisition of larger meanings that can be carried away.

I wish now to shed a bit more light on why the smoothing out ordinarily achieved by theory can be a malady that derails proper learning. Ironically, this is a hard point to explain without getting theoretical about it. It is also more than a bit ironic that I should insist so strongly on persistent reading, in a book that focuses on six books that ambition to summarize and distill larger bodies of learning within their smaller scope. This book too, despite my ambition to encourage a reading of the classics, in effect replaces its chosen texts by reducing them to examples. Nevertheless, there is a question to be asked, if the work of reading is not be supplanted by ideas or by discussions of reading. How to do the work of reading, so as to stay continuously close to the text? But this is a question a worthy author, Ludwig Wittgenstein, has already pondered.

Muddling Along with Wittgenstein

I have long thought of Wittgenstein as illuminating the work I do. Indeed, whenever in the past thirty-five years I have studied Mīmāṃsā case reasoning, I have thought of him as in important ways an intellectual stylist akin to some of the best Mīmāṃsā thinkers. He and they thwart efforts to escape examples and texts built of examples too quickly, in the quest for enduring meanings.

Mādhava's *Garland* and Wittgenstein's *Investigations* are both most extraordinary pieces of hard reading that notably slow us down. They share certain virtues: persistent interest in the particular; the pragmatic deferral of theory (without much in the way of theoretical argument against theory); respect for logic, though in a practical manner that stresses understanding the text at hand; resistance to generalizations; and preference for provisional strategies by which to "collect" ordinary wisdom on how language is already successful in practice. And so Wittgenstein, like Mādhava, directs us to put aside larger conceptual questions that are not of interest, and to commit ourselves rather to a learning that persists in the study of cases, all the way to an end to reading that will usually turn into rereading.[1]

In trying to hold together the many strands of this book, I have been consoled by these familiar words from Wittgenstein's preface:

> It was my intention at first to bring all this together in a book whose form I pictured differently at different times. But the essential thing was that the thoughts should proceed from one subject to another in a natural order and without breaks. After several unsuccessful attempts to weld my results together into such a whole, I realized I should never succeed. The best that I could write would never be more than philosophical remarks; my thoughts were soon crippled if I tried to force them on in any single direction against their natural inclination.—And this was, of course, connected with the very nature of the investigation. For this compels us to travel over a wide range of thought criss-cross in every direction. The philosophical remarks in this book are, as it were, a number of sketches of landscapes which were made in the course of these long and involved journeyings.[2]

Remarks that are sketches, rather than any smoother completion to thinking; an attention to words that follows their natural inclinations; traveling the paths of thoughts that criss-cross in every direction: this is a kind of writing that is not easily finished with.

If we do not read and write in a proper way, we end up distracted by the expectation that we can experiment for a time and then give up on it: "The existence of the experimental method makes us think we have the means of solving the problems which trouble us; though problem and method pass one another by."[3] Wittgenstein hopes rather to leave us with a *Philosophical Investigations* that is an uneasy whole, that really cannot be introduced succinctly, outlined neatly, or summarized in a way that obviates the need for further reading. What he gives us instead is an unruly text with many lines of thought and seemingly stray (and often unanswered) questions that make readers stumble and stop now and then. Wittgenstein's reluctance to let go of the particular is mirrored in his revision of what counts as philosophy and how philosophizing relates to the particulars of our experience, our learning, and our speaking. His commitment to particulars serves as an enduring therapy conducive to intellectual and spiritual health, such as becomes immunized to generalizations. This Wittgensteinian therapy returns us to what both the Christian and Hindu traditions have told us for a very long time: we never master the texts we read, but only enter again and again into spaces that force us to read and think in unusual ways, now across religious margins. The six texts placed together in this volume compose a rough, hard-going terrain for reading that can be traversed only slowly.

Let us now look a little more deeply into what Wittgenstein is up to, with respect to his notion of philosophy, the poetic turn in his writing (and thus in the reading), and his pedagogical goals.

Resisting Generalizations

For the first of these goals I rely on the essay "Philosophy" by G. P. Baker and P. M. S. Hacker.[4] They guide us into the intentions underlying the intense, disciplined thinking and writing we find in the *Investigations.* Key is to see that Wittgenstein is setting aside what is ordinarily understood to be philosophy: "We must reject the old idea of the great Western philosophers that there are two kinds of problems in the field of knowledge: the essential ones, which it is the task of philosophy to investigate, and the inessential, quasi-accidental ones, with which the empirical sciences deal."[5] We need rather to realize that philosophy is not "a cognitive discipline with a genuine subject matter" that one masters, and the sum total of which would make it at least a respectable field in the humanities or perhaps in some branch of cognitive studies. Rather, we must undo such philosophizing: "Our whole way of thinking must be rotated, so that we abandon the illusion that logical investigation can yield insight into the a priori order of the world and the necessary depth structure of all thought and language."[6] Using words that might well please a Mīmāṃsā or Vedānta intellectual, he insists that "there are no great essential problems, only great and compelling illusions of such problems."[7] Familiar philosophical problems, earnestly considered and argued for centuries, in fact signal "an awareness (not typically a self-conscious one) of a disorder in our concepts."[8] Since our problems are neither empirical nor theoretical, they cannot be solved directly, but rather are to be disentangled "by ordering those concepts." This disentanglement is in turn achieved by a "grammatical investigation"[9] into how language actually works, on the visual and audible surface of things: "Their product is not insight into or knowledge of the essence of the world or the workings of the human understanding or the hidden essence of language, but the dissolution of the problems and an overview of (some part of) the web of language."[10]

Shifting scenes: the *Garland* too manifests no anxiety about the efficacy of words, their ability to engage the world in its ordinary form or in the extraordinary rearrangements that form sacrificial text and practice. Mādhava's relentless quest to detect the reason key to each of his 907 cases manifests the same confidence: when texts and actions are properly understood, there are hardly any issues left that merit second-order theorizing. We read, and read again, and are the better for it, instructed, taught truth, and (as we shall see in chapter 5) drawn to participate religiously in new ways.

Wittgenstein is distancing himself from nearly irresistible cravings that afflict and distort even the better work of philosophy. Baker and Hacker enumerate six of these cravings that may plague all of us who are anxious to establish and defend the significance of our work. First are the cravings for generality and unity more appropriate to science than philosophy:[11]

> 1. We have a craving for generality, which is a spur to scientific ingenuity in devising ever more powerful and general theories . . . we follow this urge to generalize when struggling with conceptual problems, and all too commonly demand generality where only particularity is meet.
>
> 2. We have a craving for unity, which informs our scientific endeavors, in which we seek to subsume the greatest multiplicity of phenomena under a single all-encompassing law.

My six texts show themselves generative of fresh insights large and small, not just for the times of their composition, but now too. Like the *Investi-*

gations, they do so not by elevating human thoughts, words, and activities to a condition apart from the places where we live religiously, but by patiently dwelling amid those details again and again. And so we must endure the odd insights that make them worth reading. To stay focused on the required study, we must resist the temptation to summarize ("Just tell us what the book is about! We don't have time to read all the dense texts you give us!") in a way that drains particulars of their significance, as if to absolve us of the requirement to understand them.[12]

Baker and Hacker describe how Wittgenstein also exposes the tendency to complicate simple matters by metaphysical overlays upon language that lead us to articulate wrong questions in search of a certainty we cannot have:

> 3. We have a metaphysical urge to seek necessities where there are none. We project features of our forms of representation onto reality, think we discern the necessary structure of language or of the world, and then try to explain the illusory necessities. "The greatest danger in philosophy comes from the metaphysical tendency that completely distorts grammar."

What Wittgenstein wants us to understand therefore resists explanations that may seem more interesting than the texts before us. Seemingly honest questions, of the kind thought to be particularly suited to philosophy and theology, push us to look for deeper meanings:

> 4. The urge to explain phenomena, to answer the question, "Why?," is the root of the scientific endeavor to render nature intelligible to us. We transfer the craving for explanation to philosophy. . . . We are the oblivious to the fact that there are problems, both within philosophy and in other domains (e.g., anthropology, aesthetics), that are resolved by an arrangement of the data which will render them perspicuous and make it possible to apprehend formal relations between them.

We tend to ask very large questions, despite the fact that we already have in front of us words—spoken, written—that, once arranged properly, do quite well in guiding us through the intellectual and spiritual mazes of our lives: in Wittgenstein's case, the workings of ordinary language, and in my case, the ordinary texts of instruction, doctrine, and participation such as we are reading in this book. Intelligibility resides nearby, in the refined arrangement of details, in the particular words before our eyes: "tradition" is often the best—or least lacking—answer as to why we do something. This is why the configurations of topics and assertions in our texts are irreplaceable. This is not to deny that it does little simply to give the *Garland* to readers, as if to say, "This is the book—with 1,536 two-line verses, with an auto-commentary Mādhava added to it—read it!" Indeed, my chosen texts themselves, and this book too, are intended to be helps to the reading's all-important first steps, but one must practice, learning patiently how to read.

Baker and Hacker next expose the tendency to certain more poetic and even quasi-religious overtones, to which both Wittgenstein and Mādhava are resistant:

> 5. We have a myth-making tendency, a proneness to erect mythologies instead of simply describing phenomena. This is obvious in our disposition to personify forces of nature, and the mythologies that mankind has woven around such personifications. What is less obvious is the fact that there is an entire mythology embedded *in our language,* a mythology of the mind as a space, of time as a river, of space as a receptacle, of introspection as a form of perception, and so forth. In philosophy we are all too prone to be taken in by such turns of phrase.

There is much that we would have to say about myth's explicit and framing role in religious traditions and in my six texts, so as to be fair to Wittgenstein's criticisms and to the traditions themselves. But luckily the point here is rather more modest. Wittgenstein, who rarely discusses religion directly, is focused on myth's unhealthy tendency to distract us from what we actually say and do. Reading religiously or not, we need to cultivate a certain wariness regarding the imbedded and unnoticed tropes that shape our ways of speaking, lest we confuse our manner of speaking with what we are more immediately talking about. My six authors do not think of themselves as aiming at better myths. Rather, they seek to illumine great textual traditions in the present moment, so that they can fulfill their instructive role, teach truth, and draw readers into the life of what they read. In any case, reading the six texts *together* upsets the myths and unexamined habits underlying *each* of them as Hindu and Christian, Sanskrit and Latin, Tamil and French texts.

Baker and Hacker finally take note of Wittgenstein's concern about the distracting yearning for definitions and access to the essences of which they speak:

> 6. Ever since Plato . . . philosophers have craved definitions, which will exhibit the essential nature of what falls under them . . . Wittgenstein thought this to be misguided. Definitions do not disclose essences, they determine them. They give rules for the use of words, not insights into the language-independent essence of things.[13]

It is difficult indeed to speak honestly and carefully, so as to teach and write with a certain discipline. Speaking and writing with discipline is important. But as philosophers from Socrates to Wittgenstein have noticed, the quest for better definitions can end in sophistry, words about words that make us neglect the set of references by which such words have meaning. Like the questions and answers of a catechism, or the doctrines of a theological treatise, definitions pertain not so much to what things are, but to how they are to be spoken and practiced. We need to keep returning to each text and to what it actually says, how it works, and what its words might accomplish in the presence of attentive readers. Exercises in this mode—in the *Investigations,* in any of our texts—aid us in stepping away from the fictions we impose on language when we let go of the direct work of attentive study and instead play around in the rather less useful realm of abstract ideas.

The Poetic Gesture

Marjorie Perloff has written insightfully on Wittgenstein's striking conception of his own writing, his deep care for his manner of writing, and how he wants his text to be read. Referring to Wittgenstein's preface, she observes that the *Philosophical Investigations* is "really only an album," "a medley, a commonplace book or loose collection of disparate items, collaged together *kreuz und quer* (criss-crossed) without much thought of the controlling structure"[14]—or, I might add, in despair over the idea of such control. She draws an analogy with poetry:

> Wittgenstein describes the method whereby he ordered the "remarks, short paragraphs, of which there is sometimes a fairly long chain about the same subject" into the larger structure of the book. Wittgenstein's writings enact their central motive: words and phrases can be understood only in their particular context, their use. Not what one says but how one says it is the key to doing philosophy. And that, of course, is what makes it poetry as well.[15]

Such poetry—words catching and holding readers' active attention—is key also to the *Garland,* and indeed to this book, for which I have created a special rough context that, if ignored, leaves the book with the appearance of an imperfect patching together of various texts.

Referring to Wittgenstein's *Culture and Value* in particular, Perloff notes how he emphasizes the need for slow reading: "Sometimes a sentence can be understood only if it is read at the right tempo. My sentences are all to be read slowly."[16] Or again, "Thoughts rise to the surface slowly, like bubbles,"[17] and ought not be hurried, were that even possible. She sees how Wittgenstein points to a disciplined slowness: "The necessity, in an information age, of slowing down the reading process, was central to the thinking of many of Wittgenstein's contemporaries . . . the term *ostranenie* (estrangement, defamiliarization) was always associated with slowing down the reading (or viewing) process in art." And so, she observes, quoting Wittgenstein, "To say 'Philosophy must be written only as one would write poetry'[18] is to be aware of the need for density and resonance—rather than logic and sequential argument—in the verbal construct."[19] My suggestion here is that the goal of density and density's resonances lies at the heart of each of our six texts. They waste no words but expect the words that remain to be noticed, thought through, internalized by readers. Such texts spare us only the difficulties arising in the superfluous, the irrelevant, the distracted, the overly general.

Here we may recall our reading of the *Garland.* It is poetic in form, written in tightly metered verses, and is possessed of an artful, hard-won density that resists efforts to understand any of it too quickly, too easily. Every word counts. What Perloff says, again citing Wittgenstein, might well apply to Mādhava: "poeticity" depends upon "the conviction that 'language is not contiguous to anything else. We cannot speak of the use of language as opposed to anything else.' For if one begins with the actual words spoken or written, word choice and grammar are seen to be everything."[20] By extension, we can likewise read the *Sentences* and *Perspectives,* the *Admirable Secret* and the *Linked Verses* (our pair yet to come), according to their authors' choices in what to say and not to say in their work of covering vast amounts of material in as small a place as possible.

Accordingly, Perloff cautions against imagining that one will eventually be able to leave behind all the laborious details: "'progress' is too strong a word here, for, as Wittgenstein puts it in a 1930 Lecture, 'Philosophical analysis does not tell us anything new about thought (and if it did it would not interest us).' Rather, 'Philosophy is the attempt to be rid of a particular kind of puzzlement.'"[21] The progress involved is to find our way back to the present moment, by our reading and learning to read. Indeed, Perloff adds, "The limit of language manifests itself in the impossibility of describing the reality that corresponds to (is the translation of) a sentence *without simply repeating the sentence.*"[22]

For this disclosure of what is in a sense already obvious, examples and comparisons are essential:

> Analogies thus provide sometimes positive, sometimes negative, reinforcement: in either case, they lead us to revise our previous understanding of this or that fixed notion. It is this processive, self-corrective, and even self-canceling nature of Wittgenstein's propositions—their deployment of language as "a labyrinth of paths",[23] their use of countless

> examples, anecdotes, narratives, and analogies—that gives the text its poetic edge. . . . However much the individual exempla in the text are open for discussion and debate, the unstated axiom governing them is that "language is not contiguous to anything else," and that accordingly, the meaning of a word is its use in the language. And the text enacts that theorem, presented as a non-theorem, at every turn. Showing, not telling, is the mode.[24]

Processive, self-corrective, even self-canceling: Wittgenstein's goal is a certain manner of hands-on, text-grounded learning that leaves no alternative to a notable intimacy between writer and reader, bonding in the intimacy of a reading wherein all extraneous questions evaporate.

Dallas High comments on the *use* at the heart of Wittgenstein's writing: "Because the writing of the later Wittgenstein wishes not to offer understanding without personal involvement and puzzlement or 'to bring light into one brain or another' even in the work's own 'poverty and in the darkness of this time,' there is clear propriety for *'using' rather than commenting* upon the writings, *working through* some of his thoughts and puzzles rather than summarizing them, *applying his insights* rather than grouping, categorizing, or classifying them."[25] Stanley Cavell discusses the "confessional" mode of Wittgenstein's thought, his intent to break the hold of the past over the present, the dead over the living. While a wholesale indictment of the past is inadvisable, Cavell's conclusion is to the point: "Because the breaking of such control is a constant purpose of the later Wittgenstein, his writing is *deeply practical and negative,* the way Freud's is. And like Freud's therapy, it wishes *to prevent understanding which is unaccompanied by inner change.*"[26] Slow reading, I suggest, is the necessary work that leads to such change, in religious and interreligious reading. Thus Mādhava and Appayya Dīkṣita, Lombard and Canisius, all sought to instigate inner change by their writing and by the work into which they invite their readers. Louis de Montfort and Manavāḷamāmuni, our authors in chapter 5, will speak to the same point.

Writing so as to Teach

The concerns for philosophical method and pedagogy are inseparable: as we read, so we think. Wittgenstein worries therefore about our time-consuming distractions from language as it works right before our eyes—on our tongues, unto our ears. We are distracted, and we end up thinking, teaching, and writing at length about matters that are themselves the offspring of our misunderstanding of what we are up to and how we learn. As we have already seen, his remedy lies practically in a style of his writing that compels dedicated readers to learn and understand different things, differently.

In *Wittgenstein and the Philosophical Investigations,* Maria McGinn characterizes that pedagogical practice as follows:

> understanding Wittgenstein's method and its connection with the form of the text is the key to understanding the *Investigations.* . . . Wittgenstein himself emphasizes over and over again that it is a method or a style of thought, rather than doctrines, that characterizes his later philosophy. It is, moreover, his insistence that his philosophical aims do not involve him in putting forward 'any kind of theory' (*PI* 109) that makes the question of method, and of how to read his remarks, such a difficult one, for it suggests that we cannot approach the book in the usual way, with a view to finding and extracting the views which are expressed in it.[27]

Not in the usual way: the temptation is to impose order on Wittgenstein's seeming disorder by ordering and thematizing his work, talking over it rather than working it through. Learning in the particular is what matters, and it must be done slowly, without short cuts.

Thus too, in an unexpectedly similar way there is no quick way around the *Garland,* the *Perspectives,* the *Sentences,* and the *Catechism.* They "work" as they are, even if they themselves claim humbly to stand in for older, larger traditions. I have stressed over and again that my presentation of a few apt passages seeks only to make easier the first reading. It does not replace the work of reading the whole of each text, however long that takes. Wittgenstein, McGinn argues, "attempts, not a systematization of the rules that govern our use of words, but an evocation of the distinctive patterns of use that characterize our employment of them; it is by making ourselves aware of these distinctive patterns of use that we clarify the grammar of our concepts." He does this "to make us aware of the clash between our philosophically reflective idea of how a concept works and the way it actually functions"[28]—or, as I put it, the clash between what we think our traditions say and how they function as read, learned, and passed down. The directness of reading seems simple, but it has great effect, serving to deflate the great questions about religions by gentle persistence in acts of reading that respect religious texts and yet transgress their margins by reading other texts at the same time.

McGinn offers her version of the malady and diagnosis as Wittgenstein sees them:

> It might be helpful to identify the attitude that makes us so resistant to Wittgenstein's idea that we must concern ourselves with describing

> language-in-use by a special name, since it is of central importance in the underlying dialectic of Wittgenstein's later philosophy. I shall call it the theorizing or theoretical attitude. It is this attitude that Wittgenstein means to characterize when he says that 'we feel as if we had to penetrate phenomena' (*PI* 90). It is vital to our coming to understand Wittgenstein's later philosophy that we come to see the significance of this attitude and the nature of Wittgenstein's opposition to it.[29]

The return to details can be off-putting:[30]

> One of the difficulties in understanding the *Investigations* is that this switch from looking towards the construction of a model or a theory, back towards a concern with the details of particular cases of our ordinary practice of employing language, is so difficult to accept. The style of thought involved in undertaking a grammatical enquiry seems to go in quite the wrong direction, for its direction is the very opposite from the one that the theoretical attitude makes us want to go in. For while we feel that our question can only be answered by the construction of an account that explains what a given phenomenon consists in, Wittgenstein wants us to look at the intricate details of concrete instances of our practice of using language.[31]

A return to the details of particular cases; spending time with particular words and paragraphs; an inquiry that annoyingly keeps heading back to the particular without generating explanatory theories: this practice is at the heart of *Reading the Hindu and Christian Classics.*

Thus the importance of learning from the master's stubborn resistance to generalization:

> Wittgenstein expresses this idea that his method tries to turn us in a direction that we are unwilling to follow at a number of points. . . . [But] we will miss the whole point of Wittgenstein's philosophical method if we attempt to extract from his remarks a series of philosophical claims about what constitutes meaning, understanding, sensations, and so on. Not only is Wittgenstein not concerned with the construction or elaboration of philosophical theories, but whatever claims we might extract from his remarks are not to be understood as the point of the work. Thus he himself gives clear warning that any such attempt to extract "theses" will produce, not gold, but banality: "If one tried to advance theses in philosophy, it would never be possible to debate them, because everyone would agree to them" (*PI* 128).[32]

Returning to "the intricate details of concrete instances of our practice of using language" ensures the survival of reading as essential. The book is never replaced by the idea of the book or a quicker tabulation of what the books contain.

For maximum benefit, we must work through the whole of any given text rather than speeding things up by excerpting passages that support points one wishes to make:

> We must, therefore, resist the attempt to sum up, or to state philosophically exciting conclusions, and allow instead for a series of clarifications to take place in which "the philosophical problem . . . completely disappears" (*PI* 133). In this way, we never lose sight of the fact that "the work of the philosopher consists in assembling reminders for a particular purpose" (*PI* 127); the dialectical structure of the work—seen in the interaction of Wittgenstein's different voices—is thereby acknowledged as an essential part of his method, and is not seen as a mere stylistic device which obscures the general views that are being surreptitiously advanced, and which our exposition must somehow draw out.[33]

Texts that summarize—such as my six texts, and indeed this book itself—serve their role well if they are mistaken as replacements for the texts they cite and summarize.

This is why the work of reading, and comparative reading, does not in any near moment come to a halt, so as to give way to theories and theologies of religions. Instead of a well-intentioned pluralist account of religions as a justification for comparative work, we must instead keep traveling in what may seem a stubbornly wrong-headed direction: back to the text, again and again, that we might keep reading. There is no portal opened except by way of reading—my book as a start, but then reading deep into the vast library of such texts that are now, more than ever in history, available to us.

Criss-crossing Back and Ahead

My hope is that by the readings begun in this book, though in so many ways divergent from what Wittgenstein is up to—so big, so ambitious of specific and proper instruction, so Catholic, so Hindu—we can approximate a style of thought "that eschews the abstract theorizing which . . . lies at the root of philosophical confusion"[34]—and then, too, eschews the forms of quick reading that skate over the details and leave the great books in the background, there to be quoted but no longer actually read. In such a manner, we can leave behind us a host of theological and interreligious confusions as well.

As we read and reread our instructive, doctrinal, and (soon to follow) participatory texts, we need to learn and then write with an acute awareness that writing about them or from them—drawing out a page or two here and there of each text, as I have done—is at best a provisional exercise meant to inspire readers to do likewise. One needs to learn Christian doctrine or Hindu ritual reasoning, for instance, from the text up. For this certain humility is required: neither the author nor the reader can master the method and the outcome. Again, the preface to the *Investigations:* "My thoughts were soon crippled if I tried to force them on in any single direction against their natural inclination." Let the reading proceed, and see where it leads.

This detour has been intended to shed light on the work of *Reading the Hindu and Christian Classics* in its substantive second, third, and fifth chapters. I admit that this can be done only from an oblique angle, since Wittgenstein and our authors do not share a particular philosophical or theological project, and there is much to divide them. Tradition and its truths are not only literary matters, the content of faith matters. It is not only the healing of philosophy that is at stake in the books I introduce here. The *Garland,* the *Sentences,* the *Catechism,* the *Perspectives*—and soon, the *Admirable Secret* and the *Linked Verses*—all aim at realities older and deeper than Wittgenstein takes up in his argument with philosophical peers. And yet my intuition is that his understanding of philosophy, his poetic manner of writing, and his pedagogical intent—all subversive of generalization and abstraction—help make the case why our reading must be slow, patient, meticulous, and open-ended. It would be marvelous, for example, were readers, before going to chapter 5, to go back and reread earlier chapters now: after Wittgenstein.

FIVE

Words of Participation

The Invitation to Inspired Speech

At the start of chapter 1 I recounted taking the *Garland* off the shelf in order to read it, of necessity slowly and over a long period of time: a great obligation accidently incurred with abundant fruits but hardly a chance of an audience. In the course of this study, I found myself learning so much that I was at a loss as to what to do with what I was learning. With that first learning in mind, I reflected more deeply and widely on the practice of close reading, slowly done, as a necessary manner of study. Reading the *Garland* led me to recall the Catholic catechetical tradition and to reflect on the power of instruction in a complete vocabulary of the divine-human relationship as believed and practiced. Recognizing that truth is at stake in such reading led me to seek out further texts that lead readers toward truth in its doctrinal form, thought through and argued in a communal context. So I took up the *Perspectives* and the *Sentences,* two massive texts that still claim to serve the needs of beginners. After reading them in chapter 2, I circled back in chapter 3 to the dynamic of instruction, now reading the *Garland* alongside the *Catechism* of Peter Canisius. Comparative themes arose, regarding the nature of the human as distinct from and related to the divine, the unity and plurality of the world, and the extent of sacrificial and moral rules in religious and ordinary life. Chapter 4 diverted our attention for a moment to the *Philosophical Investigations,* to confirm that there is a certain nontheoretical solidity behind the claim that there is no way forward but the work of patient study.

Participation as the Fruit of Study

Our texts instruct, and they disclose truth. But traditions intent upon knowledge and truth want more than the intellectual assent of their readers. Rather, instruction and doctrine are meant also to draw readers into the communities they visit in their reading, become participants who reenact as their own the words they read. This eventuality becomes all the more apparent when spiritual classics actively draw readers into participation by words that appeal to heart as well as mind.

To show this dynamic at work, I turn now to my final pair of texts for slow reading, two vernacular devotional classics intending to inspire readers to participate wholeheartedly in the mysteries at hand, in and just beyond words: Louis de Montfort's eighteenth-century French-language *Admirable Secret of the Most Holy Rosary* (*Le Secret Admirable du Trés Saint Rosaire*) and Maṇavāḷamāmuni's fourteenth-century Tamil-language *One Hundred Linked Verses on the Holy Word of Mouth* (*Tiruvāymoḻinuṟṟāntāti*).

The *Admirable Secret* takes up the familiar prayer practice of the rosary, in order to detect within that practice the entirety of the Catholic faith intellectually, imaginatively, and practically enhanced. Montfort hopes that his readers will be drawn into the mysteries of the birth, death, and resurrection of Christ dramatized in the decades of the rosary and recollected during the recitation of its Lord's Prayer and many Hail Marys.

The *Linked Verses* by style and content intensifies, in the small confines of one hundred verses, the intellectual and affective energies of the thousand verses of the most highly venerated *Holy Word of Mouth.* The hundred ten-verse songs of that text (about which I say a little more later on) are in turn revered as the unparalleled flood of passionate words arising in the ecstatic experience of the Tamil saint Śaṭakōpaṉ, a flood in which listeners find themselves immersed. Arising in Maṇavāḷamāmuni's meditations on the *Holy Word,* the *Linked Verses* offers a straight path into the *Holy Word* and the spiritually charged world of Śaṭakōpaṉ.

These are two texts, then, that expect for their readers a heightening of experience and a participation in revered words arising from experience. They may turn out to be more demanding and perhaps off-putting than the instructive and doctrinal challenges of the four texts considered in previous chapters.

At the Heart of Catholic Piety: Praying the Rosary

The *Admirable Secret* is a text of 120 pages in the French edition of Montfort's works, and 74 pages in a common English edition.[1] Its author, Louis Grignion de Montfort (1673–1716), was primarily a pastor who traveled for years as a rural preacher. His accomplishments were in part practical. He founded the Daughters of Wisdom, a congregation of nuns dedicated to the care of needy children and the sick. He is best known for the *True Devotion to the Blessed Virgin,* which serves well as a larger frame for the Marian piety vital to all his writings. He also gathered a group of priests dedicated to continuing his mission and the spread of devotion to Mary, a society that came to be known as the Missionaries of the Company of Mary or, more commonly, the Montfort Fathers. In addition to the *Admirable Secret of the Most Holy Rosary,* we have too Montfort's *Holy Methods for Reciting the Rosary Drawing upon Oneself the Grace of the Mysteries of the Life, Passion and Glory of Jesus and Mary* (henceforth *Holy Methods*), a short and practical text instructive on how to structure one's prayer and prayer times. Employing ordinary and accessible French, Montfort wrote the *Admirable Secret* in order to give practical advice on how to draw Catholics back more fervently to a practice they thought they already knew well, now with a heightened sense of the wholeness of faith everywhere latent in each small prayer.

The Rosary as Object, Prayer, Practice

But let us first recall "the Catholic rosary." Materially, a rosary is a connected circle of fifty beads marked off in sets of ten by an extra bead separating each decade from the ones before it and after it. Usually, rosaries also have, attached to the circle, a short string of extra beads, often just three or five, that end in a crucifix. Three prayers comprise all the words of the rosary, the first two of which we saw playing a role in the *Catechism:*

> Our Father, who are in heaven, hallowed be your name; your kingdom come, your will be done on earth as it is in heaven. Give us this day our daily bread; and forgive us our trespasses as we forgive those who trespass against us; and lead us not into temptation, but deliver us from evil. Amen.
>
> Hail Mary, full of grace, the Lord is with you. Blessed are you among women, and blessed is the fruit of your womb, Jesus. Holy Mary, Mother of God, pray for us sinners, now and at the hour of our death. Amen.
>
> Glory be the Father, and to the Son, and to the Holy Spirit, as it was in the beginning, is now, and will be forever. Amen.

A Hail Mary is prayed on each of the fifty beads, with a Lord's Prayer before the first decade, and on the intervening single beads between decades. On a set of five beads adjunct to the circle, an opening Lord's Prayer and three preliminary Hail Marys are said, and a "Glory Be." According to Montfort, the Creed is to be recited while holding the crucifix.

The fifty Hail Marys upon the fifty beads of the rosary are ideally recited thrice daily, each decade linked to scenes from the fundamental Christian story:

> The Joyful Mysteries: Annunciation, Visitation, Nativity, Presentation in the Temple, Jesus at age twelve found in the Temple;
>
> The Sorrowful Mysteries: Agony in the Garden, Scourging at the Pillar, Crowning with Thorns, Carrying of the Cross, Crucifixion;
>
> The Glorious Mysteries: Resurrection; Ascension; Pentecost; Assumption of Mary; Mary's Coronation as Queen of Heaven.

Excepting the last two glorious mysteries, the mysteries are all taken directly from the Gospels.

This instance of popular repetitive prayer was highly prized by Montfort precisely as rich in Christological and Marian motifs. In his view, it is a premier instance of devotion that also encapsulates in the simplest and most intense of forms the tradition as a whole. What is taught by way of instruction in the catechisms and investigated in doctrine is now enacted in the recitation of the rosary. Recitants are now participants in the divine-human drama that they may have earlier already learned and studied.

Montfort's 1st "Rose" (chapter) merges practice and meaning, announcing the mysteries in their ethical import:

> The rosary is made up of two things: mental prayer and vocal prayer . . . mental prayer is none other than meditation on the chief mysteries of the life, death and glory of Jesus Christ and of his most blessed Mother. Vocal prayer consists in saying fifteen decades of the Hail Mary, each decade headed by an Our Father, while at the same time meditating on and contemplating the fifteen principal virtues which Jesus and Mary practiced in the fifteen mysteries of the rosary. In the first rosary, of five decades, we honor and reflect on the five joyful mysteries; in the second, the five sorrowful mysteries; and in the third, the glorious mysteries. So the rosary is a blessed blending of mental and vocal prayer by which we honor and imitate the mysteries and the virtues of the life, death, passion and glory of Jesus and Mary.[2]

The 2nd Rose traces its lineage back through tradition to Mary herself, addressed throughout the Hail Mary. Montfort claims its direct reception by St. Dominic, the famed preacher and reformer:

> Since the rosary is composed, principally and in substance, of the prayer of Christ and the angelic salutation, that is, the Our Father and the Hail Mary, it was without doubt the first prayer and the first devotion

of the faithful and has been in use all through the centuries, from the time of the apostles and disciples down to the us. It was only in the year 1214, however, that the rosary in its present form and according to the method we use today was given to the Church by the Blessed Virgin to St. Dominic as a means of converting the Albigensians and other sinners.[3]

All the words of the Hail Mary are taken to be divinely inspired utterances: the words of Gabriel to Mary ("Hail Mary, full of grace . . ."), and of Elizabeth to Mary ("Blessed are you among women . . . ," to which the Church appended a doctrinally charged closing invocation ("Holy Mary, Mother of God . . ."). The words of the Lord's Prayer are of course taken from Jesus's Sermon on the Mount in the Gospel according to Matthew, chapter 6, where Jesus gives them to his listeners as an exemplary prayer.

With such first-person origins, the garland of words fashioned in the particular form of the rosary takes on a particular force and energy within the Church. By it, recitants enter right into a lineage of believers linked closely to the persons to whom the prayers are addressed. Each daily recitation reenacts sacred speech reaching back to the words of Gabriel and Elizabeth. Drawing on older accounts, Montfort elaborates the drama of the medieval revival of this piety, Dominic's receiving of the rosary during a time of great difficulty:

I will tell you the story of how he received it, as Blessed Alan de la Roche reports it in his famous book *De Dignitate Psalterii. Saint Dominic, seeing that people's crimes were hindering the conversion of the Albigensians, withdrew into a forest near Toulouse, where he spent three days and three nights in continual prayer and penance. During this time he did nothing but groan and weep and lacerate his body with blows of his discipline. Finally, he collapsed, half-dead.*[4]

While Montfort does not dismiss heretics so abruptly as does Canisius, we cannot but observe here the matter-of-fact way in which Albigensians are portrayed as in need of conversion. Mary's intervention saves the day, as she teaches the efficacy of the rosary even within a dispensation ordered to the saving work of Christ:

At this point our Lady appeared to him, accompanied by three princesses from heaven, and said to him, "My dear Dominic, do you know which weapon the Blessed Trinity uses to reform the world?" "Oh, my Lady," answered Saint Dominic, "you know far better than I do, because next to your Son Jesus Christ you have always been the chief instrument of our salvation." Then our Lady replied, "I want you to know that, in this kind of warfare, the principal weapon has always been the Angelic Psalter (or

Rosary), the foundation-stone of the New Testament. Therefore, if you want to gain these hardened souls for God, preach my Psalter."[5]

Dominic thereafter is a conduit in his era of this privileged living word:

> Inspired by the Holy Spirit, instructed by the Blessed Virgin as well as by his own experience, Saint Dominic preached the rosary for the rest of his life. He preached it by his example as well as by his living word, in cities and in the countryside, to people of high station and low, before the learned and the uneducated, to Catholics and to heretics. The rosary, which he said every day, was his preparation for every sermon and his refuge after preaching.[6]

The point is therefore to attest not only to the authenticity of the rosary's words, but also to its efficacious transmission, alive and potent in the lifetime of any and all readers.

Readings in Montfort's *Admirable Secret of the Most Holy Rosary*

The *Admirable Secret* over and over makes the case for the daily recitation of the rosary as the vehicle for sharing its potent sacred power. Montfort readily concedes that the practice is repetitive and always in danger of becoming rote. But he also thinks that the repetitive practice can be deepened and purified by the cultivation of right attitudes of mind and heart, and by hearing fervent appeals such as those everywhere in the *Admirable Secret.* He seeks to inspire his listeners and instill new confidence, that they might return with fervor to what might have become overly familiar, seemingly commonplace, or out of date. He enhances and intensifies the significance of the familiar prayers by showing that there is inscribed in them every key doctrine of the faith, now recast not as something to think about, but as something to do by way of daily recitation. The rosary was not meant to replace other practices, such as the sacraments or a life of love and service, but it was to serve as a gateway to a deeper and more intense living of the Christian life.

The success of this manner of affective appeal is a matter of persuasion, and persuasion is necessarily very much a matter of taste, supported by reason, authority, etc. Writing that encourages spiritual advancement cannot be timeless or context free. Montfort's florid language, effective in its time, indeed seems out of date as we encounter it now. If with respect to our earlier texts, we needed to learn to study carefully and patiently teachings and doctrines not fully aligned with twenty-first-century dispositions, and without rushing to critique, the *Admirable Secret* requires of us a different kind of suspension, lest due to matters of taste we miss or dismiss the appeals Montfort so fervently poses to readers. He certainly makes his direct appeal with great energy and purpose. In the preamble to the *Admirable Secret,* Montfort addresses his audience in four groups: priests (with a "white rose"), sinners (with a "red rose"), seekers after mystical advancement ("with a mystical rose bush"), and children (with "a little rosebud").

The white rose is a plea to priests, that they see the theology and practice of the rosary as in harmony with their mission to preach: "Beware, please, of thinking of the rosary as something of little importance, as do ignorant people, and even several great but proud scholars. Rather, it is truly great, sublime, and divine. Heaven has given it to us, to convert the most hardened sinners and the most obstinate heretics." Tradition testifies to God's consistent graciousness with respect to the rosary, which offers "grace in this life and glory in the next." Its authority is ancient and consistent: "The saints have practiced it, and the Popes have endorsed it." Few know its secrets well, but once its secret power has been revealed to a director of souls, "he will say the rosary each day and will teach others to recite it." In turn, "God and his blessed Mother will pour abundant grace into his soul, that he may be an instrument of God's glory; and his word, though simple, will do more good in one month than that of other preachers in several years."[7] Encouraging priests to practice what they preach, Montfort too enlists the authority of tradition in support of his message. He promises to speak not from his own experience, though he says he has much he could say, but from convincing and even erudite tradition: "I think it will be quite enough for this little summary that I am writing if I tell you a few ancient and authenticated stories. For your sake, I include several passages in Latin, drawn from good authors which prove what I have outlined for the faithful in French."[8]

To sinners he offers a red rose. The rosary offers an escape from their self-destructive behavior. For those who pray, divine chastisements will be nothing more than thorns on the beautiful rose of faith restored: "If you are faithful in saying it even unto death, I do assure you that, despite of the greatness of your sins 'you shall receive a never-fading crown of glory' (*I Peter* 5.4), you will receive a crown of glory that never fades."[9] Indeed, it is never too late:

> Even if you are on the brink of the abyss, even if you already have one foot in hell, even if you have sold your soul to the devil like a magician, and even if you are a heretic as obstinate as a devil, sooner or later you will be converted and will amend your life and save your soul, provided that—and I reemphasize what I am saying and the terms of my counsel—you say the rosary devoutly every day until death for the pur-

> pose of knowing the truth and obtaining contrition and pardon for your sins. You will see in this book many stories of great sinners who were converted through the power of the rosary.[10]

"Please read and meditate upon them:" do this, and it will make a difference.

Montfort assures those already devout and spiritually advanced in other ways that theirs will be an entire mystical rose bush. The rosary is not merely an added practice, but one that enriches the daily spiritual practices already in place:

> Devout souls, illumined by the Holy Spirit, you will not mind my giving you this little mystical rose bush from heaven to be planted in the garden of your soul. It will not harm the sweet-smelling flowers of your contemplations. It is sweet-smelling and entirely divine, and will not in the least interfere with your carefully planned flower-beds. It is pure and well-ordered, and inclines all to order and purity. If it is carefully watered and properly attended to every day as is necessary, it will grow to such a marvelous height, and its branches will have such a wide span that, far from hindering your other devotions, it will maintain and perfect them.

He proposes a potent equation that even mystics could hardly ignore:

> This mystical rose bush is Jesus and Mary in life, death and eternity.[11]

Nothing could be more basic to the mystical life than participation in this holy practice.

Finally, even children can take it up, Montfort thinks, and so he offers them a little rosebud, the story of a child who wanders off with the Virgin Mary:

> At the end of the third day they found her at the front door looking extremely happy and pleased. Naturally they asked her where on earth she had been, and she told them that the lady to whom she had been saying the rosary had taken her to a lovely place where she had given her delicious things to eat. She said that the lady had also given her a baby boy to hold, that he was very beautiful, and that she had kissed him again and again.

He claims the direct testimony of an eyewitness:

> The father and mother, who had been converted to the Catholic faith only a short time before, sent at once for the Jesuit Father who had instructed them for their reception into the Church and who had also taught them devotion to the rosary. They told him everything that had

happened, and it was this priest himself who told me this story. It all took place in Paraguay.

If children listen to this story and take to heart his words, their lives and practice of the rosary will likewise lift them up into the mysteries of God even during this life:

> So, dear children, imitate these little girls[12] and say your rosary every day as they always did. If you do this, you will earn the right to go to heaven to see Jesus and Mary. If it is not their wish that you should see them in this life, at any rate after you die you will see them for all eternity. Amen.[13]

The entire opening section ends with an appeal to all: "Therefore, let all people, the learned and the ignorant, the just and the sinners, the great and the small, praise and honor Jesus and Mary night and day, by the holy rosary. And so, 'Greet Mary who has labored much among you' (*Romans* 16.6)."[14] The *Admirable Secret* is itself just a book, but it is presented by Montfort as an exhortation grounded in a long lineage of preachers and practitioners who vouch for the efficacy of this practice. He hopes that readers will learn from his instruction on the deeper theological and spiritual meanings of the rosary but then realize his teachings in their lives by committing to the regular recitation of the rosary. The *Admirable Secret* is therefore a bridge between understanding and participation.

Fifty Beads of Instruction

Montfort fills the ensuing forty-nine chapters ("roses") to confirm the links of the rosary with insightful exegesis, right theology, and fervent piety. In the first decade (roses 1–10), he recounts inspiring pious stories about the origins of the rosary, intended to demonstrate its fruitfulness to well-disposed listeners. The second decade (roses 11–20) illustrates "the surpassing merit of the rosary" by attention to the prayers of which it is comprised, making clear the connections:

> 11 The Creed, said on the crucifix
>
> 12–14 An exegesis of the Lord's Prayer, said at the start of each decade
>
> 15–16 The Hail Mary: the words addressed by Gabriel to Mary ("Hail Mary, full of grace . . ."), followed by Elizabeth's words ("Blessed are you among women . . ."), concluding with the anti-Arian words of the early Church ("Holy Mary Mother of God . . .")
>
> 17–19 Pious stories confirming the importance of the Hail Mary
>
> 20 An exegesis of the words of the Hail Mary

The third decade takes up the joyful, sorrowful, and glorious mysteries as a set of largely biblical stories that are to be contemplated and appropriated with special attention to the efficacy of recitation:

21 The mystery of salvation, across the fifteen mysteries

22 How meditation on the mysteries makes us resemble Jesus

23 How the rosary is a memory of the life and death of Jesus

24 How it is a great means of perfection

25 The riches of holiness arising from it

26 The sufficiency of the rosary compared with all other practices

27–29 The fruits of the rosary

30 The indulgences linked to the rosary

The fourth decade (roses 31–40) further details the "surpassing merit of the holy rosary as seen in the wonders God has worked through it," by drawing in still more pious stories illustrative of the benefits of regular recitation. Montfort writes with a religious imagination populated with apparitions, miracles, and salutary stories that inspire and warn, and with them, he seeks to enflame readers similarly inclined.

Theology and inspirational narratives cannot on their own suffice, if willing practitioners are neglectful of temporal and physical concerns. The fifth decade (roses 41–49) is therefore still more practical, instructive regarding how to pray the rosary worthily despite distractions, with attention to bodily posture, time and place, and circumstances favoring private or communal recitation:

41 Intentions required for saying the rosary properly, with right intentions

42 Praying with attentiveness to God's voice

43 Overcoming distractions by focusing and resisting temptations

44 Fighting distractions by meditating on its mysteries

45 Proper space, time, posture

46 Communal, choral recitation

47 Seriousness in prayer and joining a confraternity

48 Further instruction on perseverance

49 Further details regarding indulgences

These details of course pose further challenges to readers, who are invited to experiment on such matters, to act rather than considering them merely in theory. Without such a commitment to doing, what the practice is about and where it leads cannot be really understood.

Better Theology, Better Practice

Here too, it is important to turn to the reading of the text, and so now I offer two in-depth examples, one theological, the other practical. The first pertains to Montfort's exposition of the Creed, and here he plays his role as theologian. In the 11th Rose, he emphasizes the importance of the Creed, to be prayed on the crucifix at the start of every recitation:

> The Creed, the Symbol of the Apostles, is said on the crucifix of the rosary. It is a holy summary and abridgement of the Christian truths. It is a prayer that has great merit, because faith is the root, foundation and beginning of all Christian virtues, of all eternal virtues, and of all prayers that are pleasing to God. "Anyone who comes to God must believe." (*Hebrews* 11.6) It is necessary that the person who would approach God by prayer begin by faith. The greater his faith the more force and merit his prayer will have in itself, and the more it will glorify God.[15]

If the Creed provides a foundation for prayer, great power dwells in professing faith even in the simplest form, "I believe":

> I shall not stop here to explain the words of the Apostles' Creed, but I cannot resist saying that the first words, "I believe in God," confirm the acts of the three theological virtues of faith, hope and charity. They are wonderfully effective as a means of sanctifying the soul and smiting the devil.

Vivid testimonies reinforce the point:

> It was with these words that many saints overcame temptations, especially those against faith, hope or charity, be it during their lifetime or at the hour of their death. They were also the last words of St. Peter the martyr. He managed to trace these words in the sand with his finger, when his head was divided in two by a blow of a heretic's sword, as he was about to expire.[16]

The faith enunciated in the Creed, uttered with grace and in charity, clears the way for the mysteries that follow:

> Just as faith is the only key which opens up for us all the mysteries of Jesus and Mary contained in the rosary, it is necessary to begin the

> rosary by saying the Creed with great attention and devotion. The more our faith is alive and strong, the more merit our rosary will have. This faith must be vivified and animated by charity: if one is to recite the rosary well, to recite the rosary properly it is necessary to be in God's grace, or at least seeking it.[17]

Montfort may be speaking from his own experience when he notes that this faith is also a bulwark against troubles sure to arise.:

> This faith must be strong and constant, that is, it must not be looking for sensible devotion and spiritual consolation in the practice of the rosary; nor should one give it up because the mind is flooded with countless involuntary distractions, or because one experiences a strange distaste in the soul or an almost continual and oppressive fatigue of the body. Neither feelings, nor consolation, nor sighs, nor transports, nor the continual attention of the imagination are needed. Pure faith and good intentions are quite enough. *Sola fides sufficit.*[18]

The Creed inaugurates every recitation of the rosary, and the rosary enacts that faith over and again. Doctrine comes alive in the prayers of recitants.

My second example draws on the 42nd, 43rd, and 44th Roses and turns still more directly to practice. The 42nd, drawn partly from the *Rosier Mystique* of Antoninus Thomas (as my italics show), begins as a call for attentiveness in prayer:

> *In order to pray well, it is not enough to give expression to our petitions by means of that most excellent of all prayers, the rosary, but we must also pray with great attention, for God listens more to the voice of the heart than to that of the mouth. To be guilty of willful distractions during prayer would show a great lack of respect and reverence; it would make our Rosaries unfruitful and fill us with sins. How dare we ask God to listen to us if we ourselves do not pay attention to what we are saying?* Or if, while we pray to his redoubtable majesty which makes all tremble, we voluntarily run after a butterfly? *Far from that person will be God's blessing, which is changed into a curse on those have with negligence done the things of God: "Cursed be the one who does God's work negligently."* (*Jeremiah* 48:10)[19]

Distractions are inevitable but ought not be allowed to diminish the value of prayer:

> In truth, you cannot say your rosary without having a few involuntary distractions; it is even difficult to say one Hail Mary without your ever restless imagination distracting you from the object of your attention. But you can recite it without voluntary distractions, and you must take

> all sorts of precautions to lessen involuntary distractions and to focus your imagination.

Montfort then dramatizes the entire scenario, heightening what is to be gained in recitants' affective commitment to praying the rosary all the way through despite obstacles. The potential is great:

> To this effect, put yourself in the presence of God, and believe that God and his Blessed Mother are watching you, and that your guardian angel is at your right hand, taking your Hail Marys, if they are well said, and using them like roses to make crowns for Jesus and Mary.

But so too the danger:

> And, just the opposite, at your left hand is the devil, ready to devour every Hail Mary and to write them down in his book of death, if they are not said with attention, devotion, and modesty. Above all, do not fail to offer up each decade in honor of one of the mysteries, and to represent for yourself, in your imagination, our Lord and his holy Mother in the mystery you are honoring. (n. 120)[20]

He closes the 42nd Rose by repeating Thomas's pious report on Mary's readiness to intervene directly:

> *We read in the life of Blessed Hermann of the Order of the Premonstratensians, that when he would say the rosary attentively and devoutly while meditating on the mysteries, the holy Virgin used to appear to him resplendent in light and with breathtaking majesty and beauty. But, as time went on, when his fervor cooled and he fell into the way of saying his rosary hurriedly and without giving it his full attention. she appeared to him again, her face furrowed, sad, and displeased. Hermann was astonished at the change in her, and the holy Virgin explained, "I appear this way before your eyes, such as I am in your soul, because you treat me more as a woman vile and worthy of contempt. Where is the time when you would greet me with respect and attention, meditating on my mysteries and praising my greatness?"*[21]

Colloquy of this sort—direct conversation with the one to whom one addresses ordinary prayers—is common in the *Admirable Secret.* The words of the rosary come directly from scripture and tradition and speak directly to the reality of Mary present and attentive. Recitation puts one in touch not only with those words, but directly with her as well. She then speaks on her own.

The 43rd Rose again concedes that the rosary's repetitiveness might encourage distractions. Montfort urges perseverance but asserts too that the rosary perfects its readers even in the crucible of boredom. In the 44th Rose, he condemns the temptation to race through the rosary, neglecting its deeper meanings; here the analogy between slow learning and slow reading and now slow praying is apt. To counter this temptation, recitants can try slowing down at select points marked by a + , taking an extra breath so as to slow things down in a way conducive to meditation:[22]

> Our Father who art in heaven, + hallowed by thy name, + thy kingdom come, + your will be done + on earth as it is in heaven. + Give us this day + our daily bread, + and forgive us our trespasses + as we forgive those who trespass against us, + and lead us not into temptation, + but deliver us from evil. Amen. +
>
> Hail, Mary, full of grace, + the Lord is with thee, + blessed art thou among women, + and blessed is the fruit of your womb, Jesus. + Holy Mary, Mother of God, + pray for us sinners, now + and at the hour of our death. Amen. +[23]

Composed of many words and subject to many repetitions, the rosary matures through mindfulness and heads toward a kind of simplicity, ever purer and more intense. Recollecting the rosary's theology and vulnerable to its effects, recitants pray with an increasingly widened consciousness and awakened heart, and come to dwell in its divinely and humanly populated universe.

Key to Montfort's exposition is its instructive force, linking the rosary to the mysteries and doctrines of the faith. But he often and quickly reverts to a strategy of pious appeal. Thus he tells the vivid and unusual story of three sisters who pray the rosary with varying degrees of piety and attention, each meriting a different reaction from the Virgin Mary when she appears to them. The more lax the sisters are, the more disheveled, wan, and displeased Mary shows herself to be when she appears. When the lax sisters have been properly chastised and then return to proper practice, they finally learn to pray together piously and with full attention. The question Montfort hopes his readers will take up is an obvious one: Which sister are you like? How would the Virgin look if she appeared to you? The rediscovery of devotion can always occur, it is never too late:

> At the end of this second year, on the same day of the Purification, our Lady, clothed in a magnificent robe, and again attended by St. Catherine and St. Agnes, wearing crowns, appeared to them in the evening. She said to them, "Be assured of the kingdom of heaven, and you will all have the great joy of going there very soon." The three of them cried, "Our heart is ready, our dear Lady, our heart is ready." Then the vision

> faded. That same night they became ill and sent for their confessor, and received the last sacraments, thanking him for the holy practice he had taught them. After compline, the holy Virgin to them appeared with a large company of virgins and had the three sisters clothed in white robes. All three of them went forth while angels were singing, "Come, spouses of Jesus Christ, receive the crowns which have been prepared for you for all eternity."[24]

In a somewhat alarming manner, the culmination of their devotion is thus a quick ascent into heaven. But the moral is mundane:

> Learn many important truths from this story: 1) How important it is to have a good director who inspires holy practices, especially that of the holy rosary; 2) How important it is to say the rosary with attention and devotion; 3) How kind and merciful is the Blessed Virgin to those who are sorry for the past and are firmly resolved to do better; 4) How generous she is in rewarding us in life, at death, and in eternity for the little services that we render her with fidelity.[25]

Montfort wants to achieve results among a wide range of readers, and so his style is homiletic, exhortative, and down to earth, particularly when he goes beyond Roche and Thomas and speaks in his own voice. Though rich in insight and affect, the "roses" do not require great effort on the listener's part. If readers simply listen, savor the simple appeals and instructions, and in the course of slow reading become inspired to take up the rosary and pray, that is sufficient. The *Admirable Secret* itself is best assessed then in terms of what readers do after they have stopped reading.

Perfecting the Practice

None of the instruction or doctrine matters, if readers do not put down the *Admirable Secret* and pick up the rosary. If they do, they will benefit from advice on how to pray it well. It is not surprising then to find right after the *Admirable Secret,* in the standard editions in French and in English, a small text entitled *Holy Methods,* which offers instructions on how to pray the rosary with amplified awareness and heightened affect. Here too Montfort offers basic advice but also some artful complications that require disciplined mindfulness on the part of recitants. The instructions further integrate recitation with reflection on the mysteries of the faith and also draw practitioners into the contemplative space of direct encounter with Jesus and Mary.

The first method, for example, adds "a special prayer at the beginning (of the whole rosary), and a prayer at the beginning and end of each decade." At the very beginning, we find this one:

> I unite with all the saints who are in heaven and with all the just who are on earth. I unite with you, my Jesus, to praise your holy Mother worthily and to praise you in Her and by Her. I renounce all the distractions that may come to me during this rosary. Holy Virgin, we offer you this Creed to honor the faith you had upon earth and to ask you to share with us that same faith. O Lord, we offer you this Our Father to adore you in your oneness and to acknowledge you as the first cause and the last end of all things. Most Holy Trinity, we offer you these three Hail Marys to thank you for all the graces which you have effected in Mary and which you have given to us through her intercession.[26]

Thereafter, at the start of the first decade, one is to pray,

> We offer you, Lord Jesus, this first decade in honor of the mystery of your Incarnation. Through this mystery and the intercession of your holy Mother we ask for deep humility of heart,

while at the end of the decade recitants make a request:

> May the grace of the mystery of the Incarnation come into my soul and make it truly humble.

At the start of the second decade, recitants pray,

> We offer you, Lord Jesus, this second decade in honor of the Visitation of your holy Mother to her cousin Saint Elizabeth.

By this mystery and through Mary's intercession,

> we ask for a perfect love of our neighbor.

At the end of the decade, the example of Mary and Elizabeth inspires this prayer:

> May the grace of the mystery of the Visitation come into me and make me truly charitable.[27]

All fifteen decades are similarly enhanced and intensified by opening and closing prayers that similarly draw recitants into the reality of the mysteries and from there to applications appropriate to daily life.

A second and rather more complex method inserts a fresh Christological dimension right into the Hail Mary itself.[28] Where the prayer simply says, "Blessed is the fruit of your womb, Jesus," several words are added each time to remind recitants of the mystery at hand. Thus,

In the 1st decade, ten times over, "blessed is the fruit of your womb, *Jesus becoming human,*"

in the 2nd, "blessed is the fruit of your womb, *Jesus sanctifying,*"

in the 3rd, "blessed is the fruit of your womb, *Jesus born in poverty,*"

in the 4th, "blessed is the fruit of your womb, *Jesus offered up,*"

in the 5th, "blessed is the fruit of your womb, *Jesus holy of holies,*"

in the 6th, "blessed is the fruit of your womb, *Jesus in his agony,*"

in the 7th, "blessed is the fruit of your womb, *Jesus scourged,*"

in the 8th, "blessed is the fruit of your womb, *Jesus crowned with thorns,*"

in the 9th, "blessed is the fruit of your womb, *Jesus carrying his cross,*"

in the 10th, "blessed is the fruit of your womb, *Jesus crucified,*"

in the 11th, "blessed is the fruit of your womb, *Jesus rising from the dead,*"

in the 12th, "blessed is the fruit of your womb, *Jesus ascending to heaven,*"

in the 13th, "blessed is the fruit of your womb, *Jesus filling you with the Holy Spirit,*"

in the 14th, "blessed is the fruit of your womb, *Jesus raising you to life,*"

in the 15th, "blessed is the fruit of your womb, *Jesus crowning you.*"

By such practice, the new titles of Jesus become more deeply rooted in the mind and heart of recitants. It also melds together more intensely the pieties of Jesus and Mary. It is not easy to say the prayers, contemplate the mysteries, be ready for encounter with Mary, and at the same time add new titles for Jesus. One has to pay attention, to remember and incorporate the changes, since the additions will become habitual only by repetition over many days. Doing all of this at once requires great clarity of mind and intention, the ruling out of distractions and a great deal of practice, so that all of this becomes so deeply internalized that it begins to happen by a rhythm now natural to the life of recitants: readers become able to put aside the *Admirable Secret* and the *Holy Methods* and participate fully yet very simply in this daily practice.

When Montfort succeeds in winning over his readers, he accomplishes a great deal. The *Admirable Secret* is an extended homily (*praedicatio*) that weaves together theology, devotion, efficacious action, and instructions on actual practice, along with pious stories and the promise of benefits, so as to expand recitants' understanding of what is going on theologically, spiritually, and morally in praying the rosary and as a result of it. The whole of the faith is now present in a circle of beads, fingered one by one. There are certainly other ways to implement and live out the faith, but Montfort finds in the rosary a portable and simple primary practice rich in faith, hope, and charity. Meanings are added and affects deepened, but what is true and good remains as unchanging as the number of beads. It is now available; you already know it; so *do* it.

An Aside of a More Personal Sort

A confessional moment: what is closest to home is sometimes hardest to make peace with, so readers will bear with me if I close this section by adding a personal reflection. In my childhood, the rosary was still a regular part of life at home and in school. I have known its prayers since earliest childhood. Even today, I own a rosary, often carry it with me when traveling. Not infrequently, at a parish or when visiting a school or convent (particularly in India), I come across small groups still praying the rosary together. I rarely join in; perhaps the group seems too pious, too earnest, and I am in a hurry. It also matters that almost no one I know (as far as I know) prays the rosary each day. So, in a rather direct sense, I have been one of those priests addressed by Montfort, and called back to the practice. While I am not fully persuaded by his words and cannot but begin to deconstruct his pieties and his inspirational stories, I am listening. I have been touched by, and cannot forget, the deep fervor and solid learning and intelligence underlying his appeals, as "pious and romantic" as they may be. If his book has not already done the work of drawing me back to the daily practice of the rosary, perhaps later on the connections may be made complete. After all, slow reading's effects too take their time.

Maṇavāḷamāmuni's *One Hundred Linked Verses on the Holy Word of Mouth*

Even as I read the *Admirable Secret* and pondered its practical meanings, I was also sifting through the store of Hindu texts I had worked with over the decades. I was seeking a Hindu text that would, differences notwithstanding, resonate well with Montfort's text, similarly using words intensely, skillfully, and beautifully, so as to draw readers into the practices lifted up and praised there.

There are of course very many Hindu texts that invite readers to move beyond learning tradition and recognizing truth into a conversion of life and deep participation in what is recited and sung, written and read.

Such texts appeal to the heart as well as the mind, as they break open, expand, and intensify psychological and bodily experiences, and induce committed readers to abandon neutrality and participate in what they are reading. It was easy enough to think of the Upaniṣads, the *Bhagavad Gītā,* numerous manuals of daily worship, handbooks of yoga, and vernacular works by great singers and poets that captivate listeners in large part by the beauty of their sentiments.

In the end my choice turned elsewhere, in search of the accessible piety of the vernacular. I have studied the Śrīvaiṣṇava tradition of Tamil-language south India for many years. This fascinating tradition, well over a thousand years old and yet thriving today, draws together the Sanskrit writings of the Vedas, the Upaniṣads, the Vedānta, etc., and the vernacular Tamil poetry of the saints known as *al̲vārs* ("those immersed [in God]," who composed passionate verses praising Nārāyaṇa (Viṣṇu, known also as Rāma, Kṛṣṇa, and in other forms), often along with his divine consort Śrī Lakṣmī.

I have found this poetry to be a most beautiful and impassioned route into the realities of love and love's commitments. Among the many Śrīvaiṣṇava texts with which I am familiar, a text I have known about for many years came to mind: Maṇavāḷamāmuni's *Hundred Linked Verses on the Holy Word of Mouth.* As noted in chapter 1, this fourteenth-century devotional work distills in 100 intense verses the 1,102 verses of the ninth-century sacred masterpiece, the *Holy Word of Mouth* by Śaṭakōpan̲. By its style, images, and sentiments, and by its beauty, the *Linked Verses* catch hold of the *Holy Word* as a work of poetry that too is beautiful as literature and powerful as spiritual utterance. Catching readers' attention, the *Linked Verses* serves as a conduit opening the way into Śaṭakōpan̲'s still larger and more beautiful devotional universe, itself a lens through which to begin to see God.[29] Like the *Admirable Secret,* the *Linked Verses* plays a modest role, drawing readers into a devotional practice—recitation, singing—that is partly replicated in slow and attentive reading.

The Great and Wondrous Challenge of Śaṭakōpan̲'s *Holy Word of Mouth*

To appreciate Maṇavāḷamāmuni's accomplishment, I must first say something about Śaṭakōpan̲'s *Holy Word.*[30] This is the most influential among the works of the āḻvārs. As mentioned, it is comprised of 1,102 verses divided into 100 songs of 10 verses on a theme.[31] The *Holy Word* draws easily, though unsystematically, on the mythology of Vaiṣṇavism, including great narratives of Kṛṣṇa, Rāma, and other divine descents (*avatāra*) to earth. It also attends constantly to the natural and the sacred geography of south India. Since Śaṭakōpaṉ presumes that his listeners already know of such matters, his songs never provide details sufficient for the absolute beginner. Expected listeners are always already in the midst of things. As poetry, the *Holy Word*'s success depends on its cumulative effect on those who hear it, attracted perhaps first of all by the form, and then by the content. Although hearing the songs, even memorizing them, is ideal, for centuries and deep within tradition there has been a commitment to the study of their beautiful, dramatic, and theological meanings. Reading cannot do everything, and translations such as mine inevitably fall short, but, I hope, we can still find our way into the *Holy Word* and become participants in its devotional universe.

Here then is a selection of fifteen verses, a small bouquet of my own, that may serve to open the *Holy Word* for readers who have not encountered it before. My hope is that each speaks for itself and without annotation beyond the titles I have added:

THE MYSTERY OF THE TRANSCENDENT GOD

Who possesses the highest, unsurpassable goodness? That One.[32]
Who cuts through confusion and graces the mind with what is good? That One.
Who is the overlord of the ever-wakeful immortals? That One.
At His luminous feet that sever affliction, bow down and rise up, my heart.[33]

LET GO, AND GO

Let go of everything, and after letting go then
Let your life-breath go to Him who owns all letting go.

LOVING THE ASTONISHING GOD

Accessible to those who love Him, for others hard to find, He is amazing.
The lady in the lotus takes pleasure at His feet so hard for us to gain, yet
Because He stole the churned butter, His waist was bound to the grindstone—
Oh! How vulnerable!

TELL HIM OF MY MISFORTUNE

Beautiful winged gentle heron, be kind.
You and your beloved—so lovely are your wings!—have mercy on me,
Be my messengers to the One riding the eagle with fiery wings.
Even if He locks you in a strong cage when you get there—
If that is your lot, what can you do?

HE DWELLS IN THE TIRUVEṄKAṬAM TEMPLE

For all time, in all places
We must always offer untainted service
To our father's father's father,
That lovely light over Tiruveṅkaṭam where cascades roar.

THERE IS ONLY ONE GOD

When there was nothing, neither god, nor world, nor life, nor anything else at all,
He made the four-faced god and all the other gods with him, and gave the world its life's breath.
This first Lord dwells in lofty Kurukūr, where jeweled terraces rise like mountains:
Apart from Him, why seek another divinity?

ALONE IN THE NIGHT

The city sleeps, the whole world lies in intense blackness, the waters are still,
As one long night stretches out.
Our Lord who ate the whole earth, who lay upon the snake bed, does not come.
Alas, who now will save the life of this stubborn sinner?

NO WAY TO REPAY YOU

I've performed no ascetic deeds, I've no subtle knowledge, but still
I cannot bear to leave You even once, Lord on the snake bed,
Father enthroned in the temple in Śrīvaramaṅkalanakar
Where lotuses bloom in the mud amid ripening paddy:
Apart from You, I am nothing.

HIS PARADOXICAL NATURE

He becomes poverty and wealth, hell and heaven,
Enmity and friendship, poison and ambrosia,
The great Lord reaches wide in myriad forms, and He rules me too.
I saw Him in the temple at sacred Viṇṇakar where the clans prosper.

HER SOLE NOURISHMENT

"My rice for eating, my water for drinking, my betel for chewing, my Lord Krishna!"
Her eyes flood tears, she keeps on crying, and

She searches for Kōḷūr, His city abundant in excellence surpassing the whole world, and
That is surely the place my young doe will enter.

AT THE HOLIEST TEMPLE, THE DECISIVE MOMENT

Mouth wide open, You ate earth, O Lord of incomparable fame,
Form of light bathed in everlasting radiance, tall One, Your servant's life breath,
O Lord of the Tiruveṅkaṭam temple, sacred mark on the brow of the world:
Call me, so that Your servant, descendant of an old clan, might reach Your feet.

HIS WORD, MY WORD, HIS WORD

How can I sing of Him? Become one with my dear life,
He makes me sing His sweet songs that I sing in my own words, and
By his own words my astonishing One now sings Himself,
First among the three deities who sang before me.

WE BECOME ONE

Beyond thought, peerless One, by His grace I have placed Him in my heart and I hold Him there,
And that too is His sweet grace, and so He makes me realize
That all mind, all breath, all body, and even the infinite are mere waste.
In the end, He ended up entirely as me Himself.

DON'T LEAVE ME

Kṛṣṇa, You have no compassion at all. When You come near my full breasts,
At Your touch I flood with a joy that never crests, beyond even the heavens.
It encompasses, submerges all I know, but then it ends like a dream.
Desire enters me, right into my inner self but, alas, this self cannot bear it
When so sweetly You leave me. Do not go to herd the cows, lest I die.

SURROUNDED

Surrounding, inside, filling, exalting everything, unlimited great source;
Surrounding that, and greater still, the good blossoming light;
Surrounding that, and greater still, the radiant joy of knowledge;
Surrounding that, and greater still, my desire for You,
But surrounding me, that too you finish off.[34]

Each of these verses is part of a set of ten verses on the same theme, as ten times over, the theme is expressed anew. Each individual verse opens up into an ever richer poetic creation that spreads out in more verses and more songs until the whole of it comes alive in the listener's mind and heart.

Songs from Experience

All the songs of the *Holy Word,* Śrīvaiṣṇava tradition tells us, well up from deep experience. For example, three earlier saints—Bhūtāḻvār, Poykaiyāḻvār, and Peyāḻvār—are said to have acquired their capacity to compose in a single night. The first of them takes shelter in a small shed, against a raging storm, and lies down. The second arrives, and they sit next to one another. A third squeezes in, and all three share the small space, now of necessity standing. But then they are amazed to find themselves further pressed by an unexpected and unseen fourth—the untimely wayfarer who turns out to be the Lord. Once they realize this, tradition reports that they spontaneously composed their verses, one hundred each, in praise of him. Experience overflows in speech that draws listeners and readers back into the original experience.[35]

Tradition tells us that from birth, Śaṭakōpaṉ refused to eat or drink or utter a word.[36] After his despairing parents finally left the infant under the great tamarind tree at a local temple, he is said to have dwelled there, deep in meditation, for sixteen years. During those years he was enlightened by the deities of all the holy temples, purified in his search for the Lord he desired, finally to be awakened by another saint, Maturakavi, who provoked him into song. He then poured out nonstop first the 194 verses of his three smaller compositions, and then the 1,102 verses of the *Holy Word.* Infused with his great passion, such verses aim to set on fire those reflecting slowly and attentively on them.[37]

In the eleventh verse of each song Śaṭakōpaṉ anticipates the transmission of his experience to others who will make his words their own and thus come to participate in his experience. Many of these eleventh verses simply rejoice at the prospect of sharing the verses by memorization and singing, probably through a manner of communal recitation in some ways similar to that accompanying the rosary. The following are particularly vivid examples that draw together the saint, his lord (named Kṛṣṇa, Keśava, Madhusūdana), and his audience:

> In wrath He destroyed the hordes of the great demon's clan, and so
> Śaṭakōpaṉ of bustling Kurukūr with its crowds wisely sang of Him
> In this set of ten from among a thousand—and so
> Crowds of devotees sing, join the dance!

Those skilled in teaching these ten verses from the thousand
Sung by Śaṭakōpaṉ of Kurukūr about Keśava whose blessed praise never ends—
To them Keśava shows country and city for their own good,
So they can flourish and gain freedom. Their destiny is to rule over all three worlds.

Praising, dancing, serving the pure jewel-colored Lord, banishing disease,
Śaṭakōpaṉ of unfailing rich Kurukūr of ancient, unerring praise
Sang an unerring thousand verses, including these ten about possession:
Those who worship, sing and dance them will feel no touch of sorrow.

Those who set their hearts on the Kōlūr temple and recite these ten verses
From the thousand sung by Śaṭakōpaṉ of Kurukūr where blossoms fill the gardens
When he cried out for Madhusūdana, our most sure treasure—
They will rule the bright radiant world.

"Come, enter right beneath my feet and flourish, servants": thus says the peerless Lord as he offers His grace, and about Him
Śaṭakōpaṉ of Kurukūr amid the plentiful paddy fields has refined these thousand verses:
Anyone holding onto anyone holding onto these ten about Tiruveṅkaṭam
Will be enthroned in high heaven.[38]

Again and again the poet invites his listeners to participate in what they hear, sharing the songs in communities those very songs create. The entrée into participation lies in the beauty of the Tamil combined with the religious energy of its themes. The words have power, but it is still up to the listeners (and later, the readers) to receive and interiorize them so as to become actors in this divine-human drama. Here we are close to the logic and affect of the rosary, but since the *Holy Word* is a very large work, many have sought an easier point of entrance to it, and this we find in the *Linked Verses.*

Insight and Form in the *One Hundred Linked Verses*

Maṇavāḷamāmuni's *Linked Verses* stands out as for our purposes an ideal instance of the work of distillation and intensification, primed to draw readers into active participation.[39] Its 100 verses are keyed to the 1,102 verses of the *Holy Word,* one verse for every ten-plus-one verses of the original. It imitates the *Holy Word*'s end-beginning style (*antāti*), by which the last word of each verse is repeated or at least echoed in the first word of the next. Composed in Tamil, the *Linked Verses* replicate the style and power of the songs and speak beautifully and effectively to newcomers and to those who also know the *Holy Word* well. Maṇavāḷamāmuni's verses recognize Śaṭakōpaṉ's singular experience as the wellspring of his poetry, and then too as the source for the experiential transformation of the devotee willing to learn from Śaṭakōpaṉ and from himself as intermediary. He draws listeners into meaning and manner of the *Holy Word,* to participation in its drama, by way of his own lovely words. Medium and message are perfectly conformed to one another, outside from the devotion celebrated in these verses.

Readers have long appreciated the beauty of the *Linked Verses.* The ancient theological commentator Piḷḷailokaṃjīyar, who lived several centuries after Maṇavāḷamāmuni, praised the composition for its sweet and lovely Tamil, and for its success in getting to the core of every song of Śaṭakōpaṉ by way of verses that merit repeated listening and deep meditation.[40] In his introduction to his brief word-by-word explication of the *Linked Verses,* the eminent twentieth-century scholar P. V. A. Annangarachariar similarly praises the work's harmony of content and style. Even by sound, he notes, the *Linked Verses* wonderfully replicates the *Holy Word:* "For every decade of the *Holy Word,* Maṇavāḷamāmuni captures the vital inner meaning. When one sees the beauty of this composition, it is hard to fathom it by heart or mind. . . . No work of such abundance had appeared before."[41]

We find a similar assessment of the *Linked Verses* in two old verses prefixed to the work in standard editions. They emphasize Maṇavāḷamāmuni's intention to enter deeply into the Tamil songs of Śaṭakōpaṉ, the *māṟaṉ* (chieftain, prince) whose *Holy Word* is sacred scripture for his community:[42]

> For the sake of those who yearn night and day for experience, the noble Maṇavāḷamāmuni
> Wove together every word and meaning in these hundred linked verses on the *māṟaṉ*'s sacred text.
>
> Maṇavāḷamāmuni of abiding fame graced us with inner meanings as he so sweetly sang his hundred linked verses on the holy words of mouth:[43]
> Drink deeply without ceasing, my heart!

Śaṭakōpaṉ's passionate, heartfelt songs arise from his experience, such as overflows in the mother tongue. Maṇavāḷamāmuni drinks deeply of those same words and from that experience composes his own songs, which in turn draw in listeners who, by insight and with pleasure, are drawn all the more directly into the *Holy Word.* Disciplined in delight, along pathways of experience and the enjoyment of the sung word we come near to the essence of things, twice and thrice over.

Savoring the *Linked Verses*

Given the intimate union of form and matter in the *Linked Verses,* I can only give a feel for Maṇavāḷamāmuni's achievement, sampling his text, beginning with his verses on the first ten songs. He first draws a parallel, already familiar in his tradition but still bold, between revelation in the Sanskrit Veda and revelation in the *Holy Word.* The artistry of the Lord ("He") and artistry of Śaṭakōpaṉ (the *māṟaṉ*) are in harmony:

> That all might see the highest reality as it really is, he sang the lofty Veda;
> That all humans might flourish without confusion, the *māṟaṉ* sang, and there lies deep-rooted freedom. (I.1)[44]

The second and third verses echo *Holy Word* I.2 and I.3 in begging listeners to let go of the world and take hold of the Lord:

> "The world, free of everything else, should by love reach the Nārāyaṇa's feet that are praised by all."
> Thus the compassionate *māṟaṉ* of famed Kurukūr graciously sang these ten verses
> That the world might flourish. (I.2)

> To those who are devout the highest is ever accessible, He was born right here that He might give freedom to all. People of the world!
> With growing love the *māṟaṉ* explains, "Give yourself!" and by his word, the solid prison of births is at last done away with. (I.3)

I.4 focuses on the woman's desperate love, painfully evident in her plea that nearby birds should carry her message where she herself cannot fly:

> The saint asked the lovely plumed birds, "Go, speak of my behavior to Him who holds the discus, tell Him, 'Agitated, pining away, she seeks her beloved.'" Such a flood of devotion! (I.4)

Maṇavāḷamāmuni wants his words to draw willing readers into the *Holy Word* and thereby into this astonishing desire for God.

The next several verses speak more vividly of the saint's suffering and surrender, experiences that become a grace for all:

> He plunged deep inside the bountiful Lord and once there thought deeply about His greatness, and about the paltry state of his own life breath.
>
> He grew weak and thought to give up everything—such was the *māṟaṉ*—
> But by His insistent generosity the Lord still enfolded him in love. (I.5)
>
> The *māṟaṉ* sang beautifully of the faultless Lord—"He is not hard to worship!"—
> And did this so well that he ended rebirths for the good people of this world. (I.6)

The remaining four verses in Book One make the teachings more personal to Maṇavāḷamāmuni himself and thus also to his listeners. By a sentiment that Canisius and Montfort would recognize, he indicates that knowing the Lord is inseparable from loving and serving him:

> Generous by nature, the holy Lord makes it possible to rejoice greatly in the lofty Heavens with no rebirth. He is so very sweet to those who belong to Him:
> All this the *māṟaṉ* makes known—and so, my heart, run, reach his feet, our treasure! (I.7)
>
> The tall Lord has become one with humans with nothing but restless hearts, deeds, and words, and
> That the world might know and contemplate service at His feet,
> The *māṟaṉ* showed his excellence, how in Him all things abide and flourish. (I.8)

Even to catch hold of the songs of Śaṭakōpaṉ, who himself is at the feet of the Lord, draws active participants into service at the feet of the Lord:

> The Lord delights in those who know these things, and He joins with them in every limb.
> By love the *māṟaṉ* caught hold of His essence, and if we sing the words he sang
> The Lord's radiant feet will rest on our heads too. (I.9)

To praise the saint is to come close to the Lord's grace, since their intentions are inseparable:

> Holding His war discus and conch He came into the world, and for no reason at all gave Himself to us: seeing all this with clarity the *māṟaṉ* put it into words,
>
> So let me put my head at his feet, let my mouth praise him! (I.10)

Maṇavāḷamāmuni is participant in of the drama of which he sings: cannot his listeners do the same? As he ponders Śaṭakōpaṉ's songs, he is drawn into more direct experience of the Lord and from there his verses arise, and those who savor them join that community of human and divine lovers.

Words of Loving Surrender

I offer as a second example the ten verses Maṇavāḷamāmuni composes for the sixth book, *Holy Word* VI.10. While the songs do not explicitly announce any progression toward the climactic surrender that occurs in VI.10, the commentators find here an implied narrative of increasing desperation, such as leads the saint to take refuge decisively in song VI.10. Maṇavāḷamamuni too does not make any such narrative explicit but simply catches the deep sentiment of each song taken on its own, and the effect of this focus is cumulative.

In VI.1, the saint sends messengers as he had done earlier in the *Holy Word,* yearning for that quintessential and intimate moment of devotion, life at the Lord's feet and even at the feet of those at the Lord's feet:

> "Dear birds, report my behavior to Rāma who ever dwells in the
> Tiruvaṇvaṇṭūr temple!"
> It was with overflowing love that the *māṟaṉ,* Kari's son, sent messengers:
> People of this world, venerate his feet! (VI.1)

Taking on the guise of a young woman, the saint argues with his lover, Kṛṣṇa:

> "Kṛṣṇa won't come here—He's over there with his dazzling women!"
> When he notices this, he loses himself, and in a woman's state he pushes
> back, feigning displeasure and crying,
> "I'll be with you no more!" Thus sings Kurukai's king. My heart, worship
> at his feet! (VI.2)

He is amazed at the paradox of a Lord so far yet near, and this gives his words an expansiveness that floods over those who take his song to heart:

> "He unites with us with great strength, as when he conquers enemies—
> Such are his contrary powers!" Thus the Tamil *māṟaṉ* gave praise that
> had no bounds.
> Those skilled in his word can teach even the heaven-dwellers. (VI.3)

Mad with love, he is recklessly given over to his Lord, in an extravagant love that turns out to be contagious for those who take to heart what is sung:

"The lovely deeds of Kṛṣṇa, the dance in rounds and all the rest:
I've a heart to praise them ceaselessly, caring not for day and night," thus the provocateur[45] sang with joy:
My heart, dive into the sweet honey of his words! (VI.4)

By the ancient and flawless grace of the Lord
The *māṟaṉ* ever sang flawlessly of his virtues, and
He dove once more into that flawless experience,
Abiding there in joy, dazzled by love. (VI.5)

Those listening to Maṇavāḷamāmuni's verses are invited to plunge into the mystery at their core:

Because he did not get to live entirely immersed in the Lord, he grew weak,
And no longer caring he let go of all that was his, and
Abandoned his own self altogether. All this the *māṟaṉ* put into song.
Come my heart, experience all this flawless perfection! (VI.6)

"My rice for eating, water for drinking, nut for chewing: my Lord, Kṛṣṇa!"
Eyes aflood, the *māṟaṉ* went to the Lord at His home on earth, Tirukōḷūr,
Where His radiant feet shine—for us too. (VI.7)

When once more in VI.8 the saint sends messengers, Maṇavāḷamāmuni intensifies his appeal:

The *māṟaṉ* told the birds flocking across the whole bright earth,
"Go, sing my sorrows to the Lord," and thus he sent messengers even to heaven.
So people of this wide world, come, reverence him! (VI.8)

He cries out with a desperation that paradoxically will set free all those who take his words to heart:

The *māṟaṉ,* Kari's son, cried to the Lord with inconsolable desire, such as heaven had never seen, and
When they heard him, their hearts melted and they too were ruined.
But if you recite this word, the world will be saved. (VI.9)

More than once Maṇavāḷamāmuni appeals to his own heart, and thus too also to the heart of any listener ready to share in taking refuge with the saint, just as he had taken refuge with the Lord:

The Lord dwells in lofty Veṅkaṭam's temple, that He might save the world—

And right there, before the Lady on the lotus, the *māṟaṉ* joyfully took refuge at His lotus feet.
My heart, let those feet be your refuge too! (VI.10)

"Those feet:" perhaps the Lord's, but perhaps too Śaṭakōpaṉ's and now—as Maṇavāḷamāmuni cannot say in his humility—his feet too.

The connoisseur of Śaṭakōpaṉ's songs will of course enjoy reading the full 110 verses of the ten songs in the sixth book of the *Holy Word.* But to those who do not know the *Holy Word,* or have no time for the whole of it, Manavāḷamāmuni offers a vital link. By his gracious words he draws readers into Śaṭakōpaṉ's words and thence directly to the Lord, who stimulates all such words. Montfort might understand so holy a lineage. After all, he related how the Virgin Mary gave the rosary—itself composed of the words of Gabriel, Elizabeth, and the earliest Church—to St. Dominic, who gave them to innumerable Christians seeking through those words a deeper and more direct relation to Mary and to Christ. For those willing to learn, both Manavāḷamāmuni and Montfort have the same message: read with your heart, and you will become part of what you read.

As Words End, There Is Love

I end this engagement with the *Linked Verses* by citing the last six verses of the whole of the *Linked Verses,* marking songs in the *Holy Word* that by tradition climax in Śaṭakōpaṉ's ascent to the Lord. The saint's words reach their fullness as he makes words of what he has seen around him. Now it is all grace:

The *māṟaṉ* witnessed the deeds of those who love Kṛṣṇa's feet, and he sang all this in brief,
That he might complete his teaching to the people of this world:
All this is due to his illustrious grace. (X.5)

Śaṭakōpaṉ testifies how the Lord took hold of him and amazed him coming to find *him,* and Manavāḷamāmuni speaks only of this, creating a holy passage for those wishing to take refuge with the Lord:

By grace the Lord reached into the depths, and by love desired the *māṟaṉ*'s so very dark body.
He yearned to take it with Him into the wide heavens:
The *māṟaṉ*'s fine word reports all this in bare simple words. (X.6)

The Lord of simple words loved him to excess, even more than He loved His own fine body.

> When the *māṟaṉ* saw His trick, he let go of himself and reached His feet.
> He is our steadfast, holy one. (X.7)

As their final union approaches, both the Lord and the saint become a sure refuge, as do the saint's words—and those of Manavāḷamāmuni. He continues to sing, surprised still even at the final moment:

> With clarity he saw how the holy Lord was pleased with himself, and so he asked,
> "But why did You place me in this confusing world? Why do You confuse me so much?"
> But then He confused our famed *māṟaṉ* once again—by embracing him. (X.8)

> And when the Lord embraced him and showed him the ancient path to heaven, he experienced it, deep inside he lived it, and
> So he sang the way for all those at his feet: crown him with ape-flowers, our wise sage! (X.9)

The words, after all, have become the instrument of a saving story that seems beyond the reach of listeners, yet as near as the words they hear:

> Our sage, the *māṟaṉ,* he cast aside all the joys he had sung before, and he grieved alone,
> But finally filled with supreme love he became one with the king of the lady in the lotus, exalted on high. (X.10)

Those who take the time to accept this invitation become part of a great drama of love, loss, and grace, even if right now they cannot realize for themselves the final homecoming. Words nearly get us there—but not yet all the way. Nevertheless, Maṇavāḷamāmuni's words are channels of his own insights and experience and now become portals for those taking the time to learn them well. They get readers as far as possible just now, in the in-between moment where we must dwell for now.

On the Way

At the end of my reflections on the *Admirable Secret,* I confessed my enduring ambivalence toward that quintessentially Catholic text and its appeal that readers participate regularly in the praying of the rosary. I could see that I was included, but that participation could not (yet) become a daily reality. Now there is no gain in avoiding the parallel question: shall we be caught up in the passions of the *Linked Verses,* and thereby drawn into the beautifully woven verses and experiences of Śaṭakōpaṉ too, so as to pray with them? I am not quite there yet either, for different reasons than those that have kept me from a full return to the rosary: the world of Śaṭakōpan̲ and Maṇavāḷamāmuni is not quite my world, nor are their pieties and practices and holy places quite my own. As a Catholic, I am from somewhere else, and the catechisms and doctrines and pieties of my tradition, composed by those who have never read the *Linked Verses* or the *Holy Word,* testify that my Lord is arrives differently. This is obvious. But the salient point here is that the study of the *Linked Verses* and the *Holy Word* sets in motion for careful and patient readers a process that will not be halted by decisions and postponements one makes while still reading, even if the *Linked Verses* are unlikely to be my pathway to heaven.

The *Admirable Secret* and the *Linked Verses:* Risking a Double Intensity

The rosary as elaborated and intensified in the *Admirable Secret* resonates with the *Holy Word* as distilled and opened up in the *Linked Verses:* both instruct readers, illumine the true and the holy, and invite them to participate in that which they read. The *Admirable Secret* unpacks the meanings and sentiments of the rosary; the *Linked Verses* distills into a smaller, sweet garland the *Holy Word.* Had they become friends, Montfort and Maṇavāḷamāmuni might have agreed that by patient, humble, and intense recitation—of the rosary, of the *Linked Verses,* each opening up into mysteries greater than their own words—recitants become part of a holy drama. The Hail Mary, illumined and elaborated in the *Admirable Secret,* gives voice once again, now, to the angel, to Mary and Elizabeth, and to ancient traditions. The *Holy Word,* awakened once again in the *Linked Versions,* is recognized yet again as God's word in human words, sung by the Lord, by the āl̲vār, and by Maṇavāḷamāmuni. Such words stand between the infinities of their starting points and destinations.

Repetition is key in both cases, since neither the rosary nor a garland of verses has an ending. The rosary is never recited for a final time, just as the mysteries enunciated in its living words never become merely past items of historical interest only. What is needed are patient readers vulnerable to the implications of what they read over and over. These are readers who willing to slow down, patient in returning again and again to the texts, to be reformed and transformed by them. Montfort could not claim eternal relevance for his words, but in our world there is still a place for the appeals of a latter-day Montfort. The *Linked Verses* too is never sung for a last time, since the drama of the Lord and his *māran̲* is acted out in worship and recitation over and again, every ending a new start. There is always a role for Maṇavāḷamāmuni, his words leading listeners and readers back to the great songs, even if in new eras and in the languages of the global stage, another Maṇavāḷamāmuni might be needed.

At this point in *Reading the Hindu and Christian Classics,* the virtues of slow learning turn out to be holy virtues. Instructed in the faith (chapters 1 and 3) and drawn critically into its truth (chapter 2), readers can now participate too, by a slow reading that is nothing but loving attention to these words and the practices they inspire. We can, with due respect, read our way into each and then into both of these religious universes, when we have available to us texts such as the *Admirable Secret* and the *Linked Verses.*

Is it really so easy? Certainly, there are reasons to hesitate. We must ask whether the prior instruction and prior thinking through doctrine that I have so highly commended do not make it impossible to come to any such text of participation without a proper education in its particular traditions and truths. Authority and authorities create the frame in which the possibility of active engagement may occur, and readers may find themselves neither knowledgeable enough nor convinced enough of the truth of what they have learned. The *Catechism* and the *Sentences* stand in the background of the recitation of the rosary as elucidated by the *Admirable Secret;* the *Garland* and the *Perspectives,* or texts very much like them, prepare the way for the recitation of the *Linked Verses.*

But if we have done the kind of work recommended in chapters 2 and 3 of this book and have managed to hold and keep together the two instructions and two doctrines, we will already be experienced in the balancing act that is required for the still bolder step taken here. If we have studied, or begun to, we will find the rosary and Maṇavāḷamāmuni's verses resonating in our memories together, and we will find ourselves on the edge (or precipice) of praying the rosary *and* singing Maṇavāḷamāmuni's verses, participating because we have learned our texts well and taken them to heart. Those who respect boundaries and have learned in a careful and attentive manner know better how to negotiate, in the text, the coherent path to be traveled now twice over. Such a path is now possible, though steep, to be ascended only by those caught up in the loves they have read. Montfort and Maṇavāḷamāmuni are even now still teaching us a way forward, by the virtues and dispositions embedded in their exhortations: be instructed twice over, learn the truth twice over, be smitten twice over by beauty. Hearing together the *Admirable Secret* and the *Linked Verses,* for a time let mind follow heart.

SIX

Reading (and Rereading) the Hindu and Christian Classics

Digesting Wisdom

In the preceding chapters I have commenced the reading of six great texts, intending to sketch out for myself and my patient readers the prospects for a full reading of them:

The Garland of Jaimini's Reasons
The Collection of Right Perspectives on Our Position
The Sentences Articulated in Four Books
The Greater Catechism
The Admirable Secret of the Most Holy Rosary
One Hundred Linked Verses on the Holy Word of Mouth

When read slowly and carefully, in parts and then as wholes, these texts educate, orient, and captivate (willing and patient) readers by instruction in the faith, engagement with truth in its doctrinal form, and participation in the realities all facilitated by the words of such texts and the traditions they condense and make available so intensely. Currents of Catholic and Hindu tradition course through this book in the form of these great texts, their distinctive voices never homogenized or erased—because such blurring of particularities is hardly possible for those who actually read. Yet after study no reader will be able to think of them as merely separate from one another. In the reading, each mingles with the others over and again in the minds of readers, as they are instructed, versed in the truth, and drawn to participation. An odd but respectable introduction to Catholicism and certain forms of Hinduism has taken place. Reading the *Sentences, Catechism,* and *Admirable Secret* offers a rather direct tutorial in three moments in traditional Catholic learning. The *Garland,* the *Perspectives,* and the *Linked Verses* open the way to three more distinct moments in a traditional Hindu learning that coheres not by a single lineage of teaching and teachers, but by way of the cultivation of dispositions of mind and heart manifest in harmonies of practice, insight, and self-surrender. When such classics are slowly read and appropriated anew, right next to one another, their proximity gains a certain naturalness, has its own staying power, and bears fruits neither tradition can yield on its own.

As we go back and spend the time it takes to learn from traditions we know, or thought we knew, such learning restores to us solid grounding, in part due to the power and solidity and endurance of what we learn, and in part due simply to the work of careful and slow reading. It affords us a deeper grasp of our own traditions (insofar as we have such allegiances); it also turns out to be splendidly conducive to an analogous learning in another tradition, as we read back and forth across religious borders.

Going deep into the reader's own tradition need not stifle the disposition to learn from other traditions. Quite the opposite: depth in hitherto familiar territory gives new energy and focus to reading across and beyond familiar boundaries. Similarly, doing the hard work of learning from another tradition by careful study affords to us a freedom and a sophistication on our way home, that we might learn more deeply even in the place where we began in the first place. The slow and patient reading of such texts side by side creates a multidimensional learning that may surprise all concerned, yet without a loss of respect for either text at issue, and without a flattening reduction of the texts to mere resources for the study of other, contemporary matters.

As admitted already in chapter 1, this classical learning is practically speaking the domain (and therefore duty) of those who have the time and energy for sustained study. But it is not the preserve of academics with the leisure to read. Anyone who has access to a library can progress in such learning, since what is needed is as easily available as old books sitting on dusty shelves, quietly awaiting new readers: no high-tech equipment needed. Even small gestures toward such learning can contribute to the larger edifice of a learning that begins in the work of individual readers but must end as the work of whole communities, and then too many such communities working together. Quietly and without drama, attentive and patient readers with every level of opportunity begin to transform their respective traditions, from the inside out.

Rereading as New Reading

Reading is hard to start, but it is harder to leave off. Finishing this book does not give me license to put aside the six texts, as if there is no more to learn. Finishing the writing instead permits me to return to the prized reading I have been talking about, and now all the more fully. I benefit from further study, reading each fully and then a second and third time, the deeper knowledge of each affecting how we reread the others: the point of reading, were I to go in this direction, would be to circle back to my starting points. I could start again with the *Garland's* opening,

> In accord with the usage of the injunction, "Personal study must be undertaken," is this reflective study not to be undertaken, or is it? Thus the doubt.
>
> Some say: Study is known from ordinary experience to be a means to understanding something. There is no restriction, just as with threshing. For this reason, it is not plausible that this study be enjoined.
>
> No. As with the unprecedented result (*apūrva*) of a new moon sacrifice, this command is restrictive with respect to the unprecedented result of ritual action and thus determinative of its meaning/purpose. For this reason what is enjoined is indeed to be undertaken. (I.1.1)

So too, the first question of Canisius,

> *Who is to be called a Christian?*
>
> Those who profess the salutary doctrine of Jesus Christ, true God and human, in his Church. The true Christian is one who damns and detests all those cults and sects, which are outside the doctrine of Christ and outside the Church, wherever found among the nations, that is, Jews, Gentiles, Muslims, and heretics. This person is one who firmly submits to this doctrine of Christ.

Such is the dynamic of slow reading: in the most mundane and undramatic way, it leads one along very unpredictable paths that one might otherwise never travel at all. The reading is never done with; it is fresh because it honors what is old; instructed, exposed anew to truth, drawn into deeper participation, readers risk and gain everything, by what had seemed a safe path to say, the reading of old books.

Back to the Library: The Reader's Choice

I have chosen very good texts for this project, but they are surely not the only ones by which one might proceed. The more we read, the more refined our tastes become, perhaps a bit narrower too. We come to expect more from what we read, and seek out books similar to those we already know. This narrowing is for the better, provided we do not take our painstakingly acquired insights to be normative, as if to impugn the taste of others or to provide them with some mandatory and exclusory reading list. Communities do want to identify canons of best readings, but there is no chance today that we can finalize such lists.

And so, despite my choice of these six classics, the necessary work of slow reading need not depend on just those texts. Indeed, the fact that they form an "accidental canon" is essential to the power unleashed in the reading of them. These texts were not chosen to reflect a necessity prior to the text, nor to support a given theme. Other texts too can be chosen and will work well, if readers read attentively and pay attention to the dynamics of the readings that are to be taken together.

For instance, readers may wish to read works similar to those I chose but less formidable and readily available in English. Such texts can serve as plausible substitutes with which to begin the slow learning I have suggested. For example,

> If not the *Garland* (available only in Sanskrit), then the *Preliminary Rules of Mīmāṃsā* (*Mīmāṃsā Paribhāṣa*) of Kṛṣṇa Yajvan, in the translation of Swami Madhavananda;
>
> If not the *Greater Catechism* (available, among many versions, in a recent German translation, and in a seventeenth-century English translation), then Canisius's *Small Catechism* in the translation by Ryan Grant;
>
> If not the *Perspectives* (available in English) then the *Crest-Jewel of Discrimination* of Śaṅkarācārya, in a translation such as that by Swami Madhavananda;
>
> If not the *Sentences* (available in English translation), then Thomas Aquinas's *Compendium of Theology,* in a translation such as that by Richard J. Regan;
>
> If not the *Admirable Secret of the Rosary* (available in English translation), then the *Abandonment to Divine Providence* by Jean Pierre de Caussade, in a translation such as that by E. J. Strickland;
>
> If not the *Linked Verses* (available only in Tamil), then Maṇavāḷamāmuni's *Book of the Yearning Soul* (*Ārtiprabandham*), translated by Anand Amaladass as *Deliver Me, My Lord.*[1]

These simpler texts cover *some* of the same ground as the ones I have been reading, and for similar purposes, even while bringing forward other insights and values.[2] They too instruct readers, confront us with truth in its doctrinal form, and draw us into the practices implied by right understanding. They also provide a good grounding for returning later on to the texts I have put forward.

But if my six cases—my original list, or the substitutions I have suggested—are promising, readers may well find that other cases too come to the fore. They may choose similar formative and informative texts from other erudite traditions, according to their own interests and inclinations, the traditions they belong to or are deeply familiar with. This will be fine particularly if readers pick a text, ideally at a bit of a distance in time, geography, culture, language, and religion. Whatever the choices made, getting started in sustained reading is the main thing, choosing texts that claim a certain comprehensiveness, and thereafter reading them slowly, patiently, and fully, over and over again, until beginning to enjoy the deeper formation through study that I have been advocating.

Reading the Talmud after Hinduism, for Example

Readers can study still other traditions alongside one another: Rabbinic Judaism and Hinduism; Islam and Buddhism; Daoism and Orthodox Christianity; indigenous traditions of Africa and of the Americas. Let us consider for a moment an example of the first of these.

One might, and very pertinently, attend to the slow reading practices and conversations of Rabbinic tradition. It seems to me, with only limited familiarity, that the Rabbinic way of reading might stimulate and provoke new ways of readings among Western Christian readers, much has the Mīmāṃsā has done in this book. Not much work has been done in this regard, though I point readers' attention to a recent essay by Shoshana Razel Gordon-Guedalia, "Sagi Nahor—Enough Light: Dialectic Tension between Luminescent Resonance and Blind Assumption in Comparative Theology." In that essay Gordon-Guedalia engages "in comparative theological examination of two ritual-legal systems, Mīmāṃsaka and Rabbinic," because these "share 'measures' of hermeneutic reasoning—tools for culling ritual law from respective Urtext, each expanding into vast commentarial corpora, each yielding distillation into terse legal codes in the medieval period." Proper comparison using these tools allows one to think anew about each tradition:

> Can one suspend current sensibilities when exploring cosmologies of old—and if so, should one? Can one nimbly leap from home tradition to another and return with system-specific integrity intact—and if so, towards what end? And how might the latter relate to Jewish Temple priestly acts on behalf of others, or on behalf of themselves and their own families, as per careful Rabbinic linguistic parsing of prooftexts from Leviticus?[3]

Gordon-Guedalia properly locates herself in her Jewish tradition but also explains too her distinctive interest in Mīmāṃsā. She then engages at length in an experimental study that forms the major middle portion of the chapter, "Rabbinic and Mimamsaka Lenses on Ritual Efficacy and Agency." This reflection on ritual seeing—and blindness—begins in Talmudic study, draws on Maimonides's medieval explication of "wearing" and "seeing," and finds in Mīmāṃsā's exegesis of rules regarding the seeing of melted butter (ghee) in the course of a sacrifice (a seeing that rules out the participation of the blind) a particularly useful illumination of the rules for seeing and their interpretation:

> This rabbinic case articulation, in that it takes the "seeing" component further—to the question of whose seeing is essential, is greatly enhanced by the mīmāṃsaka discussion as to the ghee. The latter discussion put pressure on the ritual string discussion, in that it poses a third paradigm of thought. The idea that the strings must *be seen,* and not necessarily by the ritual *gavra* or *kartṛ,* makes deeper sense now that the idea of ontological change needed to effect the ghee is considered.

An interesting contrast is established:

> Although the prevailing stance in the case of the ghee is that inability to gaze bars agency to perform, (and there does not seem to be a suggestion of an*other* gaze as sufficient), while in the *tzitzit* string case, the prevailing stance is that of *as long as they are seen by anyone*—the "gaze" upon the ghee and strings cases in conjunction, illumined new layers of comprehension and possibility, worthy of future study.

Further questions can then be posed:

> Are we saying that a gaze—any gaze—ontologically changes the strings? And we may ask of the mīmāṃsaka case, for example: Are we suggesting that there might be a way to tag team ritual performance, whereby an*other* gazer may complete that final stage, thus enabling ritual completion for the blind actor? And might that final gaze, made by *other* acting in his stead, be conceptually similar to the categorization of priestly acts expressed in alternate Sanskrit verb types: *parasmaipada* connoting acts on behalf of others, and *ātmanepada* on behalf of self?[4]

We cannot dwell further on the details here; to understand more fully Gordon-Guedalia's persuasive insight—the light shed on Rabbinic rules by care for Mīmāṃsā rules—would require preliminary instruction of a kind I am not prepared to offer. But the example indicates another carefully defined route into the slow and patient interreligious study I have been advocating. In this way the very focused project of this book, engaging certain Christian and Hindu examples, can be of use to readers who are inclined to explore other traditions and canons of great theological texts that similarly can be opened.[5]

Readers of this book may envision a much wider range of further studies that might follow. There will always be still more options, regarding Islamic or Buddhist or African indigenous traditions, and on and on. The possibilities are enormous, the matter is urgent—and for that reason it becomes all the more important to slow down, reading carefully and patiently, engaging whole books and not just apt quotations from them. We need to take as much time as needed to find our bearings through the study of theological and philosophical books drawn from various traditions, finding in them a grounding for our own necessary smaller, more specific learning projects.

Small Truths, but Still Worth Learning

Such reading may be inspired by the simple fact—often neglected—that we can pick up texts from many different cultural settings—and just read them.[6] There is no limit. But possibility does not inevitably turn into an imperative to act in this way: we can read, but will we? Since slow learning—patient, quiet, for the long run—rarely sees benefits in the short run, such readers do well not to seek to sensationalize what they do. The hard work turns out to be a kind of spiritual activity, grounded in faith but also in the simple conviction that in the long run acts of careful, attentive learning go deeper and endure longer than quick glances at texts and short-lived opinions about books, methods of reading, power dynamics, and alternative ways of learning. The great texts of many cultures and religions, however different from one another, converge in the work of successive generations of good readers who trust in the underlying human and divine foundations of the intelligibility of what we read: God is known through study, and the great library of human speaking and writing through the ages begins at least to make available the knowledge of God that we very much need again today. We accumulate a plethora of insights, as certain themes and words about them recur and then are patiently held together in memory. Truth is deepened in the reading, not dissipated by endless interpretation; written as doctrine, recognized truths create bases for further constructive theologies now indebted to two or more traditions at once.

If we have held together in our minds what we have been reading, possibilities such as these multiply:

After reading the *Sentences* and the *Perspectives:* Creation of the world, angels, and humans in the image of God, written and read next to that differentiation within *Brahman* that makes individual names and forms (functionally) possible.

After reading the *Sentences* and the *Perspectives:* The distinction between angels and male and female humans, written next to the distinctions among individual self, lord, world, and *brahman.*

After reading the *Sentences* and the *Perspectives:* The human person as natural and free, written and read next to the scripturally and ritual marked actor whose extra- and pre-ritual state is of only marginal importance.

After reading the *Catechism* and the *Garland:* The kind of instruction that will successfully shape individuals who will be full members of their communities, masters of the vocabulary and ideas that count most forcefully for those communities.

After reading the *Catechism* and the *Garland:* The role differing teaching traditions play in shaping the lives of those who study the great texts in the long run, and the lives of those just now learning them for the first time.

After reading the *Catechism* and the *Garland:* The dynamics of vice and virtue, sin and forgiveness, placed alongside measured sacrificial commands and prohibitions of wider or narrower application, each guiding the lives of attentive readings in particular ways.

After reading the *Admirable Secret* and the *Linked Verses:* The ways in which humans who encounter God through study move then from reading to recitation and prayer, ever intensifying the immediacy of encounter and its transformative effects.

After reading the *Admirable Secret* and the *Linked Verses:* The ways in which the recurring recitation of prayers can intensify a vital and dynamic relationship with God.

Each of these insights—and others that might be drawn—arise from the readings done in the preceding chapters and are formulated in accord with specific points in the readings. (Of course, readers of this book may wish to formulate other claims instead.) Crucial though is the need for vigilance, an attentiveness to the fruits of study that is adequate to the dense work of reading that ends in those fruits. Yet the reading I have in mind is also unrelenting, because it expects no closure in the short run, only a series of smaller moments of completion, as each book is read and put aside for a moment, before it is opened again. We write, but none of our own writings can be the final word. Books lead to more books.

Later on in our shared human history, we will be on surer ground in settling upon a recognized canon reaching across traditions. Now it is too soon, given the uneven ground on which traditions are heard or ignored, studied or neglected, and taken seriously or trivialized. At the moment we can only participate in the great corrective demanded of us, the return to the practices of study that have sustained our many religions and civilizations for millennia. The best we can do at the moment is create new venues for this rejuvenated project of instruction, doctrine, and participation, that younger readers in particular might not be afraid to be slower readers whose writing draws patiently, humbly, and with daring upon the great texts that have been sitting on our shelves all these many years.

Notes

Foreword

1. Johann Wolfgang von Goethe, *Conversations of Goethe with Eckermann and Soret,* trans. John Oxenford, 2 vols. (London: Smith, Elder, 1850), 2: 218–19.
2. Friedrich Nietzsche, *Daybreak: Thoughts on the Prejudices of Morality,* trans. R. J. Hollingdale, intro. Michael Tanner (Cambridge: Cambridge University Press, 1982), 5.
3. Alan Booth, *The Road to Sata: A 2000-Mile Walk through Japan* (Harmondsworth: Penguin, 1986), 180.
4. T. S. Eliot, "Tradition and the Individual Talent," *Selected Essays,* 3rd ed. (London: Faber, 1951), 13–22; I. A. Richards, *Practical Criticism: A Study of Literary Judgment* (New York: Harcourt, Brace and World, 1929).
5. William Empson, *Seven Types of Ambiguity* (London: Chatto and Windus, 1930).
6. Cleanth Brooks, *The Well Wrought Urn: Studies in the Structure of Poetry* (New York: Reynal and Hitchcock, 1947).
7. See, for example, Jonathan Culler, *On Deconstruction: Theory and Criticism after Structuralism* (Ithaca: Cornell University Press, 1982).
8. On this theme, see Kevin Hart, *The Trespass of the Sign: Deconstruction, Theology and Philosophy* (Cambridge: Cambridge University Press, 1999).
9. See William Warburton, *Essai sur les hiérogylphs des Égyptiens,* trad. et notes Léonard des Malpeines, *précédé de "Scribble (pouvoir/écrire)"* par Jacques Derrida *et de "Transfigurations (archéologie du symbolique)"* par Patrick Tort (Paris: Aubier-Flammarion, 1977).
10. See Jacques Derrida, "Scribble (Writing / Power)," trans. Cary Plotkin, *Yale French Studies* 58 (1979), 129.
11. See Bernard of Clairvaux, *On the Song of Songs,* trans. Kilian Walsh, intro. M. Corneille Halfants (Kalamazoo, MI: Cistercian, 1971–80), Thomas Aquinas, *Commentary on the Gospel of John,* trans. Fabian Larcher and James A. Weisheipl, intro. and notes Daniel Keating and Matthew Levering, 3 vols. (Washington, DC: Catholic University of America Press, 2010); Origen, *The Song of Songs: Commentary and Homilies,* ed. R. P. Lawson (New York: Newman Press, 1957); and Origen, *Commentary on the Gospel According to John,* trans.

Ronald E. Heine, 3 vols. (Washington, DC: Catholic University of America Press, 1989–93).

12. On the motif of "religious reading," see, in particular, Paul J. Griffiths, *Religious Reading: The Place of Reading in the Practice of Reading* (Oxford: Oxford University Press, 1999).
13. James Garden, *Comparative Theology; Or the True and Solid Grounds of Pure and Peaceable Theology. A Subject very Necessary, though hitherto almost wholly neglected. Proposed in an University-Discourse. And now translated from the printed Latin copy, with some enlargements by the author* (Edinburgh: T. and W. Ruddimans, 1735), 3–4.
14. See, for example, Karl Rahner, "Anonymous Christians," *Theological Investigations,* trans. David Bourke (New York: Seabury Press, 1974), chapter 6.
15. See Francis X. Clooney, ed., *The New Comparative Theology: Interreligious Insights from the Next Generation* (London: T. and T. Clark, 2010).

Preface

1. The video recording of the lectures is available online at the University of Virginia website for the Richard and Page-Barbour Lectures.
2. Nor did I follow the plan of the lectures exactly. Chapters 1 and 3 arise from the first lecture, chapter 2 from the second, and chapter 5 from the third. Chapter 4, my nod to Wittgenstein, was not a substantive part of any of the three lectures, though we might hope that his ghost-presence was felt throughout.

ONE Remembering How to Learn in a Forgetful World

1. Mādhava was a south Indian scholar in the court of the Vijayanagar empire that flourished in south India in the thirteenth to sixteenth centuries. Tradition holds that he become a renunciant and took the name Vidyāraṇya, became head of the Śṛṅgeri Math, a famed center of meditation and learning in the Vedānta tradition, and continued his teaching and writing. In addition to the *Garland,* Mādhava also wrote a series of texts explicitly marked by his name: the *Parāśara-Mādhava,* a commentary on the *Parāśara Smṛti;* a long appendix to that text, the *Vyavahāra-Mādhava;* a text on ritually relevant calendric issues and time, the *Kāla-Mādhava;* and, possibly, the famed *Discernment regarding Liberation While Alive* (*Jīvanmuktiviveka*), on the life of the renunciant, freed from ritual obligations. The *Garland* shares with these works a commitment to the details of practical and prescriptive texts, a respect for the complexity and plurality of realities to be taken into account, and a determination to explain with extreme economy what is at the heart of any given vexed case. On Mādhava and the multiple texts attributed to him, see Clooney, "Mīmāṃsā for the Mīmāṃsakas."
2. See Clooney, "Mādhava's *Garland.*"
3. The king quickly decided that some further explanation was needed. He praised Mādhava for composing the *Garland,* but asked for further explanation: "He indeed who lived by wisdom and was clear on all the *śāstras* composed this

weighty garland of reasons in the school of Jaimini. Vīraśrībukkabhupati praised the work in the middle of the assembly, but then instructed Mādhava, 'You must make an elaboration for it'" (Introductory verses 4ab). The *Elaboration* more than quadruples the length of the work, hence the fullness of the three volumes in the 1892 edition.

4. Composed in a rising Vijayanagara empire that was intent on organizing every aspect of life, the *Garland*'s work of concise summary seems to have met key requirements appropriate to its era. Its consolidation of knowledge—achieved in Mādhava's own slow and patient study—ensured that beginners might learn economically and easily, even while at the same time it gave the assurance that traditional knowledge was coherent and simple enough to be stated simply. It is also a safeguard against oblivion, since once learned, it puts one in touch with every aspect of an ancient and great school of erudite wisdom. The Mīmāṃsā interpreter is a scholar of the law who sifts through precedents in order to discover the underlying reason for things, a key that is specific to one case or set of cases while yet shedding light on related and new cases even in very disparate fields. Many have been bolder still in extending Mīmāṃsā principles to nonreligious law cases, though this is not a unanimous viewpoint. See Kane, *History of Dharmashastra,* 1283–84.
5. The *Garland,* introductory verses 7 and 8. Throughout, translations from the *Garland* are my own. Note: since the work is available only in Sanskrit and in various editions, I don't think page numbers are needed.
6. The *Garland* is by no means the only Mīmāṃsā text that aimed at digesting tradition. Other Mīmāṃsā thinkers too wrote thematic treatises, which may be characterized as inward- or outward-directed. Śālikanātha Miśra's *Prakaraṇa Pañcikā* (*Exposition of the Sections*) is an early entry in the latter category, raising issues in argument with the Buddhists regarding the nature of knowledge and its authority, and language (10: 39–40). The *Mānameyodaya* (*The Arising of What Is to Be Known and the Means of Knowing*) of Nārāyaṇa Bhāṭṭa Pāda (1590) is a major Mīmāṃsā contribution to the pan-Indian debate on the *pramāṇas.* By contrast, Pārthasārathi Miśra's *Nyāya Ratna Mālā* (*Garland of the Gems of Reasoning*) focused on key issues that mattered to the Mīmāṃsā thinkers in dispute among themselves, such as the usefulness of Vedic study to the nature of injunctions, and the distinction between obligatory and optional rites. Interesting too as works furthering the goals of Mīmāṃsā are the thematic treatises that attempt to get at the essential issues in Mīmāṃsā by a more concentrated focus. Here one can turn to the *Artha Saṃgraha* (*The Collection of Meanings*) of Laugākṣi Bhāskara (1700) and the *Mīmāṃsā Nyāya Prakāśa* (*Light on Mīmāṃsā Reasons*) of Āpadeva (1700), both of which seek to discern and state the key Mīmāṃsā teachings on word and language in a most precise and refined form. Though attentive to grammatical issues, these works are inward-looking formulations of Mīmāṃsā reasoning that resist the temptation to recast Mīmāṃsā by the categories of outside systems. Others produced treatises that likewise aimed at the main internal themes of Mīmāṃsā. The most introductory of these is the *Mīmāṃsā Bāla Prakāśa* (*Light on Mīmāṃsā for Beginners*) of Śaṅkara Bhāṭṭa

(1550–1650), a text that seems an early and provisional effort in the field, while the *Mīmāṃsā Paribhāṣa* of Kṛṣṇa Yājvan (1600–1650) covers some key themes and then just the first five books of the *Sūtras,* but in a relatively simple and straightforward manner. R. Thangaswami Sarma's *Mīmāṃsā Mañjarī* (*Bouquet of Mīmāṃsā*) is a recent (later twentieth century) Sanskrit-language contribution to this textbook literature and indeed a masterful survey of the entirety of the tradition. It is important to notice that most topics in these texts are very much internal to the Mīmāṃsā and as such are not easily accessible to those unfamiliar or uninterested in what is of interest to Mīmāṃsā thinkers in the bulk of their work. But the reasoning, like jurisprudence grounded in particular cases but then more widely pertinent, can be extended to analogous situations. Still another, and most interesting, genre marks the effort to reduce the tradition to a more manageable form, to get straight, in as brief a way as possible, what each of the twelve books of the *Sūtras* (and its subsections) are about—and to do so in correspondence to the order of the *Sūtras* and its cases ("sites," *adhikaraṇas*) as identified by Śabara. The *Mīmāṃsā Nyāya Saṃgraha* (*Collection of Mīmāṃsā's Reasons*) of Mahadeva Vedāntin (1700) is a very useful work, particularly now as expertly edited and translated by James Benson. Appaya Dīkṣita's *Pūrvamīmāṃsāviṣayasaṃgrahadīpikā* (*Lamp Shining on the Collection of the Topics of Pūrva Mīmāṃsā*) is a brief prose treatise covering the entirety of the *Sūtras*' topics in a brief number of pages. These are elegant accomplishments, simplifications possible only because of the erudition of their authors. All these texts introduce the Mīmāṃsā, usually with an epistemological or metaphysical slant. But the *Garland* is a most perfect instance in the genre of case analysis and unparalleled in its concision. It ambitions no originality, rather only to complete and perfect the Mīmāṃsā tradition of ritual analysis by creating a perfectly adequate summation of the tradition. It is succinct without being obscure, efficient in reducing vast learning to (relatively) simple expression, patient with complexity even while bringing into the spotlight the sought-after maxims of ritual reasoning.

7. See Clooney, *Thinking Ritually.*
8. Clooney, "Mīmāṃsā as Introspective."
9. I draw here on the introduction to Mādhava's own *Elaboration.*
10. Here and throughout, I am thus following a particular strand of Mīmāṃsā thinking that stays very close to the cases. I do not attend to the philosophical layers of discourse later on woven around the *Sūtras,* but I do not dispute that those are of greater interest to many scholars.
11. Though grounded in the substance of Vedic sacrifices and the texts governing those sacrifices, Mīmāṃsā analysis does not, except on very particular points, offer useful guidance on how actually to do rituals. If we do not practice such rituals, this does not in itself disqualify us from the study of the interpretive practices. Rather, the emphasis is on clear reasons, clearly articulated, but without ever leaving behind the Vedic context. The many cases address problems in the exegesis of rites and texts prescribing ritual practices and obscurities in the interpreting of word and act and in the working through their logic.

12. Paraphrased from the introduction to Mādhava's *Elaboration,* verse 29. Unfortunately, in the course of the whole *Garland,* the *Elaboration* very rarely identifies the kind of connection linking cases to one another, and as a result readers have to determine this connection.
13. I also have more to say on case reasoning in my reflection in chapter 4 on the complicated and irregular writing that comprises Ludwig Wittgenstein's *Philosophical Investigations.* In his preface he tells us that his writing "compels us to travel over a wide range of thought criss-cross in every direction."
14. I omit some *sūtras.* Since Mīmāṃsā texts are most easily cited by *adhyāya* (book), *pāda* (chapter), and *sūtra,* I do not add page references. For the sake of clarity in the translation of *sūtras,* notoriously laconic, I have had to add a word on occasion and have uncluttered the translations by omitting most parentheses marking such additions.
15. See my comments on these verses in Clooney, Mādhava's *Garland."*
16. See Clooney, *His Hiding Place,* and Clooney, "Mīmāṃsā as Introspective."
17. And yet, although this is not a book about the *Garland,* it is entirely infused with what I have learned from years of studying the *Garland.* Due to it, I have cultivated an ever stronger preference for the slow, sure, concrete, and particular, and a suspicion about ways of thinking that leave details aside for the sake of generalizations that in turn make further study unnecessary. The *Garland* has served also to set a rather high bar in choosing the texts considered here: introductory; aimed at synthesis; needing to be read beginning to end; and training readers to think about particular things in a new way, to read more slowly, content for a (long) moment "to find everything in the book," and to keep a healthy distance from generalizations that make the reading unnecessary.
18. Annunziata and Quite, *First Communion Catechism,* 12.
19. Even as I have chosen the Catholic and Jesuit Canisius, I do not dispute the importance of other catechisms, such as Luther's pioneering catechisms and the famed *Heidelberg Catechism* or, on the Catholic side, the catechisms of the Council of Trent and of Canisius's Jesuit colleague, Robert Bellarmine.
20. As numbered in *A Catechism of Christian Doctrine.*
21. My emphases.
22. Because I wanted also to turn to the matter of truth in its doctrinal form, I have also refrained from writing a book, otherwise worthy, filled with these traditions' recommendations on slow reading.
23. Information on the primary texts used, and on available translations, can be found in the bibliography. The *Garland* and the *Linked Verses* have not been translated into English thus far; Canisius's *Catechism* was translated into English, and many other languages, in the seventeenth century, but there is no modern English translation of his *Catechismus Maior,* which I am using here (in its post-Tridentine version). I refer to the texts in what seems in each case the simplest way: by case (*adhikaraṇa*) number in the *Garland;* by section of the *Catechism;* by page number (Sanskrit, English) of the *Perspectives;* by page numbers in Silano's translation of the *Sentences;* by chapter (or "rose") in the *Admirable Secret;* and by verse number in the *Linked Verses.*

24. In chapter 2, we learn from Rosemann's scholarly readings of Peter Lombard.
25. Rosemann, *Understanding Scholastic Thought,* 96.
26. I mention *lectio divina* only here in this volume. While I highly favor this slow, contemplative study, I do not wish to co-opt the term for the intellectually intense manner of study I have in mind here.
27. Rosemann, *Understanding Scholastic Thought,* 96.
28. Rosemann, *Understanding Scholastic Thought,* 97.
29. Rosemann, *Understanding Scholastic Thought,* 101.
30. Rosemann, *Understanding Scholastic Thought,* 98.
31. A decade ago, in a book entitled *Beyond Compare* (Clooney) I studied the dynamics of learning in classic texts of two great theologians, that of the fourteenth-century Hindu and Śrīvaiṣṇava Vedānta Deśika, by way of his *Essence of the Three Mysteries,* and the sixteenth-century Catholic Francis de Sales, by way of his *Treatise on the Love of God.* Both de Sales and Deśika gave priority to the transmission of knowledge from teacher to student, in coherent traditions that prized classic texts and teachings and passed them down. Both thought that religious intellectual work in large part was a matter of learning, with intelligence and imagination, to be just the channel through which tradition flows a generation further. In *Beyond Compare* I referred also to Pierre Hadot's *Philosophy as a Way of Life,* on the rich and fully engaging practice of philosophy as a way of life, and Paul Griffiths's *Religious Reading,* on the important distinction between a secular, consumerist reading and properly religious reading. Both promote a way of reading that works within the bounds of a tradition's self-presentation, respects its priorities and rules of interpretation, and is open to the formative goals thought to arise from the reading. To think imaginatively in and beyond traditions one knows well is the way forward. But there is no way to become the best of readers except by reading patiently, diligently, and with a cultivated openness and indeed humble vulnerability to what one reads.
32. For a very brief preview of the fuller experiment of this book's chapter 4, see Clooney, "Mādhava's *Garland,*" 590–93.

TWO Words of Truth

1. That truth is at stake pertains even to the *Garland,* which, more by omission than commission, rules out alternate ways of finding meaning in texts and purpose in actions. Absolute realities such as a supreme deity or Vedānta's brahman or even Buddhism's cosmological and psychological truths are put aside as distractions from the text, in order that the truth *in* Vedic text and practice remain central: for Mādhava and his tradition, truth abides in the word that is studied: it is neither merely verbal, nor merely beyond words.
2. In his fine essay "Reading the Bible with Eyes of Faith: The Practice of Theological Exegesis," Richard Hays has written persuasively on the kind of reading that is textually attentive yet adept in recognizing and accepting the truth of and in what is studied. He aptly emphasizes the necessity of a theological reading of the Bible. He sketches a mode of reading that allows faith, truth,

reason, and practice to remain mutually interactive and in that way pertinent. By contrast, if study is removed from its communal and theological contexts for the sake of neutral learning, or learning committed rather to an academic community at best uncommitted religiously, there is a danger that "the very project of studying something called the Bible becomes intellectually incoherent" (Hays, "Reading the Bible," 11). Hays characterizes theological exegesis as "a complex practice, a way of approaching Scripture with eyes of faith and seeking to understand it within the community of faith" (11). He identifies twelve marks of this praxis, of which the following eight are most pertinent to this chapter: 1. "Theological exegesis is *a practice of and for the church.* We lavish our attention on the biblical texts because these texts have been passed on to us by the church's tradition as the distinctive and irreplaceable testimony to events in which God has acted for our salvation." 2. "Theological exegesis is *self-involving discourse.* Interpreters who read the Bible theologically approach the text with an awareness that we are addressed and claimed by the word of God that is spoken in the text, and we understand ourselves to be answerable to that word." 4. "Theological exegesis attends to *the literary wholeness of the individual scriptural witnesses.*" 5. "Theological exegesis can never be content only to describe the theological perspectives of the individual biblical authors; instead, it always presses forward to *the synthetic question of canonical coherence.*" 6. "Theological exegesis does not focus chiefly on the hypothetical history behind the biblical texts, nor does it attend primarily to the meaning of texts as self-contained works of literature; rather, it focuses on these *texts as testimony.*" 7. "*The language of theological exegesis is intratextual in character.* In intratextual theological exegesis, our interpretations will remain close to the primary language of the witnesses rather than moving away from the particularity of the biblical testimony to a language of second-order abstraction that seeks to 'translate' the biblical imagery into some other conceptual register." 10. "Learning to read the text with eyes of faith is a skill for which we are trained by *the Christian tradition.* Consequently, theological exegesis knows itself to be part of an ancient and lively conversation." 11. "Theological exegesis, however, goes beyond repeating traditional interpretations; rather, instructed by the example of traditional readings, theological interpreters will produce *fresh readings,* new performances of Scripture's sense that encounter the texts anew with eyes of faith and see the ways that the Holy Spirit continues to speak to the churches through the same ancient texts that the tradition has handed on to us." 12. "Finally, when we speak of theological exegesis, particularly when we acknowledge the Spirit's role, we must always remember that we are speaking not chiefly of our own clever readings and constructions of the text but, rather, of the way that God, working through the text, is reshaping us" (Hays, "Reading the Bible," 11–15) The last three points are most pertinent to the work of this book, capturing as they do the dynamics of instruction, creativity, and the (re)location of individuality in community that are essential to slow learning as a religious practice.

3. For a recent explanation of mine on why I am not interested in pluralist the-

ologies of religions—if anything, I am prone to an "including theology"—see Clooney, "Fractal Theory."

4. Its fuller name is *Śāstrasiddhāntaleśasaṃgraha, Collection of Perspectives on the Right Positions in the Instructive Scriptures.*
5. Or, "Because the instructive scriptures are the source of it."
6. I am using here the summary given in Bhāratītīrtha's fourteenth-century *Garland of Vyāsa's Reasons,* as a key aid in summarizing the key topics of each book and its chapters.
7. Throughout, I use these equivalents: *adhyāya* = book; *pāda* = chapter; *adhikaraṇa* = case;. I leave *sutra* untranslated.
8. In the famed *tat tvam asi* of the *Chāndogya Upaniṣad* VI, which is taken to map the identity of *brahman* as the object of meditation (*tat*) and of the meditator (*tvam*).
9. *Garland of Vyāsa's Reasons,* introductory ślokas 5–8. I have added the numbers marking the chapters in each book.
10. See Modi, *Critique of the Brahmasūtra;* Clooney, *Theology after Vedānta.*
11. On the *Garland of Vyāsa's Reasons,* see Clooney, "On the Style."
12. From the preface to Dīkṣita, *Śāstra-Siddhānta-Leśa-Saṃgraha* (1973) by S. R. Krishnamurti Sastri, xi. Sastri helpfully outlines *Perspectives* and marks its main topics, which are aligned with the topics of the four books of the *Sūtras* (listed earlier): "The *Śāstra-siddhānta-leśa-saṃgraha* consists of four chapters. The first chapter discusses such important topics as the nature of Brahman, the distinction between *Īśvara* and *Jīva*s, the problem of the causality of the world, the nature and the locus of *māyā-avidyā,* the nature and scope of injunction in respect of the Vedāntic study. The second chapter focuses its attention on the problem of Scripture versus perception and the authority of Scripture, the nature of dream and erroneous cognition. The means to liberation is the chief topic of discussion in the third chapter. The fourth chapter is concerned with Jīvanmukti, the nature of liberation in the context of *eka-jīva-vāda* (the position that there is just one individual self) and *aneka-jīva-vāda* (the position that there are multiple individual selves), the nature of the removal of ignorance, and so on" (xi–xii).
13. By Śaṅkara, the leading teacher of Advaita Vedānta.
14. Ramesan, *Śrī Appayya Dikshita,* 97.
15. The detailed table of contents for the *Perspectives* in the Sanskrit edition runs about thirty pages. It is a gem in itself, a fine distillation of the various right interpretations of issues taken in the *Perspectives.* It is presumably by the editors of the Sanskrit edition, Sastri and Veezhinathan. In my summary, I follow the numbering of thematic sections given in the table of contents, though omitting some details and grouping the sections under my own subtitles.
16. Throughout, I generally translate *avidyā* (pertaining to the individual) as ignorance but leave *māyā* (pertaining to the cosmos) untranslated, for the want of a satisfactory English translation.
17. From the preface to Dīkṣita, *Śāstra-Siddhānta-Leśa-Saṃgraha* (1973) by S. R. Krishnamurti Sastri, xi.

18. S. R. Krishnamurti Sastri, in the introduction to Dīkṣita, *Śāstra-Siddhānta-Leśa-Saṃgraha* (1973), xi. In his introduction to the English translation, S. S. Suryanarayana Sastri observes: "The *Siddhāntaleśa* is much more than a catalogue of varieties of advaita doctrine. The author's mind has reacted on the views expounded, and some evidence of it is found in the way he arranges the views on each topic. The order is not necessarily chronological, though it may be so in a few cases. In the very first topic, for instance, the first view expounded, that study of the Vedānta is an *apūrva-vidhi,* is that of the author of the *Prakaṭārtha,* while the last view, that there is no injunction at all, is that of Vācaspati; and Vācaspati was certainly earlier than the author of the *Prakaṭārtha,* who abused the former in vile language for his alleged slavish adoption of Maṇḍana's views. The arrangement of the views is so made that, in most cases, each prior view comes in for criticism from the exponent of the next; criticism is thus immanent, though rarely out of the mouth of Appayya himself" (Dīkṣita, *Sastra-Siddhānta-Leśa-Saṃgraha* (1935), 4).
19. For another image, that of branches, leaves, and fruit arising from a tree's trunk, see Clooney, *Theology after Vedānta,* 18–23.
20. Here I give page numbers in the Sanskrit, as in Sastri and Veezhinathan. Throughout, although I have not followed it closely, I also give references to the page numbers in the English translation (Dīkṣita, *Śāstra-Siddhānta-Leśa-Saṃgraha* [1935]), for readers who wish to consult a translation. These opening verses are found at Skt. 2–4; Eng. Tr., 129. When pertinent, I give pages numbers in Gotszorg's French translation too.
21. Skt. xvii–xix. The seven points offer a distillation of a section of the *Perspectives,* running to eleven pages including the *Kṛṣṇālaṃkāra* commentary of Acyutakṛṣṇānandatīrtha and comments from the editor; without the latter two elaborations, Dīkṣita's exposition of the seven positions would be no more than four pages long. Here too and throughout, my translation, with slight modifications for clarity.
22. Skt. 33; Eng. Tr. 148–49.
23. These titles are mine, based on indications given in the outline and body of the text.
24. Skt. xix–xx.
25. As above, *sūtra* I.1.2 is "That whence the birth, etc., of the world," a definition of *brahman* in terms of what comes forth from it.
26. *Māyā* is the cosmic creative power of Brahman conditioned and as it were outside itself, leading to appearances of duality, including the world as such; *avidyā* is the personal ignorance of an individual. For clarity, as above, I retain *māyā* and translate *avidyā* as "ignorance."
27. The *Tīkā* ("short commentary") referred to a number of times in the table of contents may indicate Padmapāda's *Pañcapādikā,* a partial commentary on Śaṅkara's *Bhāṣya.* Thus Sastri, 302n49, in Dīkṣita, *Śāstra-Siddhānta-Leśa-Saṃgraha* (1935).
28. The table adds that regarding this view, there is in the *Tīkā,* an interpretation not to Dīkṣita's liking.

29. Skt. 50–53; Eng. Tr. 154; Gotszorg in Dīkṣita, *Traduction du Chapitre 1,* 87.
30. Skt. 52–53; Eng. Tr. 154–55; Gotszorg in Dīkṣita, *Traduction du Chapitre 1,* 88.
31. Skt. 53–55; Eng. Tr. 154–55; Gotszorg in Dīkṣita, *Traduction du Chapitre 1,* 91.
32. Here, too, I introduce small modifications for the sake of clarity in English.
33. *Sattva* is one of the three constituents (*guṇas*) of reality, along with energy (*rajas*) and lethargy (*tamas*); as such, *sattva* is tantamount to *being* in a stable, pure form that may appear complex and tainted in this world.
34. The "Varied Light" is chapter 6 of the *Pañcadaśī.*
35. This text is a commentary on a commentary on the *Māṇḍukya Upaniṣad.*
36. These positions are found in the Sanskrit table of contents, page 21.
37. The editor attributes this position to the *Iṣṭasiddhi,* an important and famously difficult Vedānta philosophical work. This is indeed a difficult position, attributing the ignorance to Brahman, which then, mistakenly thinking itself a personal self, also mistakenly conjures the perfections of "lord" for itself.
38. Skt. 104; Eng. Tr. 176; Gotszorg in Dīkṣita, *Traduction du Chapitre 1,* 169.
39. Skt. 104–5; Eng. Tr. 176; Gotszorg in Dīkṣita, *Traduction du Chapitre 1,* 169.
40. Dīkṣita gives no summary conclusion at the end of his exposition of all ten views, but the commentator Acyutakṛṣṇānandatīrtha observes, "And so, it is established that Brahman, in the form alone of lord, is the material cause of all, because there is no superfluous inclusion of an individual self." The volume editors suggest that this position, following the *Vivaraṇa* in accord with the *Summary of the Vedānta,* was Dīkṣita's own from the start, but that he reports the other views because he deems them to merit consideration.
41. Skt. 395–396; Eng. Tr. 413.
42. Lombard, *Sentences,* Book I:5. Except where noted, the translations are Silano's.
43. Lombard, *Sentences,* Book I:3.
44. Lombard, *Sentences,* Book I:3.
45. Lombard, *Sentences,* Book I:4.
46. As Rosemann notes, Lombard exemplifies deference in the face of mystery: "Peter Lombard presents his ideas with his usual sense of humility, recognizing the limits of the human mind in coming to grasp why the human person was created as an incarnate spirit, how precisely the details of angelic nature are to be understood, or why God allowed the devil to tempt humanity, knowing as He did that we would fall. This humility produces three consequences. First, Lombard *shuns excessively speculative explanations,* attempting to keep his account of matters such as human nature in its prelapsarian state as straightforward as possible. Secondly, Peter *leans strongly to the literal reading of scriptural texts,* as we have seen in the examples of the *Genesis* account of creation and of the Fall. *Such literal readings in fact minimize the need for speculation.* Thirdly and finally, the *Book of Sentences* is *reluctant to foreclose discussion,* often preferring a multiplicity of voices to assertion of the truth of one particular human point of view" (Rosemann, *Peter Lombard,* 117).
47. Silano, in Lombard, *Sentences,* Book I:xviii.
48. Lombard, *Sentences,* Book I:4–5, citing Augustine, *De Trinitate* III.
49. Silano, in Lombard, *Sentences,* Book I:xviii.

50. Rosemann, *Peter Lombard,* 117.
51. Lombard, *Sentences,* Book I:12.
52. Rosemann, *Peter Lombard,* 62–63.
53. Rosemann, *Peter Lombard,* 64.
54. Rosemann, *Peter Lombard,* 196. See also my comments on Wittgenstein's writing style—and thus his teaching technique—in chapter 4.
55. The *Sentences* can, Silano observes, be usefully conceived of as a set of cases, mostly familiar, yet once more to be read through, one by one: "At the core of the casebook will be not the author's desiderata regarding the law, but the authorities. Statute law will have its niche, but pride of place will belong to judicial decisions, largely because these are less clear and synthetic than statute law and so better exemplify the seemingly contradictory goods that must be balanced in legal reasoning. Deciding which judicial decisions are sufficiently significant and instructive to become the source of legal doctrine is not a straightforward process. It is not simply a matter of the place of the deciding tribunal in the judicial hierarchy, since the decisions of courts of first instance stand more or less on an equal footing with those of the most exalted Supreme Courts" (Silano, in Lombard, *Sentences,* Book I:xix–xx) Though deferential toward tradition, by selectivity in cases and authorities cited, the author of a book of cases is active in shaping what is read and to what purpose: "The author of a good casebook is humbly reticent. It is not for him to trumpet his own views on all sorts of legal topics, and yet he claims and exercises the great authority to decide which, of the endless number of judicial decisions that are published every day, have important jurisprudential implications and should be taken to exemplify some issue or problem in the law from whose study students and judges can profit" (xx). The generalities are already in place, and there is little surprising regarding the doctrines at issue, regarding Trinity and Incarnation, creation and redemption. What is most fruitful pertains to the way the text is composed, its order of exposition and study. Reading the *Sentences* requires that readers discern the point of each case, and then too the teacher's point in adducing just a set of cases in a certain order. Lombard is writing for the *prudentes* (and Silano here echoes William of Tyre), those who respect the law and are able to work it through, case by case. On the *prudentes,* see Locklin, "Interreligious Prudentia," 295.
56. Here numbered by the "distinctions" (groups of related questions) dedicated to the topic.
57. Here, too, and with only slight modifications, I use the headings as given by Silano.
58. Lombard, *Sentences,* Book II:5–6.
59. Lombard, *Sentences,* Book II:68–70.
60. Lombard, *Sentences,* Book II:70–71.
61. Lombard, *Sentences,* Book II:71.
62. Lombard, *Sentences,* Book II:76–77.
63. Lombard, *Sentences,* Book II:76–77.
64. Lombard, *Sentences,* Book II:77.
65. Rosemann comments on the sensitivity with which Lombard treats this topic,

relevant then as now, as readers of *Genesis* seek to infer how women and men are to relate in society: "Explaining why Eve was created from Adam's side—not from his head or feet—(Lombard) argues that this mode of creation symbolizes the fellowship of love, as well as the equality, that was meant to govern the relationship of the sexes: 'Since woman was not destined to be either the ruler or the servant of man, but his companion, she was to be brought forth neither from his head nor from his feet, but from his side'" (Rosemann, *Peter Lombard,* 106–7). He adds a cautionary note: "Just a few distinctions after this passage, however, Peter suddenly speaks of a master-servant relationship between man and woman to illustrate the domination of the higher aspects of reason over the lower ones. This reversal is no doubt inspired by *Genesis* 3:16, a biblical verse that presents woman's subjection to man as a punishment for sin" (107). But even here, the essential dignity of the woman is defended: "As far as Eve's soul is concerned, it was not made from Adam's soul, as some heretics would have it—such as the traducianists, who also held that all the other human souls stem from Adam's—but from nothing" (107).

66. Lombard, *Sentences,* Book II:77.
67. Lombard, *Sentences,* Book II:78. The critical edition notes that Lombard is referring to Resp. *Ephesians* 5.32 and Resp. *John* 19.34.
68. Lombard, *Sentences,* Book II:80.
69. Lombard, *Sentences,* Book II:81.
70. Rosemann, *Peter Lombard,* 56.
71. As cited by Rosemann, *Peter Lombard,* 56.
72. Rosemann, *Peter Lombard,* 56.
73. Rosemann, *Peter Lombard,* 56–57.

THREE Words of Instruction

1. In *Les Origines du Catéchisme Moderne,* Jean-Claude Dhotel narrates the catechetical drive to fine-tune the level of technical expertise in accord with the intended reader: teacher or student; theologian or pastor; simple parishioner or future teacher. Yet even when catechisms were adjusted for the sake of more and less educated audiences, they did not change the truth to fit the subjective needs and interests of their intended readers. They sought rather to impart settled truths as integral wholes woven into the life of the community. The history of catechisms is interesting and complex and has been relatively well studied. *Les Origines* provides a finely detailed presentation of relevant background of early modern catechisms. Against the background of the medieval and creedal precedents, Dhotel traces the formation of the catechisms from Luther on. In "Development of Modern *Catechisms*," the third chapter of her 1970 dissertation, Sister Mary Charles Bryce, OSB, gives a clear overview of early catechisms and the place in Catholic history of the catechisms of Canisius, Bellarmine, and the Council of Trent. As Bryce points out (21–30), the work of the Church in teaching and passing on the faith is as old as the Church.
2. The Commandments, as enumerated in Canisius's *Catechism:* 1. I am the Lord

your God. You shall not have strange gods before me. You shall not make graven images, that you might worship them. 2. You shall not take the name of the Lord thy God in vain. 3. Remember that you keep holy the Sabbath day. 4. Honor thy father and thy mother, that you may be long-lived upon the land which the Lord thy God will give you. 5. You shall not kill. 6. You shall not commit adultery. 7. You shall not steal. 8. You shall not bear false witness against your neighbor. 9. You shall not covet your neighbor's wife, 10. Nor his house, nor his field, nor his servant, nor his handmaid, nor his ox, nor his ass, nor anything that is his.

3. The Creed, as divided into thematic portions: 1. I believe in God, the Father Almighty, Creator of heaven and earth; 2. and in Jesus Christ, His only Son, our Lord: 3. Who was conceived by the Holy Spirit, born of the Virgin Mary; 4. suffered under Pontius Pilate, was crucified, died and was buried. 5. He descended into hell; the third day He rose again from the dead; 6. He ascended into heaven, is seated at the right hand of God the Father Almighty; 7. Thence He shall come to judge the living and the dead. 8. I believe in the Holy Spirit, 9. the Holy Catholic Church, the communion of Saints, 10. the forgiveness of sins, 11. the resurrection of the body, and 12. life everlasting. Amen.
4. The Lord's Prayer, in a standard form: Our Father, Who art in Heaven, hallowed be Thy name; Thy Kingdom come, Your will be done on earth as it is in Heaven. Give us this day our daily bread; and forgive us our trespasses as we forgive those who trespass against us; and lead us not into temptation, but deliver us from evil.
5. Bryce enlists Thomas McDonough for the sake of a description of Luther's project: "Thomas McDonough observed that the catechism captured the very heart and soul of Luther's convictions, the core of which was his 'Law-Gospel doctrine of salvation which entailed a despair-faith experience of sin and grace.' These seemed to fall quite logically into place under the Decalogue and Gospel, which he interpreted as keeping the law—a somewhat novel interpretation of that term which literally means 'good news.' He held that in the Gospel was the command to believe (Creed), pray (Lord's Prayer), and administer the sacraments. McDonough put it that 'faith in the Decalogue is as much a part of Luther's theology as faith in the New Testament.' If this is true, the Gospel section must be seen not only as promise but also as commandment, the fulfillment of the Law" (Bryce, "Influence of the Catechism," 33–34) Bryce also notes that in the Roman Catechism authorized by the Council of Trent the order differs: the Apostles' Creed; Sacraments; the Ten Commandments; the Lord's Prayer: "Briefly overviewed, this sequence delineates what God has done for man—narrated and explained in the Apostles Creed—and what He continues to do through the communication of his own life to man through his Son in the Sacraments. The two last sections point up man's response, love for love, in prayer and leading Christian lives according to God's prescribed norms in the commandments" (15–16).
6. See Bryce, "Influence of the Catechism," 41–45, on Canisius's catechisms. Throughout, I have also consulted the edition of the *Catechism* by Filser and Leimgruber. See also Molinario, *Le catéchisme.*
7. Respectively, *The Greater Catechism: Summary of Christian Doctrine; The Lesser*

Catechism or the Smaller Catechism for Catholics; the *Smallest Catechism: Summary of Christian Doctrine Given by way of Questions, and Accommodated to the Capacity of the Simple.*

8. Dhotel, *Les Origines du Catéchisme Moderne,* 77. Translations from Dhotel are my own. But even if such a layering of texts, each presupposing the former, was Canisius's intention, the general assumption remains that the three catechisms target three groups of people distinguished by age and education. Dhotel notes too (77) that the catechisms were rather early on sorted out according to the anticipated audience, the smallest for children and the least educated, etc.
9. Similarly, the *Garland* distills tradition in a most succinct form that stands on its own, while yet offering further and richer insights to those who then reread the commentarial tradition underlying Mādhava's work.
10. Dhotel, *Les Origines du Catéchisme Moderne,* 66.
11. Dhotel observes that Canisius not only proposed alternatives to the very popular and influential catechisms of the reformers but also wrote in an appealing manner that was not incidental to his success. His *Catechism* can be distinguished from other Catholic catechisms, such as that of Edmond Auger, SJ, who wrote in order to rebut John Calvin's *Instruction et confession de foi dont on use en l'Eglise de Genève* (Dhotel, *Les Origines du Catéchisme Moderne,* 19). Calvin already had moved away from Luther's simpler primers toward a presentation of the faith that was more institutionally grounded and philosophically explained (45), and Auger too inclined in that direction. (Dhotel analyzes Auger's catechism on pages 50–64 and shows how it responds to and parallels Calvin's work.) While Auger's work had its merits—zeal, erudition, rebuttal without stooping to the harshest language of polemic—Dhotel laments its overly technical nature and concern for arguing contemporary issues rationalistically, to the detriment of a deeper attention to tradition and its more integral intellectual and spiritual teachings. Faith and works suffer separation even in a work defending their relationship, so that as a result "dogma risked being presented only as knowledge and the Ten Commandments only as duty; the whole of the catechism was a lesson to be learned rather than a school in the Christian life or, as it was said, of piety" (60). By contrast, Canisius writes more holistically and probably more confidently. He relies on the power of a positive presentation of the faith, for the sake of a Christian formation that integrates wisdom and justice. He steers away from fiercely apologetic refutations and favors a rich, positive presentation of the faith. (For a contrary view, on the *lack* of pacific nature in Canisius's *Catechism,* see Pabel, *Peter Canisius.*) If Auger depends on the rhetoric of apologetics and tends toward polemic, Canisius's writing adds up to a surer powerful recollection of tradition as a whole. See Dhotel, *Les Origines du Catéchisme Moderne,* 80.
12. Canisius's catechisms met the needs of his era and remained effective even for a long time thereafter. Pope Leo XIII's words exemplify the esteem in which the *Catechism* was held even at the end of the nineteenth century: "[Canisius] did not hesitate to descend from the heights of wisdom to the basics of writing. He undertook the instruction of children and even composed elementary writing books and grammars for their use. Indeed just as he often came back

from preaching to the courts of kings to address the people, so, after learned writings on dogma or morals, he used to compose pamphlets destined either to strengthen the faith of the people or to arouse and nourish their piety. He had wonderful success in preventing the inexperienced from getting caught in the nets of error." In its simpler forms his writing may be intended for those with minimal education, but overall their effect was to help shape the cultures of a Catholic Europe: "The *Summa* [*Catechism*] which he published for this purpose is a compact and tightly-knit work, written in beautiful Latin and not unworthy of the Fathers of the Church. This remarkable work was enthusiastically received by learned men in almost all the countries of Europe. Less voluminous but no less useful were the two [smaller] famous catechisms which this blessed man wrote for less cultivated minds: one for the religious instruction of children, the other for young men already involved in the study of the arts. These two works had such a great success among Catholics immediately upon publication that almost all professors charged with teaching the basics of the faith had them in hand. They were used not only in the schools as a spiritual milk for the children, but they were also explained publicly in the churches to the benefit of all." In light of chapter 2 readers may be disposed to agree with Pius XI, who, when he declared Canisius a doctor of the Church on 21 May 1925, wrote as follows: "He is not deficient who would compare the *Summa* of Canisius to the *Book of the Sentences,* nor the one who would say that the blessed author of the *Catechism* is for the West what Saint Cyril of Jerusalem was for the Church of the Easter" ("Non defuit qui Canisii *Summam* cum *Sententiarum Libro* compararet, nec qui Beatum *Catechismi* auctorem talem pro Occidente, qualem S. Cyrillum Hierosolymitanum pro Orientali Ecclesia fuisse diceret"). Even if we take into account the paramount authority of the *Catechism* of the Council of Trent, Canisius's work was the most famous catechism of the Catholic Reformation, going through four hundred printings and editions in 150 years. As Leo XIII puts it, "during three centuries Canisius has been regarded as the teacher of Catholics in Germany. In popular speech 'knowing Canisius was synonymous with 'preserving the Christian faith'" ("Militantis Ecclesiae," 1 August 1897). Many other catechisms might well be studied, but studying this one is a very good place to start.

13. Or, rather, just its first half: "Hail (Mary), full of grace, the Lord is with you, blessed are you among women, and blessed is the fruit of your womb (Jesus)."
14. The Commandments of the Church, given under n. 13: 1. Celebrate the stipulated feast days of the Church. 2. Reverently hear the holy office of the Mass on feast days. 3. Observe the fasts stipulated for certain days and certain times, as in Lent, on the days before solemn feasts at four times of the year, which our greater one observed in those times in the temples, and called vigils. 4. Confess your sins to your priest each year. 5. Receive the sacred Eucharist at least once in a year, around the feast of Easter.
15. The fifth part in Canisius's catechism is notably fully developed. It may best be taken as a treatise on justice, even a mapping of the Christian moral life, rather than simply another section of the *Catechism.* Sins are listed and distinguished, and family trees of sins—the major sins and the lesser sins that are their "daugh-

ters," sins in which one causes others to sin, even if not acting oneself, the sins against the Holy Spirit, and sins crying out to heaven—mapped for the sake of the reader, perhaps primarily the confessor and the moralist. In turn, virtues too are proposed and distinguished: the three kinds of good works (fasting, prayer, and mercy); the works of mercy; the cardinal virtues (prudence, justice, temperance, and fortitude); the gifts and fruits of the Holy Spirit; the eight beatitudes found at the Sermon on the Mount; the evangelical virtues (poverty, chastity, and obedience). For some, the treatise on sinful and good deeds may serve as reference for the work of spiritual direction and confessions. Indeed, the reflection on sin has a prayerful context. Dhotel notes that at the start of this long Part Five, on justice, sin, and virtue, there is an image of the crucified Christ, with the words, "The just died for the unjust, that we who are dead by sins might live for justice . . . that without fear and freed from the hands of our enemies we might serve him in holiness and justice before him, all of our days" (I Peter 2.25 and Luke 1.74–75, cited in Latin by Dhotel, *Les Origines du Catéchisme Moderne,* 74–75). Things are put in proportion: sins are to be considered carefully and in detail, but always within the frame of the larger truth of redemption. The picture Dhotel refers to can be found in the 1933 edition, on page 150. Interestingly, Part Five is the only part of the *Catechism,* at least in that edition, that has an illustration.

16. Dhotel, *Les Origines du Catéchisme Moderne,* 71.
17. *Iudaica, ethnica, mahometica, haeretica.*
18. Throughout, my translations from the Latin.
19. Some scholars in the Mīmāṃsā tradition, most notably Kumārila Bhaṭṭa and his disciples, very vigorously engaged hostile philosophies, so as to defend what they took to be the metaphysical and epistemological foundations required for the actual work of Mīmāṃsā inquiry.
20. The subsequent two paragraphs of this article, which we cannot consider here, state the relationship of the Son to the Father, the work of redemption, and the Son's superiority to and dominance over all other powers, earthly or heavenly.
21. *Iudaeis et ethnicis:* we are again reminded that Canisius's positive vision of the faith always carries with it sharply drawn borders that also exclude.
22. In chapter 5, we will see how in his treatise on the rosary, Louis de Montfort invests the words of the Hail Mary with multiple layers of scripture, doctrinal and experiential meaning, so that the simplest prayer comes to include much of the faith. Ever practical, Canisius does something of the same here, investing with greater consequence the often routine sign of the cross.
23. The threefold path: suggestion (temptation); delight (indulgence); consent (as the decision freely made, to sin).
24. In an appendix, Canisius describes at length and in detail the several families of kindred sins, including many smaller sins that, when carelessly indulged, lead the lax person into greater and more perilous sin.
25. As we keep reading the *Catechism* across its five parts, we see how far removed we are from the idea of a catechism as only a number of brief questions and brief answers listed together. Rather, we are shown the whole of the faith in detail and

as integral, and so too as it plays out in terms of the moral life. So we must resist the temptation to look merely at the answers to particular questions. The whole must be studied, slowly, and in the given order, moving from the Creed to the prayers and then to the commandments of the Church, the whole life of faith, hope, and charity mapped and explained. As students learn and take to heart the distinctions patiently enunciated by the Church, they also see Christian moral teaching in its breadth and depth, and they become clear on what applies positively and negatively in a moral life.

26. We must concede that despite its back and forth format most easily translated by questions and answers, the *Garland* is not a catechism in the ordinary sense and certainly was not written for a wide audience. Though it is highly instructive, its focus is not doctrines but sacred rules for reading properly. And, of course, the content of what is asked and the reasons adduced diverge widely from any Christian catechism. Though it is formative, it is not meant for the general populace, nor would a life conformed to it turn out to be an "ordinary life" in the sense Canisius might expect.
27. It is notable that here too Mādhava gives the pertinent text only in the *Elaboration.* It is as if to say: in the *Garland* itself, what matters is that there are such texts, not what they say in particular.
28. By contrast, as shown in chapter 5, the *Hundred Linked Verses on the Holy Word of Mouth,* composed in Tamil, largely bypasses the issue of caste. Devotion and its expression in words is for anyone willing to listen.
29. Introduction in the *Garland,* verse 2 (Mādhavācārya, *Jaiminīyanyāyamālāvistara,* 2). The characteristics are very briefly stated, discrepant from the standard ordering of the books of the *Sūtras.* I have generally followed the *Elaboration* on the passage, which elaborates the parallels in statecraft, and a clear footnote by Ramanatha Sastry and Pattabhirami Sastri (Mādhavācārya, *Jaiminīyanyāyamālā of Mādhavācārya,* 2), which makes explicit the order of attributes with respect to the books of the *Sūtras.*

FOUR Reading with Wittgenstein

1. I have more recently been comforted also by a passage I came across in reading a memoir by Benoit Mandelbrot, the "father" of fractal geometry, on the uneven terrain of some very insightful scholarship: "I never begin with a table of contents and then write chapters, sections, and sentences in the order in which they appear. Instead, I start with several already available pieces that can be counted upon to provide the structure of the whole, and I keep adding here and there. Every so often, I wake up in the morning with the overwhelming feeling that a chunk of the book is in the wrong place and had better be brought forward or back. Quite literally, a book does not approach completion until I know it by heart" (Mandelbrot, *Fractalist,* 277–78).
2. Wittgenstein, 1946 preface to *Philosophical Investigations,* which is to be found at the start (on an unnumbered page) of Wittgenstein, *Philosophical Investigations.*
3. N. xiv, Wittgenstein, *Philosophical Investigations,* 232.

4. In Baker and Hacker, *Wittgenstein.* I have omitted some of the parenthetical detailed references to Wittgenstein's works cited in the original.
5. Baker and Hacker, *Wittgenstein,* 274.
6. Baker and Hacker, *Wittgenstein,* 274.
7. Wittgenstein, *Philosophical Investigations,* 118; Baker and Hacker, *Wittgenstein,* 274.
8. Baker and Hacker, *Wittgenstein,* 274.
9. Baker and Hacker, *Wittgenstein,* 274.
10. Baker and Hacker, *Wittgenstein,* 274.
11. The six cravings are enumerated in Baker and Hacker, *Wittgenstein,* 282–83. I have altered the order of them.
12. All six books I use in this volume of course claim to be summaries themselves, but they are entrées into rather than substitutes for the older and more expansive texts distilled in their words.
13. Baker and Hacker, *Wittgenstein,* 282–83.
14. Wittgenstein, cited by Perloff, "Writing Philosophy as Poetry," 725. She observes also that Wittgenstein's "remarks" are nevertheless the result of much more intensive *dichten* than is usually thought. Etymologically, she explains, the verb *dichten* comes from the adjective *dicht* (thick, dense, packed): *dichten* originally meant 'to make airtight, watertight; to seal the cracks (in a window, roof, etc.)'—in other words, something like the Zen phrase 'to thicken the plot'" (725).
15. Perloff, "Writing Philosophy as Poetry, 715.
16. Wittgenstein, *Culture and Value,* 65; cited by Perloff, "Writing Philosophy as Poetry," 726.
17. Wittgenstein, *Culture and Value,* 72; cited by Perloff, "Writing Philosophy as Poetry," 26.
18. Wittgenstein, *Culture and Value,* 28; cited by Perloff, "Writing Philosophy as Poetry," 726.
19. Perloff, "Writing Philosophy as Poetry," 726. She adds, "Indeed, no sooner has he made the statement above than Wittgenstein adds somewhat sheepishly, 'With these words, I was also acknowledging myself to be someone who cannot quite do what he would like to do' (*Culture and Value,* 28). And a few years later: 'I squander untold effort to make an arrangement of my thoughts that may have no value whatever' (*Culture and Value,* 33)" (Perloff, "Writing Philosophy as Poetry," 716).
20. Perloff, "Writing Philosophy as Poetry," 719. The included passage is from Wittgenstein, *Wittgenstein's Lectures,* 112.
21. Perloff, "Writing Philosophy as Poetry," 719. The included passage is from Wittgenstein, *Wittgenstein's Lectures,* 35, 1.
22. Perloff, "Writing Philosophy as Poetry." The allusion is to Wittgenstein, *Culture and Value,* 13.
23. As cited from Wittgenstein, *Philosophical Investigations,* n. 82.
24. Perloff, "Writing Philosophy as Poetry," 723.
25. High, *Language, Persons, and Beliefs,* 20, my emphases; cited by Thiselton, *Two Horizons,* 4, 370.

26. Cavell, "Availability of Wittgenstein's Later Philosophy," 93, my emphases; cited by Thiselton, *Two Horizons,* 370.
27. McGinn, *Wittgenstein and the Philosophical Investigations,* 10. The pertinent passage in *Philosophical Investigations* is worth quoting in full: "It was true to say that our considerations could not be scientific ones. It was not of any possible interest to us to find out empirically 'that, contrary to our preconceived ideas, it is possible to think such-and-such'—whatever that may mean. (The conception of thought as a gaseous medium.) And we may not advance any kind of theory. There must not be anything hypothetical in our considerations. We must do away with all *explanation,* and description alone must take its place. And this description gets its light, that is to say its purpose, from the philosophical problems. These are, of course, not empirical problems; they are solved, rather, by looking into the workings of our language, and that in such a way as to make us recognize those workings: *in despite of* an urge to misunderstand them. The problems are solved, not by giving new information, but by arranging what we have always known" (n. 109). All of this might have been said by Mādhava, had he chosen to explain himself to us.
28. McGinn, *Wittgenstein and the Philosophical Investigations,* 14.
29. McGinn, *Wittgenstein and the Philosophical Investigations,* 16.
30. Just as, we may recall, the *Sentences* are thought to fall short of the desired methods and system.
31. McGinn, *Wittgenstein and the Philosophical Investigations,* 19.
32. McGinn, *Wittgenstein and the Philosophical Investigations,* 28.
33. McGinn, *Wittgenstein and the Philosophical Investigations,* 28–29.
34. McGinn, *Wittgenstein and the Philosophical Investigations,* 29.

FIVE Words of Participation

1. The *Admirable Secret* was not published in Montfort's lifetime, and in any case it is much indebted to older sources. He refers repeatedly to the *De Dignitate Psalterii,* by Blessed Alan de la Roche. Much is borrowed, verbatim, from the *Rosier Mystique de la Très Sainte Vierge* (1685) by Antoninus Thomas, OP. The *Oeuvres Complètes* helps us by putting in italics the passages of the *Admirable Secret* borrowed fully from the *Rosier Mystique.* The text of the *Admirable Secret* itself thus merits further study, to specify Montfort's contribution beyond what was said by Antoninus Thomas and also Alan de la Roche. Recent scholarship has scrutinized the likely redaction of the *Admirable Secret* and reassessed its attribution as a completed whole by Montfort. For insights into the complicated authorship of works attributed to Montfort, see Bernard Guitteny, *Grignion de Montfort* and "Le texte authentique," and Le Tourneau, "Nouvelles recherches." This important scholarship by Guitteny and others does not, however, take away from my purpose. Even if Montfort drew more heavily on earlier sources than even he admits, this strengthens the case that the *Admirable Secret,* like the five other texts studied in this book, is heavily indebted to tradition and to the distillation and easy presentation of the whole of it in a small space. Most pertinent

is the placement of persuasions and edifying tales entirely at the service of a specific, repetitive recitation practice. Enhanced understanding and a great realization of the truth lead one closer to praying the rosary. As with the *Catechism* and *Sentences,* the wholeness of the faith is encountered in a small space, even if now enriched with affective and practical impetus, integrated for the sake of the transformation of life.

2. Throughout, I use the 1988 English translation (Montfort, *Admirable Secret*) with some adjustments according to the text as given in the *Oeuvres Complètes.*
3. Montfort, *Admirable Secret,* nn. 10–11. The Albigensians sought a pure, uncompromised form of Christian identity and life and found abhorrent the corruption of the Church. They are said to have sought escape from the body.
4. Here and throughout, I italicize passages borrowed from Antoninus Thomas and la Roche.
5. Montfort, *Admirable Secret,* n. 11.
6. Montfort, *Admirable Secret,* n. 12.
7. Montfort, *Admirable Secret,* n. 1.
8. Montfort, *Admirable Secret,* n. 2.
9. Here and below, Montfort quotes the Bible in Latin, repeating it in a French paraphrase.
10. Montfort, *Admirable Secret,* n. 4.
11. Montfort, *Admirable Secret,* n. 5.
12. The girl and her older sister.
13. Montfort, *Admirable Secret,* n. 8.
14. Montfort, *Admirable Secret,* n. 8.
15. Montfort, *Admirable Secret,* n. 34.
16. Montfort, *Admirable Secret,* n. 34.
17. Montfort, *Admirable Secret,* n. 35.
18. From the *Pange Lingua* hymn.
19. Montfort, *Admirable Secret,* n. 119.
20. On the Ignatian influence on the use of the imagination regarding the mysteries of the rosary see Mitchell, *Mystery of the Rosary.*
21. Montfort, *Admirable Secret,* n. 121.
22. It is interesting that almost nothing in the 43rd and 44th Roses is borrowed from Thomas.
23. Montfort, *Admirable Secret,* n. 127.
24. Montfort, *Admirable Secret,* n. 128.
25. Montfort, *Admirable Secret,* n. 128.
26. Montfort, *Oeuvres Complètes,* 392.
27. Montfort, *Oeuvres Complètes,* 393.
28. Described in Montfort, *Oeuvres Complètes,* 397–98.
29. Maṇavāḷamāmuni wrote commentaries on the works of the great teacher Piḷḷailokācārya. His *Garland of Gems of Teaching* (*Upadeśaratnamālā*) is a record and celebration of the āḻvārs and the lineage of teachers in Śrīvaiṣṇavism. His *Twenty Verses on the Royal Ascetic* (*Yatirājaviṃśati*) celebrates Rāmānuja as the leading teacher of the tradition, while his *Order of*

Holy Worship (*Tiruvārādhanakramam*) supplements Rāmānuja's *Daily Manual* (*Nityam*) with a simpler and more practicable routine for daily worship.

30. On the *Holy Word of Mouth* (*Tiruvāymoḻi*), see Carman and Narayanan, *Tamil Veda,* and Clooney, *Seeing through Texts* and *His Hiding Place.*
31. For the mathematicians among us: the "thousand verses" is actually 1,102. Each song has an 11th verse praising the previous 10, their author, what they tell us about God, and the benefits accruing to those who learn and sing them. One song, II.7, has 12 verses. Hence the sum total of 1,102 verses.
32. Here and throughout, in my translations of the *Holy Word* and the *Linked Verses* I capitalize pronouns referring to the Lord and his actions, although in the Tamil no capitalization occurs.
33. *Manaṉ* may be translated as "mind" as well as "heart," though here I generally prefer the latter; indeed, it might best be translated as "mind-heart."
34. I.1.1, I.2.1, I.3.1, I.4.1, III.3.1, IV.10.1, V.4.1, V.7.1, VI.3.1, VI.7.1, VI.10.10, VII.9.2, VII.8.3, X.3.2, X.10.10.
35. For a summary of the basic story of the first three *āḻvārs,* see *Govindacharya, Holy Lives of the Azhvars,* 80–84.
36. A legend echoing the opening line of VI.7.1 cited above.
37. A modern retelling of Śaṭakōpaṉ's meditation and poetry, told by Algondavilli Govindacharya based on ancient sources, ends this way: "After Maturakavi has awakened the saint, the Lord reveals directly to Śaṭakōpaṉ the mysteries of God's own self and of the world. . . . Our saint was so enraptured with this awful beatific vision, was so animated and transported, felt so blessed and so afflated with divine ecstasy, that he expanded beyond the limits of his own being; and he poured forth its uncontainable contents of love and wisdom into songs, melodious and mellifluous, and brimming with all the varying phases—joys and sorrows, nights and days, of the soul in its journey towards the Divine—in its progress toward the Goal of Infinite Bliss" (Govindacharya, *Holy Lives of the Azhvars,* 204–5).

    In the famous song VII.9, Śaṭakōpaṉ himself evokes the experience of possession to trace his inspiration to its divine source. His beloved God does not speak to him directly or indirectly as Mary did to Dominic; here the saint is taken over, filled with divine presence, such that every word is the divine word: "He has exalted me for all time, and day after day made me into Himself, And by me He now sings Himself in sweet Tamil—My Lord, my first one, my abiding light: How can I sing of Him?" "How can I sing of Him? He has become one with my dear life, He makes me sing sweet songs that I sing by my own words, and By his own words this astonishing one now sings Himself, Though he is first among the three deities who sang before me." "Making clear that He is the first of all, He came, entered my tongue, was there first of all, And in these good sweet songs He sings Himself to His pure first devotees. My father, here in my mouth: can I ever forget Him?" (VII.9.1–3).
38. II.3.11, III.10.11, IV.6.11, VI.7.11, VI.10.11.
39. It is impossible here to explore the great commentarial tradition that arose in the teaching of the *Holy Word,* though I have explored the beauty of those

teachings elsewhere (see Clooney, *Seeing through Texts* and *His Hiding Place*). Those teachings, far greater in length than Montfort's *Admirable Secret,* nevertheless share with it the intent of exposing readers to the depth and power of the songs, getting them also to participate in the reality of what they hear. Those commentaries are brilliant, but vast as they are they can hardly be called summations. Some much more succinct expositions of the *Holy Word* focused on its themes and its implied theology. For example, Vātikēsari Aḻakiya Maṇavāḷa Jīyar's *Connections in the Tamil Upaniṣad* (*Dramiḍopaniṣad Saṃgati*) offers a two-line verse summarizing each song, identifying its main theological point. In addition, Vedānta Deśika's *Necklace of the Meanings in the Tamil Upaniṣad* (*Dramiḍopaniṣad Tātparyaratnāvaḷi*) offers a single Sanskrit verse for each song. This verse contains ten words, each word catching the meaning of one verse of the Tamil. In the end, we have one hundred new verses, adding up to one thousand words that capture the meanings of the thousand Tamil verses. Both works are brilliant, and worthy of study, since they encapsulate the theology of the *Holy Word* in a very manageable form. But still, written in Sanskrit, they do not with immediacy communicate Śaṭakōpaṉ's affective achievement in his native Tamil. Neither work draws listeners and readers into the deep flood of the saint's experience and its overflow into living words.

40. Maṇavāḷamāmuni, *Tiruvāymoḻi Nūṟṟantāti (Linked Verses,* 1916), 3–6.
41. Annangarachariar's introduction in Maṇavāḷamāmuni, *Tiruvāymoḻi Nūṟṟantāti (Linked Verses,* 1978), 58; my translation.
42. Freestanding prefixed verses (*taṉiyaṉs*) attributed to Periyajīyar, "the great teacher." They are found in the 1916 edition, pp. 1–2. Throughout, all translations from the Tamil are mine.
43. Or, equally possible, "As he so sweetly sang his *Hundred Linked Verses on the Holy Word of Mouth,*" thus naming the text.
44. Throughout the *Linked Verses,* it is sometimes ambiguous whether "he" is the Lord, or Śaṭakōpaṉ, or even sometimes Maṇavālamāmuni. Rather than clarifying matters by using the capital "H" for the divinity, I have left the ambiguity, since a certain fluidity seems true to Maṇavālamāmuni's point: one authority, one author's spirit, flows through all these words.
45. Literally, Paraṅkucaṉ, "who is (like) a goad."

SIX Reading (and Rereading) the Hindu and Christian Classics

1. Full bibliographical information is in the bibliography.
2. The differences, though not sufficient to counter the substitutions entirely, are not inconsiderable: the *Preliminary Rules* does not deal directly with the 907 cases taken up in the *Garland,* but only with the interpretive rules; the *Small Catechism,* by definition, omits much of the detail and the marginal citation of authorities that fill out the *Catechism;* the *Crest-Jewel* is a teaching text, not a treatise focused on doctrinal differences among Nondualist Vedāntins; the *Compendium* is a small and refined exposition, in which we do not find evident the working through of doctrine; the *Abandonment,* an apt replacement for the

Admirable Secret in terms of its spiritual power, does not so explicitly intend practice; the *Book of the Yearning Soul,* though drawing on the sentiments of the *Holy Word,* does not explicitly direct readers back to it.

3. Gordon-Guedelia, "Sagi Nahor—Enough Light," 229.
4. Gordon-Guedelia, "Sagi Nahor—Enough Light," 250.
5. For further instances of advanced Jewish-Hindu study, see Goshen-Gottstein, *Same God, Other God,* and Theodor and Greenberg, *Dharma and Halacha.*
6. See Griffiths, *Religious Reading;* Clooney, *Beyond Compare.*

Bibliography

Primary Sources

Annunziata, Sister, and Father McQuite. *First Communion Catechism*. Rev. ed. of *The Baltimore First Communion Catechism*. New York: Benziger Brothers, 1962.

Aquinas, Thomas. *Compendium of Theology* [*Compendium Theologiae*]. Translated by Richard J. Regan. Oxford: Oxford University Press, 2009.

Bhāratītīrthamuni. *Vaiyāsikanyāyamala* [*The Garland of Vyāsa's Reasons*]. Anandasrama Sanskrit Granthavali 23. Edited by Dadhicapandita Sivadatta. Pune: Anandasramalaya, 1891.

Canisius, Peter. *Catechismi Latini et Germanici. Prima Pars: Catechismi Latini*. Edited by Frederick Streicher, SJ. Rome: Pontifical Gregorian University, 1933.

———. *A Small Catechism for Catholics* [*Catechismus Minimus*]. Translated by Ryan Grant. Post Falls, ID: Mediatrix Press, 2014.

———. *Summa Doctrinae Christianae Una cum Auctoritatibus*. 4 vols. According to the 1569 edition, a new edition. Vienna: Charles Kollmann, 1833.

———. *A Summe of Christian Doctrine: Composed in Latin by the R. Father Petrus Canisius, of the Society of Jesus. With an appendix of the fall of man and justification, according to the Doctrine of the Councell of Trent*. Translated into English. St. Omer: John Heigham, 1622.

A Catechism of Christian Doctrine. Rev. ed. of the *Baltimore Catechism, No. 3: A Text for Secondary Schools and Colleges*. Patterson, NJ: St. Anthony Guild Press, 1941/1949.

Caussade, Jean Pierre de. *Abandonment to Divine Providence (with the Letters of Father de Caussade on the Practice of Self-Abandonment)*. Edited by J. Ramière and translated by E. J. Strickland. San Francisco: Ignatius Press, 2011.

Deśika, Vedānta. *Dramiḍopaniṣad Tātparyaratnāvaḷi* and *Dramiḍopaniṣatsāra*. With the commentary of Uttamur Viraraghavachariar. Chennai: Ubhaya Vedānta Granthamala, 1963.

Dīkṣita, Appayya. *Pūrvamīmāṃsāviṣayasaṃgrahadīpikā*. In Mādhavācārya, *Jaiminīyanyāyamālā (with Vistara)*, 9–22.

———. *Sastra-Siddhānta-Leśa-Saṃgraha*. Translated by S. S. Suryanarayana Sastri. Chennai: University of Madras, 1935.

———. *Śāstra-Siddhānta-Leśa-Saṃgraha of Śrīmad-Appayya-Dīkṣitendra with the Commentary Kṛṣṇālaṃkāra of Acyutakṛṣṇānanda-Tīrtha*. Edited by S. R.

Krishnamurti Sastri and N. Veezhinathan. Secunderabad: *Śrīmad-Appayya-Dīkṣitendra-Granthāvaḷi* Prakāśana-Samiti, 1973.
———. *Traduction du Chapitre 1 du Texte Sanskrit d'Appayya Dīkṣita Intitulé Siddhānta-Lesa-Saṃgraha: Compendium de Morceaux Choisis des Thèses de L'Advaita Vedānta.* Annotated and translated by Gilles Gotszorg. Lille: Atelier National de Reproduction des Thèses. Reproduction on demand of 1993 thesis.
Filser, Hubert, and Stephan Leimgruber. *Petrus Canisius, Der Große Katechismus: Summa doctrinae christianae 1555.* (Latin-German ed.) Regensburg: Schnell & Steiner, 2003.
Lombard, Peter. *The Sentences.* 4 vols. Translated by Giulio Silano. Toronto: Pontifical Institute of Mediaeval Studies, 2007–2010.
———. *Sententiae in IV Libris Distinctae.* 2 vols. 3rd ed. Rome: Editiones Collegii Bonaventurae ad Claras Aquas, 1971.
Mādhavācārya. *Jaiminīyanyāyamālāvistara or Mīmāṃsādhikaraṇamālā.* Edited by Pandit Śivadatta. Pune: Anandasrama Press, 1892.
———. *The Jaiminīyanyāyamālā of Mādhavācārya with His Own Commentary the Nyāyamālāvistara (Part I, Chapters I–III).* Edited with the Explanation of Examples and Notes by A. Ramanatha Sastry and Pattabhirama Sastry. Benares: Jaya Krishna Das Haridas Gupta, 1937.
———. *Jaiminīyanyāyamālā (with Vistara).* Bombay: Vidyaranya Vidyapeetan, 1983.
———. *The Jaiminīya-nyāya-mālā-vistara of Mādhavācārya.* Edited for the Sanskrit Text Society by the late Theodor Goldstücker and completed by Edward B. Crowell. London, Trübner, 1878.
Maṇavāḷa Jīyar, Vātikēsari Aḻakiya. *Connections in the Southern Upaniṣad* [*Dramiḍopaniṣad Saṃgati*]. As found at the end of each song of *Tiruvāymoḻi* in the volumes of the *Bhagavat Viṣayam* edition of the five classical commentaries, as edited and published by S. Krishnamachariyar. Madras: Nobel Press, 1924–1930.
Maṇavāḷamāmuni. *Deliver Me, My Lord* [*Ārtiprabandham*]. Translated by Anand Amaladass. New Delhi: Śrī Satguru, 1990.
———. *Tiruvāymoḻi Nūṟṟantāti* [*One Hundred Linked Verses on the Holy Word of Mouth*]. With the commentary of Piḷḷailokaṃjīyar. Kanchipuram: Srinivasa Accukkutam, 1916.
———. *Upadeśaratnamālā and Tiruvāymoḻi Nūṟṟantāti* [*One Hundred Linked Verses on the Holy Word of Mouth*]. With the commentary of P. B. Annangarachariar. Kanchi: Kanchigranthamalakaryalaym, 1978.
Montfort, Louis Grignion de. *The Admirable Secret of the Most Holy Rosary.* In Montfort, *God Alone,* 151–231.
———. *God Alone: The Collected Writings of St. Louis Mary de Montfort.* Translator anonymous. Bay Shore, NY: Montfort, 1988.
———. *Holy Methods for Reciting the Rosary Drawing upon Oneself the Grace of the Mysteries of the Life, Passion and Glory of Jesus and Mary.* In Montfort, *God Alone,* 233–62.
———. *Méthodes saintes pour recitant le saint Rosaire et attire sur soi la grâce des*

mystères de la Vie, de la Passion et de la Gloire de Jésus et de Marie. In Montfort, *Oeuvres complètes,.* 391–438.

———. *Oeuvres complètes de saint Louis-Marie Grigniondе Montfort.* Paris: Éditions du Seuil, 1966.

———. *Le Secret Admirable du Trés Saint Rosaire.* In Montfort, *Oeuvres complètes,* 263–89.

Śaṅkaracarya. *Vivekacūḍāmaṇi* [*The Crest-Jewel of Discrimination*]. Translated by Swami Madhavananda. Kolkata: Advaita Ashrama, 2003.

Vedāntin, Mahadeva. *Mīmāṃsānyāyasaṃgraha: A Compendium of the Principles of Mīmāṃsā.* Edited by James Benson. Wiesbaden: Harrassowitz Verlag, 2010.

Wittgenstein, Ludwig. *Culture and Value.* Edited by G. H. von Wright in collaboration with Heikki Nyman. Translated by Peter Winch. Chicago: University of Chicago Press, 1984.

———. *Philosophical Investigations.* Translated by G. E. M. Anscombe. Oxford: Blackwell, 1997.

———. *Wittgenstein's Lectures, Cambridge 1930–32.* Edited by Desmond Lee. Totowa, NJ: Rowman and Littlefield, 1980.

Yajvan, Krishna. *Mīmāṃsā Paribhāṣa* [*Preliminary Rules of Mīmāṃsā*]. Translated by Swami Madhavananda. Kolkata: Advaita Ashrama, 1987.

Secondary Sources

Alexander, Elizabeth Shanks. "Casuistic Elements in Mishnaic Law." *Jewish Studies Quarterly* 10.3 (2003): 189–243.

———. *Transmitting Mishnah: The Shaping Influence of Oral Tradition.* Cambridge: Cambridge University Press, 2006.

Baker, G. P., and P. M. S. Hacker. *Wittgenstein: Understanding and Meaning.* Vol. 1 of *An Analytical Commentary on the Philosophical Investigations.* Part 1, Essays. Oxford: Blackwell, 2008.

Bell, Richard H. "Theology as Grammar: Is God an Object of Understanding?" *Religious Studies* 11.3 (1975): 307–17.

Berg, Maggie, and Barbara K. Seeber. *The Slow Professor: Challenging the Culture of Speed in the Academy.* Toronto: University of Toronto Press, 2017.

Bhasyacharya, N. *A Catechism of the Visishtadwaita Philosophy of Sri Ramanuja Acharya.* Madras: Theosophical Society, 1887.

Bryce, Mary Charles, OSB. "The Influence of the Catechism of the Third Plenary Council of Baltimore on Widely Used Elementary Textbook from Its Composition in 1885 to Its 1941 Revision." Ph.D. diss., Catholic University of America, 1970.

Carman, John, and Vasudha Narayanan. *The Tamil Veda: Pillan's Interpretation of the Tiruvāymoḻi.* Chicago: University of Chicago Press, 1989.

Cavell, Stanley. "The Availability of Wittgenstein's Later Philosophy." *Philosophical Review* 71.1 (1962): 67–93.

Chossat, Michel, SJ. *La Somme des Sentences: Oeuvre de Hugues de Mortagne vers 1155.* Louvain: Spicilegium Sacrum Lovaniense Bureau 1923, Fasicule 5.

Clooney, Francis X. *Beyond Compare: St. Francis de Sales and Śrī Vedānta Deśika on Loving Surrender to God.* Washington, D.C.: Georgetown University Press, 2008.

———. "The Contribution and Challenge of Mīmāṃsā to the Dream of a Global Hermeneutics." In *Musings and Meanings: Hermeneutical Ripples,* edited by Nishant A. Irdayadason, 135–51. New Delhi: Christian World Imprints, 2016.

———. "Difficult Remainders: Seeking Comparative Theology's Really Difficult Other." In *How to Do Comparative Theology: European and American Perspectives in Dialogue,* edited by Francis X. Clooney, SJ, and Klaus von Stosch. New York: Fordham University Press, 2018.

———. "Divine Word, Human Word in Nammāḻvār." In *In Spirit and in Truth,* edited by Ignatius Viyagappa, SJ, 155–68. Madras: Aikiya Alayam, 1985.

———. "Fractal Theory, Fractal Practice: Theology of Religions, Comparative Theology." In *New Paths for Interreligious Theology: Perry Schmidt-Leukel's Fractal Interpretation of Religious Diversity,* edited by Paul Knitter and Alan Race. Maryknoll, NY: Orbis Books. 2019.

———. *Hindu God, Christian God: How Reason Helps Break Down the Boundaries between Religions.* New York: Oxford University Press, 2001.

———. *His Hiding Place Is Darkness: A Hindu-Catholic Theopoetics of Divine Absence.* Stanford: Stanford University Press, 2014.

———. "Mādhava's *Garland* of Jaimini's Reasons as Exemplary Mīmāṃsā Philosophy." In *The Oxford Handbook of Indian Philosophy,* edited by Jonardon Ganeri. New York: Oxford University Press. 2017.

———. "Mīmāṃsā as Introspective Literature and as Philosophy." In *The Encyclopedia of Indian Religions.* Hinduism and Tribal Religions. Edited by Pankaj Jain. New York: Springer (forthcoming).

———. "Mīmāṃsā for the Mīmāṃsakas: Distinctiveness of Style in Mādhavācārya's *Jaiminīyanyāyamālā.*" *Brahma Vidya: Adyar Library Bulletin* (Chennai) 78–79 (2014–15): 487–518.

———. "On the Style of Vedānta: Reading Bhāratītīrtha's *Vaiyāsikanyāyamālā* in Light of Mādhava's *Jaiminīyanyāyamālā.*" In *The Bloomsbury Research Handbook of Vedānta,* edited by Ayon Maharaj. London: Bloomsbury (forthcoming).

———. *Seeing through Texts: Doing Theology among the Śrīvaiṣṇavas of South India.* Albany: State University of New York Press, 1996.

———. *Theology after Vedānta: An Experiment in Comparative Theology.* Albany: State University of New York Press, 1993.

———. *Thinking Ritually: Retrieving the Pūrva Mīmāṃsā of Jaimini.* Vienna: Sammlung De Nobili Institut für Indologie der Universität Wien, 1990.

———. "Traveling the *Via Pulchritudinis*—Both Ways." In *Finding Beauty in the Other: Theological Reflections across Religious Traditions,* edited by Peter Casarella and Sirry Mun'im, 213–43. New York: Crossroad, 2018.

———. *The Truth, the Way, and the Life: Christian Commentary on the Three Holy Mantras of the Śrīvaiṣṇava Hindus.* Leuven: Peeters, 2008.

Dhotel, Jean-Claude. *Les Origines du Catéchisme Moderne: D'après les premiers manuels imprimés en France.* Paris: Aubier, 1967.

Dupuis, Jacques. *Christianity and the Religions: From Confrontation to Dialogue.* Maryknoll, NY: Orbis Books, 2002.

Galewicz, Cezary. *A Commentator in Service of Empire: Sayana and the Royal Project of Commenting on the Whole of the Veda.* Vienna: De Nobili Research Library, 2009.

Girolimon, Michael T. "Hugh of St Victor's *De sacramentis Christianae fidei:* The Sacraments of Salvation." *Journal of Religious History* 18.2 (1994): 127–38.

Gordon-Guedalia, Shoshana Razel. "Sagi Nahor—Enough Light: Dialectic Tension between Luminescent Resonance and Blind Assumption in Comparative Theology." In *How to Do Comparative Theology,* edited by Francis X. Clooney and Klaus von Stosch, 229–55. New York: Fordham University Press, 2017.

Goshen-Gottstein, Alon. *Same God, Other God: Judaism, Hinduism, and the Problem of Idolatry.* London: Palgrave Macmillan, 2016.

Govindacharya, Algondavilli. *The Holy Lives of the Azhvars.* Mysore: G.T.A. Press, 1902.

Griffiths, Paul J. *Religious Reading: The Place of Reading in the Practice of Religion.* New York: Oxford University Press, 1999.

Guitteny, Bernard. *Grignion de Montfort, missionnaire des pauvres: 1673–1716.* Paris: Les Editions du Cerf, 1993.

———. "Le texte authentique du Traite de la vraie devotion a la Sainte Vierge de saint Louis-Marie Grignion de Montfort." *Nouvelle revue théologique* 127.3 (2005): 403–26.

Hadot, Pierre. *Philosophy as a Way of Life: Spiritual Exercises from Socrates to Foucault.* Translated by Michael Chase. Oxford: Wiley-Blackwell, 1995.

Hays, Richard. "Reading the Bible with Eyes of Faith: The Practice of Theological Exegesis." *Journal of Theological Interpretation* 1.1 (2007): 5–21.

Hennessy, Kate. *Dorothy Day: The World Will Be Saved by Beauty.* New York: Scribner, 2017.

High, Dallas. *Language, Persons, and Beliefs.* New York: Oxford University Press, 1967.

Hill, Wesley. "God's Strangeness." *First Things,* no. 259 (January 2016), 15–16.

Kane, Pandurang Vaman. *History of Dharmashastra.* Vol. 5, pt. 2. 1962. Pune: Bhandarkar Oriental Research Institute, 2007.

Leo XIII. "Militantis Ecclesiae." Encyclical on St. Peter Canisius, August 1, 1897.

Le Tourneau, Dominique. "Nouvelles recherches sur saint Louis-Marie Grignion de Montfort." *Revue d'Histoire de l'Eglise de France* 91.2 (2005): 403–12.

Locklin, Reid. "Interreligious Prudentia." In *Vatican II: Forty Years Later,* edited by William Madges, 283–307. Maryknoll, NY: Orbis Books, 2006.

Mandelbrot, Benoit. *Fractalist: Memoir of a Scientific Maverick.* New York: Pantheon Books, 2012.

McDonough, Thomas M. *The Law and the Gospel in Luther.* London: Oxford University Press,1963.

McGinn, Maria. *Wittgenstein and the Philosophical Investigations.* New York: Routledge, 1997.

Mitchell, Nathan. *The Mystery of the Rosary: Marian Devotion and the Reinvention of Catholicism.* New York: New York University Press, 2009.

Modi, P. M. *A Critique of the Brahmasūtra (III. 2. II–IV): With Special Reference to Śaṅkarācārya's Commentary.* Bhavnagar: Mahodaya P. Press, 1943.

Moi, Toril. *Revolution of the Ordinary: Literary Studies after Wittgenstein, Austin, and Cavell.* Chicago: University of Chicago Press, 2017.

Molinario, Joël. *Le catéchisme, une invention moderne.* Montrouge: Bayard, 2013.

Moyaert, Marianne. *Ritual Participation and Interreligious Dialogue: Boundaries, Transgressions and Innovations.* New York: Bloomsbury Academic, 2015.

Neusner, Jacob. *Judaism as Philosophy: The Method and the Message of the Mishnah.* Columbia: University of South Carolina Press, 1991.

Novikoff, Alex. *The Medieval Culture of Disputation: Pedagogy, Practice, and Performance.* Philadelphia: University of Pennsylvania Press, 2013.

Pabel, Hilmar M. "Peter Canisius and the Protestants: A Model of Ecumenical Dialogue?" *Journal of Jesuit Studies* 1.3 (2014) 373–99.

Perloff, Marjorie. "Writing Philosophy as Poetry: Literary Form in Wittgenstein." In *The Oxford Handbook of Wittgenstein,* edited by Oskari Kuusela and Marie McGinn, 714–28. New York: Oxford University Press, 2015.

Pius XI. "Discourse on the Occasion of Declaring Peter Canisius a Doctor of the Church." *Acta Apostolicae Sedis* 17 (1925). https://www.scribd.com/document/336874765/AAS-17-1925-ocr.

Rahner, Karl. "The Prospects for Dogmatic Theology." *Theological Investigations.* Vol. 1, *Christ, Mary and Grace.* Translated by Cornelius Ernst, OP. Baltimore: Helicon Press, 1961.

Ramesan, N. *Śrī Appayya Dikshita.* Hyderabad, India: Srimad Appayya Dikshitendra Granthavali Prakasana Samithi, 1972.

Rosemann, Philipp W. *Peter Lombard.* New York: Oxford University Press, 2004.

———. *Understanding Scholastic Thought with Foucault.* Basingstoke: Macmillan, 1999.

Theodor, Ithamar, and Yudit Kornberg Greenberg, eds. *Dharma and Halacha: Comparative Studies in Hindu-Jewish Philosophy and Religion.* Lanham, MD: Rowman and Littlefield, 2018.

Thiselton, Anthony C. *The Two Horizons: New Testament Hermeneutics and Philosophical Description with Special Reference to Heidegger, Bultmann, Gadamer, and Wittgenstein.* Grand Rapids, MI: W. B. Eerdmans, 1980.

Winston-Allen, Anne. *Stories of the Rose: The Making of the Rosary in the Middle Ages.* University Park: Pennsylvania State University Press, 1997.

Index

Recent books from the Page-Barbour and Richard Lectures

Reading the Hindu and Christian Classics: Why and How Deep Learning Still Matters
Francis X. Clooney, SJ

Philosophy as Poetry
Richard Rorty

Treasure in Heaven: The Holy Poor in Early Christianity
Peter Brown

Hope without Optimism
Terry Eagleton

Structural Intuitions: Seeing Shapes in Art and Science
Martin Kemp

From Theology to Theological Thinking
Jean-Yves Lacoste, translated by W. Chris Hackett, with an introduction by Jeffrey Bloechl

Dialect Diversity in America: The Politics of Language Change
William Labov

The Witch in the Western Imagination
Lyndal Roper

Fatalism in American Film Noir: Some Cinematic Philosophy
Robert B. Pippin

The Reason of the Gift
Jean-Luc Marion, translated by Stephen E. Lewis

The Virtues of Mendacity: On Lying in Politics
Martin Jay

Fathoming the Cosmos and Ordering the World: The "Yijing" ("I Ching," or "Classic of Changes") and Its Evolution in China
Richard J. Smith